St. Patrick's People
Irish and English Catholics in Early Ohio History

Lorle Porter, Ph.D.

With
Donald Schlegel
Kathy Kreppner Graham
Pearl Gallagher Reischman

*We sing for all the unsung saints
that countless, nameless throng,
who kept the faith and passed it on
with hope steadfast and strong*

Carl P. Daw, Jr.
©1994 Hope Publishing Co., Carol Stream, IL 60188
All rights reserved. Used by permission.

"Catholics in America received acceptance only where these English and older Irish families in the country advanced and only where they lived."
—Thomas T. McAvoy, *A History of the Catholic Church in the United States*

St. Patrick's People: Irish Catholics in Early Ohio History
by Lorle Porter, Ph.D.
©2003 All Rights Reserved.

No part of this publication may be reproduced in whole or in part, stored in a retrieval system, posted on the Internet, transmitted in any form or by any means, electronic, mechanical, photocopying, recording, or otherwise, without written permission of the author.

Additional Contributors
Donald Schlegel
Kathy Kreppner Graham
Pearl Gallagher Reischman

ISBN 1-887932-87-9
Library of Congress Control Number: 2003103686

First Edition
Printed in U.S.A.

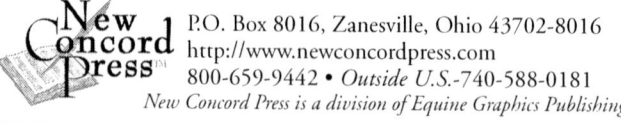

P.O. Box 8016, Zanesville, Ohio 43702-8016
http://www.newconcordpress.com
800-659-9442 • *Outside U.S.*-740-588-0181
New Concord Press is a division of Equine Graphics Publishing

Acknowledgements

I want to thank the librarians of Muskingum College for help through many years of preparation for this book. Melissa Essex of Guernsey County District Library supplied material for the Civil War section. Lydia Bonacorda of Georgetown University Library, and Father Thomas Bennett, Archivist of the Diocese of Columbus, were helpful. Sister Mary Carolyn Leslie, Archivist of the Motherhouse of the Sisters of the Holy Family in New Orleans, Louisianna, was most gracious. Ruth Biedenback Fox, Helen Sockaci, and Pearl Reischman provided photographs. Dr. Donna Edsall provided research assistance and general support.

This project grew out of a research effort to uncover Slavic immigrant records in the Cambridge coalfields, published in my book, *The Immigrant Cocoon*. Many of the early records were in St. Mary's Roman Catholic Church records in Temperanceville, Ohio. It was at that time that I met Mrs. Pearl Gallagher Reischman, a genealogist of the Gallagher Family. Pearl has helped me off and on over the years, and it is to honor her that I have completed this work. Mrs. Reischman is the great-great-granddaughter of Edmund Gallagher. Two former students at Muskingum College–Teri Hart Snyder and Kathy Kreppner Graham–did work on the history of early Catholics in this area. Another Muskingum College graduate, Bruce Yarnall, a native of the region, was most helpful. Gary S. Williams and Roger Pickinpaugh shared with me their knowledge of Noble County. Roberta Armstrong proof-read the manuscript. Toni Leland designed the book layout and cover.

Donald Schlegel, editor of the *Bulletin of the Catholic Record Society* of the Diocese of Columbus, has been a worthy disciple of Fr. Herman Mattingly, the founder of the society. Much of the primary research utilized in this book has been published in the *Bulletin*; a good deal of it is the work of Don Schlegel, who also critiqued the manuscript.

St. Patrick's People seeks to place in historical context the migration of Catholics into early Ohio. All the above-named people have had a role in bringing it to reality.

Lorle Porter
New Concord, Ohio

"Westering"

EMIGRATING TO NEW CONNECTICUT, 1817–1818.
From an engraving in Peter Parley's Recollections.

St. Patrick's People

Timeline: 7
    Catholic Experience in England/Ireland and America

A Yankee in Dixie, and a Catholic to Boot! 17
    Ohio Catholics in Galveston, Texas, 1880-1918

The Catholic Church in Colonial America 21
    English and Irish Immigrants

"Hair-buying" on the Pennsylvania/Virginia Frontier 61
    The French and Indian War

Natives and Émigrés 77
    The American Church in an Age of Revolution: Missions in Kentucky, Pennsylvania, and the West

On the Verge of "Nothingness" 93
    The Ohio Mission Field, 1790-1825

Scattered Flock, Few Shepherds 117
    Fenwick's Ohio (1825-1833) and Purcell's Ohio (1834-1845)

"New Catholics" and "Old", 1840-1900 133
    The Struggle to Remain American

Bibliography 153

Index 161

America	Europe
	1625 Charles I (Stuart)
1634 Baltimore's Maryland Colony; Andrew White and John Altham first English-speaking priests in North America; Fenwicks in Maryland	
	1640-60 English Civil War; Charles I beheaded; Cromwell's Protectorate
1642 Montreal founded by French priests and traders	
1647 Protestant uprising in Maryland; No priests in Maryland; Church underground	
1658 Lord Baltimore reinstated	
1673 Marquette's expedition in Mississippi Valley lays French claims to Midwest	
	1678 Titus Oates anti-Catholic hysteria; Catholic martyrs
1681 Robert Brooke, the first American seminarian, arrives at St. Omer, France	
	1688 Glorious Revolution in England Williamite anti-Catholic penal laws enforced; Flight of Irish as indentured servants
1689 Charles Carroll The Settler arrives; Jack Coode's Rebellion in Maryland; Anti-Catholic laws enforced	
	1690 Battle of the Boyne
	1691 Treaty of Limerick wins concessions for Catholics English government ignores treaty; British renege on promise to Irish in Treaty of Limerick. Williamite Penal laws enforced
1704 Acts to Prevent Growth of Popery; Maryland and Pennsylvania	1699–1703 Harvest failures
1708 14 disguised Jesuit chapels in Maryland; 3,000 Roman Catholics in Maryland forced underground; Catholic elite to Europe for education	

America	Europe
	1710 Drought
	1714-19 Drought
	1714-27 King George I harsh penal laws enforced
	1715 "The Fifteen" Catholic rebellion against Protestant monarchs; Taxation to crush Catholic landholders
	1720 Depression in British Isles
	1721–1723 Wet weather
	1725 Poor harvest; lawlessness terrorizes Irish
	1728-29 Potato crop fails
1731 St. Francis Xavier, Newtown, Maryland; Chapel disguised as tobacco barn	
1733 St. Joseph, Philadelphia; Fr. Josiah Greaton, SJ; Only openly-Catholic Church in English-speaking world; Bohemia Manor School, Maryland	
	1739-40 Killer frosts ruin crops Massive starvation
1741 Maryland survey: 34 chapels, 8,000 Catholics; Goshenhoppen, Pennsylvania; Conewago Chapel, Pennsylvania; German Catholic enclaves; Movement of squatters to "The Forks"	1740-41 Irish potato crop fails
	1744-45 Potato crop fails
	1745 Last Stuart "Rising" in Scotland; Some relaxation of penal code to pacify Irish
1751 Felix Hughes (Greene County) Pennsylvania begs for a priest	
1753 John J. Carroll graduates at St. Omer	

America	Europe
1754 Ann Matthews professed as Carmelite in Holland	1754–1763 FRENCH & INDIAN WAR (SEVEN YEARS WAR)
1759 Four priests function in Pennsylvania: Robert Harding SJ Theodore Schneider SJ Ferdinand Farmer SJ Matthias Manners SJ	
1761 J.J. Carroll SJ ordained in France	
1763 French allies abandon Indians; Chief Pontiac leads tribes in uprising, wiping out many frontier posts; Daniel Boone moving west	1763 Proclamation Line
1773 Boston Tea Party; Archers and Crows in Green County, Pennsylvania; John J. Carroll returns to Maryland; 23 ex-Jesuits reside in America	1770's Linen trade flattened by depression; Scotch-Irish migration heavy; Jesuits suppressed; British banking crisis; First Catholic Relief Act in England; 80,000 Catholics
1775 In Maryland, free white males with 40£ income/property can vote	
AMERICAN REVOLUTION BEGINS	
1778 Franco-American Alliance	
	1780 English depression ends
1781 British surrender at Yorktown; Lew Wetzel explores Ohio Country	
1784 John J. Carroll named Superior of the Catholic Clergy in America	

America	Europe
1785 19 priests in Maryland; 5 priests in Pennsylvania; Charles M. Whelan arrives in New York City; Estimated 25,000 Catholics in USA	
1787 Westmoreland, Pennsylvania Catholic colony; Charles Whelan in Kentucky visiting Marylander Kentucky colony; Peter Helbron pastor of Holy Trinity in Philadelphia (German parish) NORTHWEST ORDINANCE opens upper Midwest for settlement	
1789 Theo Browers, OSF at Sportsman's Hall, Westmoreland County, Pennsylvania	1789 FRENCH REVOLUTION BEGINS
1790 John J. Carroll named Bishop of Baltimore; First cotton mill in USA/beginning of Industrial Revolution; Carmel at Port Tobacco, Maryland established (First house of women religious in the USA); Refugee American nuns from Holland and Belgium	
1791 Georgetown College opens	1791-93 REIGN OF TERROR
1792 First of the French Sulpician priests arrive in America; Joseph Flaget, Benedictine; William deRohan builds Church of the Holy Cross in Kentucky settlement	1792 Additional relaxation of penal laws to pacify Irish during French Revolution
1793 Carroll informs priests that 3000 fellow priests have died in France; Frenchman Stephen Badin ordained in US; says mass at Mount Savage, Maryland, on way west	
1794 Battle of Fallen Timbers makes settlement of Ohio safe	1794 English Carmelites flee Europe; Carmelite nuns of Compiegne guillotined

America	Europe
1795 Carroll ordains Prince Demetrius Gallitzin	
1797 Zane's Trace blazes path into southern Ohio; Shehys settle in Mahoning County, Ohio	
	1798 "The Year of the French"; Wolfe Tone's disastrous Rising in Ireland; Irish gentry immigration; displaced Irish peasants starve
1799 Peter Lonergan in Waynesburg, Greene County, Pennsylvania; Peter Helbron at Sportsman's Hall assumes care of Greene County mission	1799 Napoleon controls France
1800 Ordination of William Matthews, first American native priest	
1801 Stephen Badin assumes responsibility for Kentucky	1801 Act of Union between England and Ireland; Relaxation of penal laws in England begins; English disclosure laws drive peasants into towns; Industrial Revolution underway; Napoleon sells Louisiana to US
1803 DeLongs in Ohio	
1804 Edward Fenwick OP assigned to Kentucky	
1805 Archers to Belmont County, Ohio; Dittoes and Fincks to Perry County, Ohio; Sapp Settlement in Knox County, Ohio; Gabriel Richard sent to minister in Michigan Territory	1805 Trafalgar; Britain rules the seas; Napoleon rules the continent; American ships harassed while trading with Europe; American seamen impressed by British navy
1806 Fenwick founds St. Rose of Lima convent, Springfield, Kentucky; Elizabeth Seaton confirmed into the Church	

America	Europe
1808 Brothers Enoch and Benedict Fenwick ordained ; Mount St. Mary's established in Emmitsburg; Joseph Flaget named Bishop of Bardstown, Kentucky; Edward Fenwick makes first trip up the Zane's Trace into Ohio	
1809 Mother Seaton begins her congregation of the Sisters of Charity	
1810 Michael Egan named Bishop of Philadelphia	
1811 Carroll named Archbishop of Baltimore; "Long Jim" Gallagher in Guernsey County, Ohio; Youthful "warhawks" (from the West: Ohio, Kentucky) dominate Congress; Tecumseh and The Prophet arouse renewed Indian War from Canadian base; Battle of Tippecanoe in Indiana Territory; Western produce unable to be shipped to eastern ports	
1812 WAR BETWEEN AMERICA AND BRITAIN Americans invade Canada and fail; Oliver Hazard Perry defeated British fleet on Lake Erie	1812–1814 War of 1812; Migration ceases NAPOLEONIC WAR ENDS American markets on continent dry up
1813 Creightons in Ohio	
1814 British plunder waterfront farms in Maryland, burn Washington, plunder and desecrate St. Inigoes Manor house chapel; Jesuit Order reestablished worldwide	
1815 Carroll writes to friends, describing British shelling of Baltimore; Bishop John J. Carroll dies	

13

America		Europe	
		1816	Heavy war taxes propel huge exodus
1817	Daugherty Settlement in Ohio		
1818	Edmund Gallagher family to Ohio		
1821	Diocese of Ohio created, Bishop Edward Fenwick		
1822	Dominican nuns in Kentucky; First native American foundation	1822	Irish potato crop fails
1823	Benedict Fenwick named Bishop of Boston		
1825	National Road building begins in Ohio; Ohio Erie Canal building begins	1825	Railroad building in England
1829	First Provincial Council of Baltimore	1829	Irish victory of Daniel O'Connell; Catholic Emancipation Act
1830	Dominican nuns establish convent in Somerset, Perry County, Ohio		
1831	Fenwick reports 24 priests, 22 churches	1831	Irish potato crop fails
1832	Bishop Fenwick dies	1832	Great Reform Bill in England; Middle class relief
1834	Anti-Catholic outbreak; Ursuline Convent in Charlestown, Mass. burns		
1835	St. Vincent Abbey established at Sportsman's Hall, Pennsylvania	1835	Irish potato crop fails
		1836	Irish potato crop fails
1837	German Catholic newspaper published in Cincinnati	1837	Irish potato crop fails
1839	Purcell makes first of seven recruiting trips to Europe; returns with French priests	1839	Irish potato crop fails; Zenith of Oxford Movement in England
		1842	Irish potato crop fails

America	Europe
1843 Purcell reports 50 priests in Ohio, 50,000 Catholics	
1844 Orestes Brownson converts	
1845 Brown County Ursulines established; Port cities flooded with "famine-fled" Irish	1845 John Henry Newman converts to Roman Catholicism; Irish potato production collapses; "The Great Hunger": two million emigrate, half die; one million starve in Ireland
1846 Nicholas A. Gallagher born in Temperanceville, Ohio	
1848 Jean Lamy named Bishop of Santa Fe	
	1848 European Revolts; migration hastens
1850's Railroad building in Ohio	
	1851 Irish potato crop survives
1855 John Mary Jacquet assigned to Temperanceville, Ohio	
1856 110 priests in Ohio	
1861–AMERICAN CIVIL WAR 1865	
1865 163 priests in Ohio	
1868 Diocese of Columbus founded; Sylvester Rosecrans first bishop; 154 churches, 159 priests; Nicholas A. Gallagher first priest ordained in diocese	
	1870 First Vatican Council
1882 Nicholas A. Gallagher administers Diocese of Galveston; Dominican nuns to Galveston	
1892 Nicholas A. Gallagher is third Bishop of Galveston	
1918 Nicholas Aloysius Gallagher dies	

St. Patrick's People
Irish and English Catholics in Early Ohio History

Prologue

Sarah Gallagher Malone stepped out of the Temperanceville post office into the bright fall sunshine, but with a heavy heart. Her daughter, Clara Louise, was a fourteen-year-old schoolgirl at Sacred Heart Convent in Galveston. She and her cousin, Frances Viola Schmuesser, one year older, had been studying in the Queen City of Texas for five years. They were under the care of Bishop Gallagher, Sarah's older brother. On the steps of the post office, Sarah met her niece, Mary Mame Gallagher. Mary tore open a letter from her cousin, Sister Mary St. Rita of the Convent of the Good Shepherd in New Port, Kentucky.

> Convent Good Shepherd
> Newport, Ky,
> Sept. 17, 1900
> "*The will of God is our sanctification.*" St. Paul
>
> My dear cousin,
>   No doubt you have heard by this time of the terrible calamity that took place in the city of Galveston a week ago last Saturday caused by a hurricane and tidal wave. I thought I would write to you to inform you that Rt. Rev. Uncle is safe. I know you received no word as all communication was broken off.
>   Our good Mother telephoned to the Archbishop of Cincinnati to learn if he knew anything about him, at the time had heard nothing about Uncle but shortly after a telegraph came telling the Archbishop he was safe and asking for help as soon as possible. I suppose he had to go some distance to send this message as telegraph wires were destroyed and the city was 18 feet deep in water. How delighted I was to hear he was saved. I ran to the Chapel to thank our dear, merciful Lord for having saved him from so fearful a death. The paper stated that such a calamity has never been known. Hundreds of lives were lost. The beautiful Sacred Heart Church was totally destroyed, also St. Mary's Catholic Infirmary. The Ursuline Convent collapsed and buried all the Sisters beneath its ruins. Was this not something terrible? It is a painful cross to dear Uncle after so many years of hard labor, yet we know his noble heart is capable of bearing much suffering and accepts all as the Holy Will of

God. Perhaps many souls may be converted and others inspired to love and serve God better.[1]

Sarah joyfully telegraphed scattered members of the Gallagher clan with the news: the grandson and the great-granddaughters of Temperanceville pioneers, Edmund and Anna Gallagher, had survived the worst natural disaster in American history.

On a hot, muggy Texas day, September 6, 1900, Issac Cline, the Texas section chief of the National Weather Service, received a warning that a fierce storm had struck Cuba and was heading northward. Two days later, Cline stood at his Galveston window and watched heavy sheets of rain flood the low-lying streets of the city. Then the killer storm hit with ferocity, hurling 150-mile-per-hour winds at the wooden houses along the seafront, cutting communications between the island and the mainland, and drowning avenues of escape with walls of water. Fifty-foot waves battered the coast. Cline wired his brother in Washington, DC at 2:30 p.m. with the ominous report: "'Gulf rising rapidly, half the city now under water.'" That was the last contact with the beleaguered city of Galveston until a relief party from Houston rowed out to the devastated island on September 10.[2]

They found that half the city was swept away. Seven blocks from the coast, the debris of once neatly painted houses formed a "'three-mile-long wall—100 feet thick and 20 feet high.'" Twenty-five hundred houses had been swept away, and a thousand more reduced to rubble. Between 6,000 and 8,000 people died on Galveston Island that night, making the storm the worst natural disaster in American history. Stench from decaying human and animal flesh filled the muggy air. Burial and relief work began immediately, as stunned survivors sought to halt an epidemic. Burial trenches were dug and cremation fires lit. Those fires would burn into November.

Roman Catholic Father James M. Kirwin, a native of Circleville, Ohio and a member of Bishop Nicholas Aloysius Gallagher's staff, wrote:
> It soon became so that men could not handle those bodies without stimulants. I am a strong temperance man . . . but I

---

1 Mary (Mame) Gallagher was the daughter of William Gallagher and Priscilla Creighton. She married Edward McCabe of Coshocton. Anna Gallagher was Sister Mary St. Rita, the daughter of William Gallagher's brother, James, and Mary Louise Jefferis. Letter in possession of Ruth Biedenbach Fox of Reynoldsburg, Ohio.
2 Jack Lowery, "The Storm of the Century," *Texas Highways*, August 2000, p. 48.

went to the men who were handling those bodies, and I gave them whiskey. It had to be done.[3]

What remained of St. Mary's Hospital and Chapel after the storm in Galveston.
Courtesy of the Rosenberg Library, Galveston, Texas

Kirwin's parish work—and that of all the Catholic religious on the island, was in ruins. During the storm, at Holy Rosary convent, built the previous year with funds provided by Mother Katherine Drexel, Sister Dominica opened the door to find her three blood sisters and their five children standing in the drenching rain—their home had been blown away. At Holy Rosary Church, Father Philip Keller, a native of Bavaria, halted the children's rosary hour as the winds built. When gusts blew out three stained glass windows, he hustled his charges into the three-story convent. Sister Fabian, the housekeeper, darted into the yard and freed two cows, bundling two calves into the building. At the storm's height, two hundred people crowded into the convent. Rosaries were said, confessions heard, and absolution given. At 11 p.m., the winds changed, and the refugees knew that they had been spared. For the next six weeks, the convent and school would be a refugee center.[4]

Holy Rosary's church bell was the only such bell to survive the storm. Sacred Heart Church was no more. St. Patrick's was severely damaged,

---

3 Lowery, p. 50.
4 *Holy Rosary Industrial School*, Archives, typescript. Provided by Sister Mary Carolyn Leslie, Sisters of the Holy Family, New Orleans, Louisiana.

although a statue of Mary, Queen of the Seas, was untouched. Slowly, the tales of horror emerged.

> A pregnant woman was swept from her rooftop.
> Mrs. William Henry Heideman was knocked into a steamer trunk that bobbed by on the surging water. The trunk hurtled along until it collided with a wall of the Ursuline Convent. A nun pulled Mrs. Heideman inside, and William Henry Heideman, Jr., was born just hours later.
> St. Mary's Orphanage, an assemblage of wooden buildings on the beach, was demolished in the storm. Rescue workers later found the bodies of 90 children nearby. Among the dead was a nun with nine children tied to her. The bodies of two sisters turned up at Texas City, across Galveston Bay.[5]

Frantic relief workers poured towards Galveston, but only when one railroad line was restored on September 17, could relief parties arrive in numbers. Only then did the outside world learn the magnitude of the disaster.

Newspapers in the rest of America speculated in lurid fashion on the fate of Galvestonians. Persons with relatives in the city feared the worst. In the tiny hamlet of Temperanceville, Ohio, nestled in a bowl amid the wooded hills of Belmont County, the family of Bishop Nicholas Aloysius Gallagher crowded St. Mary's Church for daily mass and rosaries said in petition for the safety of the bishop and other relatives caught in the stricken city.

Across the shattered landscape, life re-emerged. Retired army engineers began working on plans for the Galveston floodwall, which was begun in 1902 and finished two years later. In the next decade, workers would raise the streets, homes, and stone buildings to the level of the seventeen-foot wall. The three-thousand-ton St. Patrick's church would be jacked up by workmen who turned the jackscrews to the beat of a song. Galveston would return to life.[6]

In the devastated city, Nicholas Aloysius Gallagher, third bishop of the Roman Catholic Diocese of Galveston, stood amid the ruins of his church. He had spent sleepless days and nights searching for victims, comforting hysterical children, organizing relief efforts and burial parties. The results of his eighteen years in Galveston had been swept away in that many hours. Now, the gentle bishop would put his energy to work rebuilding what was lost.

---

5 Lowery, p. 50.
6 Ibid. Anonymous, *The House of Honored Men: The Bishop's Palace*. Galveston, Texas, 1981, p. 56. The floodwall successfully protected the city during the 1914 hurricane, more severe than the 1900 killer storm.

Chapter One

A Yankee in Dixie—and a Catholic, to Boot!
Ohio Catholics in Galveston, Texas: 1880–1918

On January 23, 1918, When Vicar General James Kirwin organized the solemn funeral ceremonies honoring Nicholas Aloysius Gallagher's life, it was to honor a life well spent.[7]

Sister Mary Ann (Juleann) Gallagher sat in the family pew at St. Mary's Basilica for the funeral mass for her brother, Bishop Nicholas.

---

7 Obituary, *Galveston Daily News*, January 23, 1918, p. 1. Prayer Card. Gallagher is buried under the Blessed Mother's altar in the Basilica. This is the oldest surviving Catholic Church in Texas.

Gallagher's cousin, Augustine Patrick Gallagher is the second bishop in this family. While his cousins carved out religious careers in Texas, Augustine Patrick Gallagher did the same in the Diocese of Little Rock, Arkansas.

Born to William and Barbara Reasbeck Gallagher in Temperanceville in 1871, Augustine grew up in Arkansas where his father had established a nursery business. Drawn to the church, he was educated at St. Vincent College, Cape Girardeau, Missouri, and Kenrick Seminary in St. Louis. Bishop Edward Fitzgerald, former pastor of St. Patrick's Church in Columbus (his cousin's mentor), ordained Gallagher in Little Rock in 1897. At twenty-six, Father Gallagher–a priest of four months–was sent to tend the ten Catholic families in the booming tent town of Mena, Arkansas. The entire state was a mission field. Gallagher's great ingenuity was proven when he paid off debts incurred by a previous pastor, and sought out his scattered parishioners. He would spend fifty-three years as pastor of St. Agnes, the church he built. He would tend thirteen missions scattered along 200 miles of river, riding from one to the other on a railroad handcar.

Despite the area's anti-Catholic bias, Father Gallagher served both the Catholic people and the community of Mena. His sister, Mary, tended their home and fed and housed the poor. Gallagher drew on his family heritage and built a greenhouse and stocked community gardens with plants. He developed a city park out of swampland. He was so successful that the town's leaders made him park commissioner. For his lifetime of service to the church and to St. Agnes, Gallagher was named a Domestic Prelate in 1940–a rare honor for a parish priest. "Souvenir of the Golden Sacerdotal Jubilee of the Rt. Rev. Msgr. A. P. Gallagher, V. F.," St. Agnes Church, Mena, Arkansas, 1947.

Augustine Patrick Gallagher
Courtesy Pearl Gallagher Reischman

Beside her were Sister Agnes (Clara Malone) and Sister Philomena (Frances Viola Schmuesser)–two of her seven nieces who had entered the convent.[8]

During Bishop Gallagher's four decades in Galveston, he successfully navigated reefs of politics and prejudice. The history of the Roman Catholic Church in Texas was rocky. Although Texas was part of Catholic Mexico, the vast lands north of the Rio Grande were virtually unpopulated. In 1823, in order to secure settlement, Mexican Dictator Santa Ana sought to entice American immigrants by granting huge land tracts to Stephen Austin, on condition that his settlers embrace loyalty to Mexico and to Roman Catholicism. These were difficult conditions to enforce and when, in a moment of capriciousness, the surly dictator swept away "Texicans" special privileges, Texas declared its independence. The ensuing slaughter at the Alamo fixed in Texans' minds a hatred of all things Mexican, including Catholicism. That attitude was heightened by a constant fear of Mexican invasion during the decade of the Lone Star State's existence.

Remember your prelates who have spoken to you the word of God; whose faith follow. Hebrews XIII. 7.

The Rt. Rev. Nicholas A. Gallagher
Born February 19, 1846
Ordained Priest December 25, 1868
Consecrated Bishop April 30, 1882
Died January 21, 1918

Courtesy Pearl Gallagher Reischman

The vast lands of Texas were also targeted as potential slave territory by expansionistic leaders of the American Deep South. The future of Texas thus became a key issue in the American presidential election of 1844. The new president, John Tyler, realizing that the Senate would deadlock on annexation, maneuvered through Congress a joint resolution on annexation. This tactic required but a simple majority. Thus, a slave-holding Texas was invited into the Union as the twenty-eighth state in 1845.[9] The vicious and emotionally charged War with Mexico followed.

---

8 Gallagher family vocations, drawn from Pearl Reichman genealogy and the work of Donald Schlegel, "The Dominican Sisters of the Sacred Heart Academy," *Bulletin of the Catholic Record Society* (hereafter cited as *CRS*), XVIII, #8, March, #10, October 1993.

9 Thomas Bailey, *The American Pageant, A History of the Republic*, (D. C. Heath and Company, Boston, 1956) pp. 271-3.

Once Texas became part of the United States, Pope Pius IX created the Diocese of Galveston: really all of Texas east of the Colorado River, some 700 by 300 square miles. He assigned the diocese to French missionaries. It was a blunder, as throughout the saga of Texas Independence and the Mexican War, France had attempted to secure concessions in Texas and had worked behind the scenes to prevent American annexation.[10] Thus, the French missionaries and the Mexican priests labored under grave suspicions.

Pope Pius IX
Catholic Record Society, Columbus, Ohio

The diocese's first bishop, the Frenchman, John Mary Oden, C. M., tirelessly traveled the vast empty land and built a network of forty churches that were served by forty-two priests. By the end of his twenty-five years of service, he had established five boys' schools, four girls' schools, and a college. When the French Ursuline nuns established their academy in 1846, it was the first Roman Catholic school in Texas.[11]

Oden's successor, Claude Marie Dubuis, a secular priest, and his party of sixty French religious (mostly Vincentians) arrived in Texas's port city during the American Civil War. The French Emperor, Napoleon III, was boldly intervening in Mexican politics. He replaced President Benito Juarez with an emperor: Maximilian of Hapsburg. The French soldiers brutally established a French colony in defiance of the American Monroe Doctrine. Abraham Lincoln, mired in a losing war in 1862, was incapable of any response.

Bishop Dubuis and his retinue were allowed to land in Galveston only on the promise that they would not work in support of the French or the Northern causes. The bishop quietly labored to retain the good offices of civil authorities during the difficult war years. He encouraged the Ursulines to turn their convent-school into a hospital, gaining good will among the wounded and their families.[12]

---

10 Bailey, pp. 285-6.
11 *House of Honored Men*, pp. 58-9.
12 Sheila Hackett, O. P., *Dominican Women in Texas: From Ohio to Galveston and Beyond*. (D. Armstrong Co., Inc., Houston, Texas, 1986) pp. 58-9.

At first, the Texas wartime economy flourished. Gunrunners and cotton ships sometimes evaded the Northern blockade, but most importantly, Texas beef fed the South. The Yankee victory at Vicksburg (July 4, 1863)–planned by Ohioan, U. S. Grant–ended the Texas cattle sales. The state's economy withered at Yankee hands.

The furnace of war incinerated most of the South. Texas escaped most physical damage, but not the poverty. As the final months of war ground down in Virginia, American troops–many of them Ohioans–began to occupy Texas. They were preparing for a possible invasion of Mexico. Napoleon's abandonment of his colony in 1867 made invasion unnecessary, but Texas was still an occupied, defeated, "part" of the United States.

With Lincoln dead, his merciful policy of reconciliation was buried by Radical Republicans who seized control of the Federal Government during a power struggle with Andrew Johnson. The Ohio-led "Black Republicans" imposed a humiliating military reconstruction package on the South and railroaded the three Black amendments through Congress: the Thirteenth Amendment (1865) ending slavery; the Fourteenth Amendment (1868) granting civil rights and citizenship to freed slaves and depriving Confederate leaders of those citizenship rights. President Johnson infuriated Congress by pardoning Confederate leaders on Christmas Day, 1868. During the subsequent impeachment and trial of the President, the grounds were laid for the final amendment, the Fifteenth (1870), which enfranchised male blacks. These amendments inflamed Southerners and planted deep hatred toward their agents.

Tough Phil Sheridan, a Roman Catholic from Somerset, Ohio, assumed command of the Fifth Military District (Texas) in 1867. Under military pressure, Texas began to reorganize its state government. In Washington, four-star general, U. S. Grant, assumed the presidency, a post he would hold from 1869-1876.

Major General Phil. H. Sheridan
Henry Howe, 1884

Angry but subdued, the ten southern states slowly returned to the Union under new state governments dominated by Northerners (derisively called "Carpetbaggers" in Dixie). Only in 1877, in "an act of real courage," did Rutherford B. Hayes (another Ohio general) withdraw the last of the Federal forces from Florida and Louisiana—the last states to be occupied.[13]

In 1880, Bishop Claude Marie Dubuis retired back to France. The See of Galveston was vacant. In the North, the Catholic Church was enjoying good relations with power brokers. Cardinal James Gibbons cut a high profile of urbanity as he dealt with every American president from Johnson to Harding.[14] The First Vatican Council (1870), called by Pope Leo XIII, renewed the life of the church. In the United States, Catholic colleges sprang up. Catholic University (1889) and a score of Jesuit institutions prepared a sophisticated Catholic leadership. At the same time, a huge immigration of Catholics from Central Europe was transforming the church. Gibbons and his colleagues were determined to Americanize the immigrants and secure respect for the American Roman Catholic Church.

Pope Leo XIII
Catholic Record Society, Columbus, Ohio

The Vatican, weighing the twin sources of hostility in Texas, anti-foreign and anti-Northern, followed Gibbons's call for an American prelate. It sent thirty-six-year-old Nicholas Aloysius Gallagher to act as administrator of the 25,000-member Diocese of Galveston. Sensing the delicate situation, Gallagher insisted on an installation service in Galveston, rather than his home diocese of Columbus, Ohio. He traveled by sea to New Orleans and then to the Texas port city and, in 1882, was consecrated as bishop by his old friend and mentor, Edward M. Fitzgerald, Bishop of Little Rock, Arkansas.[15]

Bishop Gallagher
Pearl Gallagher Reischman

The city that Gallagher observed on arrival was prosperous beyond his comprehension. European investors poured money into the city's

---

13 Bailey, p. 499.
14 Ibid., p. 549.
15 Schlegel, "Religious Vocations," *CRS*, XVIII #8. Fitzgerald had trained the younger priest in Columbus, Ohio.

revival. Northern investors eagerly sank funds into banks and infrastructure. (Bishop Gallagher would invest his portion of the family estate in Galveston business.)[16] Powerful political connections assured that railroads connected the island with the mainland. Congress appropriated 1.5 million dollars to construct Galveston's deep-water port. The "Queen of Texas" became a banking and cultural center for the state. By 1899-1900, it was the leading cotton port in the country. European freighters and New England sailing ships brought incredible products into the bustling city. Transplanted Greek and Portuguese fishermen sent fleets out into the gulf each morning. More European immigrants arrived regularly as ballast in the empty cotton ships.[17] Panna Maria, the oldest Polish settlement in America, thus became a part of the diocese's ethnic mosaic. Nicholas Gallagher sensed great opportunities for the church.

Opportunities and much work. The young bishop was anxious to secure an American staff to augment the aging Vincentians. He turned to his home diocese of Columbus, Ohio. Riding the train back home, Nicholas Aloysius Gallagher, son of John and Mary Ann Brinton Gallagher and a grandson of Edmund and Anna Dorsey Gallagher, recalled his life. A priest for only fourteen years, he had inherited a vast diocese with heavy fiscal and political problems. In his family's story, he found courage to deal with what might come.

Nicholas Gallagher was born on July 19, 1846 in the old stone house of his grandfather, Edmund Gallagher, in the village of Temperanceville, Ohio. He was baptized in the log church of St. Dominic that stood in the graveyard at Beaver, a half-mile from the stone house. His family's fervent Irish Catholicism flourished in the village and in the valley, where most shared that heritage. When he was ten, his pious parents were cheered by the news that the young altar boy

Gallagher Stone House, Temperanceville, Ohio
Courtesy Pearl Gallagher Reischman

---

16 Agnes Gallagher White interview, *Barnesville Enterprise*, July 29, 1990. Mrs. White was born in 1883.
17 Lowery, p. 48.

Gallagher Family Vocations

Edmund Gallagher
& 1) Anna Dorsey ——————————————— **Edmund Gallagher**
                                                        & 2) Lydia McGuinnes

- **John Gallagher**
  & Mary Ann Brinton
  - **Juleann Gallagher**
    Sr. Mary Ann: Dominican Sacred Heart
  - **Bishop Nicholas Gallagher**
    Bishop of Galveston, Texas
  - **William Gallagher**
    & Priscilla Creighton
    - **Angeline Gallagher**
      Sr. Isadore, Sr. Loretto, Florissant, MO
    - **Sarah Gallagher**
      & Joseph Hughes
      - **Constance Hughes**
        & Henry Biedenbach
        - **Sr. Mary Eloise Biedenbach**
          Franciscan Sisters, Manitowoc, WI
  - **Hannah Gallagher**
    & Edward Slevin
    - **Theresa Slevin**
      Sr. Mary Alyosius, O.P.
  - **James Gallagher**
    & Mary Louise Jefferis
    - **Anna Gallagher**
      Sr. Rita, O.P.
  - **Mary Gallagher**
    & Henry Schmueser
    - **Frances Schmueser**
      Sr. Philomena, O.P.
  - **Sarah Gallagher**
    & Michael Malone
    - **Clara Malone**
      Sr. Agnes, O.P.
    - **Genevieve Malone**
      & John Pekari
      - **Carolina Pekari**
        Sr. Mary Robert, O.P.
    - **Mary Ann Malone**
      & William McCourt
      - **Edna Rose McCourt**
        Sr. Mary David, O.P.
      - **Loretta McCourt**
        Sr. Mary Beatrice
- **Christopher Gallagher**
  & Mary Delong
  - **William Gallagher**
    & Barbara Reasbeck
    - **Augustine Gallagher**
      Msgr. Mena, AR

Right branch (from Edmund Gallagher & Lydia McGuinnes):

- **Nicholas Gallagher**
  & Mary Ann Douglas
  - **Ignatius Gallagher**
    & Rose Montag
    - **Clara Gallagher**
      Sr. Mary Charles
    - **Emma Gallagher**
      Sr. Mary Magdalene
      St. Mary Springs

A family gathering when the nuns came home to temperanceville. Standing left to right: Sr. M. David (behind center seated woman), Sr. M. Beatrice, Sr. M. Robert. Sr. Mary Agnes (seated, right corner)
Pearl Gallagher Reischman

Ohio Catholics in Galveston, Texas, 1880-1918

wanted to become a priest. They sent him to the rectory that adjoined their farm to live with their pastor, the burly, energetic French missionary priest, Father John Mary Jacquet.[18]

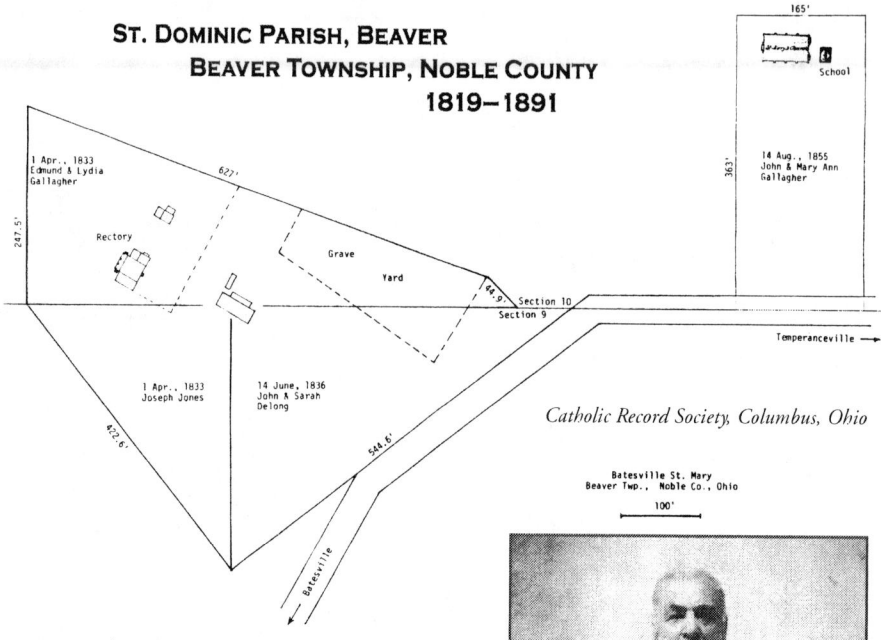

Catholic Record Society, Columbus, Ohio

Father Jacquet (called "Jack-et" by his farmer parishioners) taught Latin and Greek to Nicholas with a smattering of French and German. When the boy entered Mount St. Mary's of the West Seminary in Cincinnati in September of 1862, the sixteen-year-old was well advanced in his class.[19] Known to his classmates as "the future bishop," gentle and studious Nicholas Gallagher would be ordained in 1868 by Bishop Sylvester Rosecrans in Holy Cross Church in Columbus, Ohio,[20] the first priest born in the diocese.

Father John Mary Jacquet
Catholic Record Society, Columbus, Ohio

At twenty-two, the priest was assigned to St. Patrick's Church in Columbus, where he was mentored by Father Edward Fitzgerald. He would serve St. Patrick's–the mother church of English-speaking Catholics in

---

18 Gallagher Genealogy, Pearl Gallagher Reischman. Schlegel, "Vocations," *CRS*, XVIII #8, March 1993.
19 Agnes White.
20 Schlegel, "Vocations," *CRS*, XVIII #8, March 1993.

the city–from 1867-71, 1876-1878, and 1880-81. He was one of few priests in the newly created diocese. Many of the others were foreign-born or converts, like their bishop, Sylvester Horton Rosecrans.

That energetic bishop attempted to create a seminary, St. Aloysius, and he put twenty-six-year-old Father Gallagher in charge. However, also struggling to build St. Joseph's Cathedral on Broad Street, the bishop could not sustain both. All Rosecrans's strength went into creating a cathedral that would serve as a political statement

Sylvester Horton Rosecrans
Catholic Record Society

in Ohio's capital. Designed by his army engineer brother, General William Starke Rosecrans, St. Joseph's rose from the ground in soaring stone–a statement of Catholic permanence in the Protestant city. The day following the cathedral's dedication in 1878, Bishop Rosecrans died.

At the age of thirty-two, Nicholas Gallagher was appointed administrator of the diocese, a post he held until Bishop John A. Watterson assumed office. One year later, in 1881, Gallagher was named administrator of the Diocese of Galveston.[21]

Back in Ohio on a "begging trip," Bishop Gallagher recruited American, or at least Irish-born English speakers, for his Texas diocese. He was following the pattern of all priests in America's mission field since Andrew White had first landed at Baltimore in 1634. Most successfully, he invited twenty nuns of the Dominican Sisters of the Sacred Heart to come to Texas. In September 1882, the sisters left Somerset, Ohio aboard the Newark-Somerset-Straitsville Railroad, bound for Cincinnati. There, the bishop booked a Pullman sleeping car that became "the convent in motion."[22]

The sisters had grown uncomfortable in Ohio. Some problems festered between two congregations of nuns. As the former Diocese Administrator, Gallagher was aware of the issues between the Congregation of the Sacred Heart and their mother community at St. Mary of the Springs. Bishop Watterson did not wish to

Sr. Agnes Magevney

---

21 Schlegel, "Vocations," *CRS*, XVIII #8, March 1993.
22 Ibid. Hackett, *Dominican Women*, p. 55.

let the situation continue. He would not permit two houses of the same order to coexist in his diocese. So Mother Agnes Magevney asked Bishop Gallagher to accept her nuns. He agreed, and financed the move in 1882.[23] Bishop Gallagher also recruited members of his family for his Texas endeavor.[24]

It was a difficult adjustment for the Ohioans; the Texas climate was extreme. Malaria was common, and the Northerners were ignorant of the uses of mosquito netting. Yellow Fever struck; Dengue Fever hit in 1884. Gallagher was stricken and bedridden for three weeks. In 1885, most of the city burned. Through it all, the work of the church continued.[25]

Bishop Gallagher's greatest obstacle was his birthplace; he was "a Carpetbagger" and a man whose two brothers had died in the war wearing the enemy

Back: Hannah Slevin, Juleann Gallagher (nun) Front: Mary Schmuesser, Sarah Malone
Courtesy Pearl Gallagher Reischman

(left to right) Sr. M. Beatrice, Sr. M. David, Sr. M. Robert at diamond Jubilee, February 16, 1986.
Couretsty Pearl Gallagher Reischman

23 See Hackett for sequence of events. The key minutes of the chapter records were removed. The Dominican Sisters in Ohio were an offshoot of the first native American congregation for women, the Dominicans of Springfield, Kentucky, established in 1822. A group of four sisters moved from Kentucky to Somerset, Ohio in 1830, and there established St. Mary's Academy. Sister Rose (Jane Lynch) was one of the first postulants. After a fire destroyed their convent, chapel, and academy in 1866, the community built St. Mary of the Springs, northeast of Columbus.

Natives of Navan, County Meath, the Lynch family had long resided in Zanesville. Sister Rose served as prioress of the Somerset community from 1849-51 and 1855-73. Sister Agnes was the daughter of Eugene Magevney who was once a hedgeschool (illegal) teacher in County Fermanagh, Ireland. Magevney became a wealthy realtor in Memphis. Sister Agnes was born there in 1841. Hackett, *Dominican Women*, pp. 2-3, 14-15. A financial failure caused the new community to move to Somerset in 1879; from there, they moved on to Texas. Schlegel, "The Dominican Sisters of the Sacred Heart and Sacred Heart Academy," *CRS*, XVIII, #6-8, #10.

24 Schlegel, "Vocations," *CRS*, XVIII, #8. Frances Schmuesser mother, Mary, died in Colorado in 1895, and the girl went to Galveston in the care of her uncle, the bishop.

25 Hackett, pp. 66-67.

uniform. The imported nuns were from Somerset, Ohio, the hometown of the occupying general. And the presence of Sister Imelda was a raw wound. The nun was born Mamie Rosecrans in Keokuk County, Iowa, the daughter of Charles Wesley Rosecrans, brother of General William Starke Rosecrans. She was educated at Sacred Heart Academy in Columbus and accepted Catholicism, baptized by her uncle, Bishop Rosecrans, in 1877. At sixteen, she entered the Dominican order. Texicans who had fought against her uncle, the general, did not soon forget.[26]

Maj. Gen. William S. Rosecrans

The most outrageous thing was that Sister Imelda taught in the bishop's school for black children. Such a school had been his priority since elevation. One other had briefly existed: St. Elizabeth's School for Colored Children. It had been established by the Sisters of Mercy, but abandoned in 1882 after only one year. Gallagher encouraged the Dominicans to open another school. In September of 1887, Holy Rosary School for Colored Children opened. The following year, when the parish church was dedicated, Gallagher served as the pastor. The Ohio nuns operated the school until 1897, when the interracial Sisters of the Holy Family arrived from New Orleans to assume charge.[27]

Henriette Delille, "a free woman of color," established the order in 1841 to serve the African American community. When Henrietta died in 1862, she was known as the one "'who for the love of Jesus Christ had made herself the humble servant of the slave.'" Her order continued that mission under Bishop Gallagher's direction in Galveston.[28] Holy Rosary and St. Mary's Seminary would remain as permanent markers of the role of Nicholas Aloysius Gallagher in Galveston public life.

---

26 Edmund Gallagher died at Atlanta on July 31, 1864. William B. Gallagher died at Bolivar, Tennessee on March 10, 1865. *Official Roster of Civil War Veterans*, "Soldiers of the State of Ohio in the War of the Rebellion 1861-1865," Cincinnati, OH, 1886. Donald Schlegel, "The Dominican Sisters of the Sacred Heart," *CRS*, VIII #10, October 1993.
27 Hackett, p. 64.
28 German-born Father Phillip Keller was appointed as pastor in 1889, and with the funding of Germans, worked for twenty-four years to erect a church, convent, and boarding school. The Holy Rosary School was staffed by the Sisters of the Holy Family until 1979. In 1927, the parish high school became the first high school for black Catholics in Texas. It closed in 1941. Internet source. *Holy Rosary Industrial School*, Notes. Typescript. Sisters of the Holy Family Motherhouse Archives, New Orleans, La.

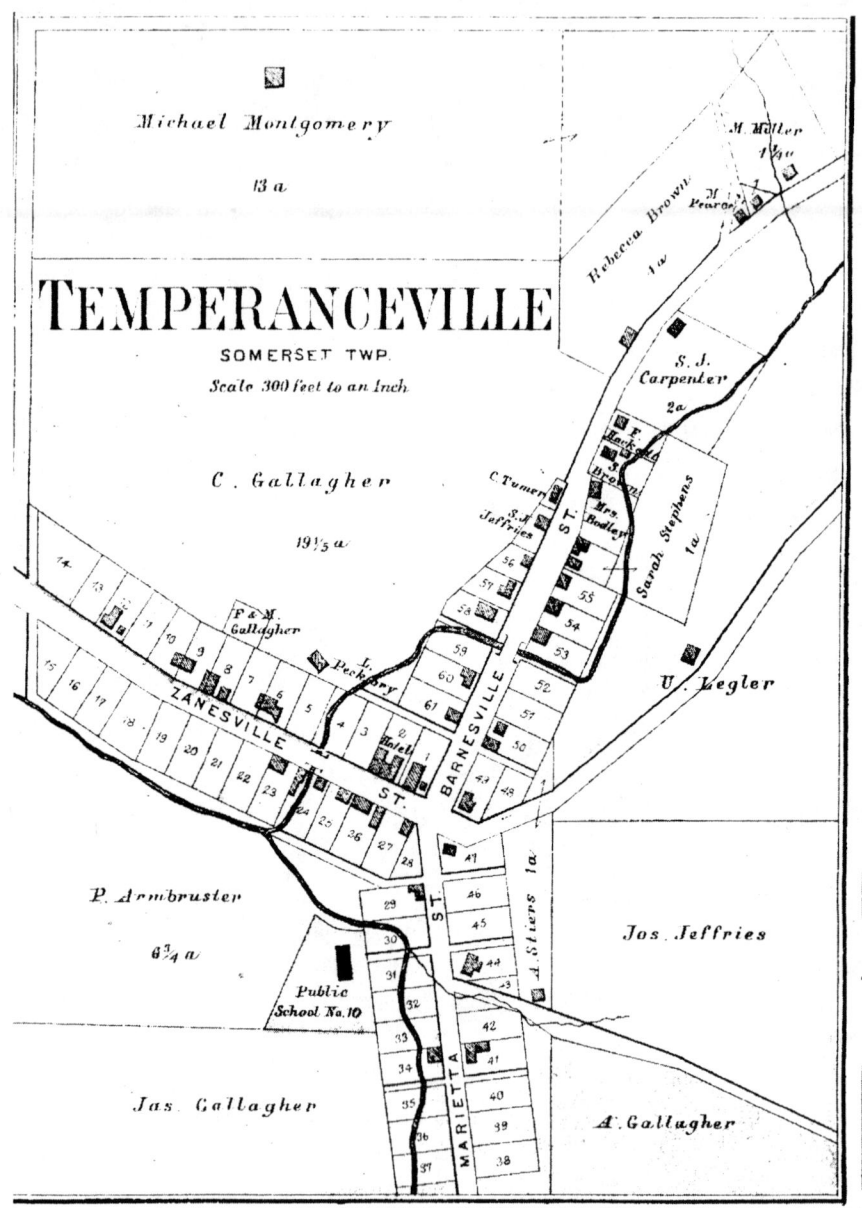

Reprinted from *Atlas of Belmont County, Ohio,* 1888
Courtesy Guernsey County District Public Library, Cambridge, Ohio

    Father Otto P. Trogus stepped out of the rectory and walked quietly to his church, St. Mary's, on the corner of the "Y" which marked Zanesville, Barnesville, and Marietta Roads in the village of Temperanceville, Ohio. The streets were quiet. It was before the 6 a.m. mass. He could expect silence, birds calling, the lowing of the villagers' cows, but by seven o'clock,

Temperanceville, Ohio, circa 1901. St. Mary Catholic Church is in foreground, next to a field with sheaves of hay.

the streets would be buzzing.

    Soon the tobacco tying shops would open and women and children would begin their tasks. William McCourt would purchase tobacco, and Clement Poulton would begin his day of making cigars, as would William C. Poulton. Anthony Pekari happily worked away, reveling in his reputation as "the professional baseball pitcher and wonderful cigar roller."[29]

St. Mary Catholic Church
Temperanceville, Ohio
Courtesy Pearl Gallagher Reischman

    Temperanceville was growing, as were most American villages and small towns in the 1900's. There was a decided shift to urban centers, no matter how small. Villagers had acknowledged that in 1891 when, after years of talk and a destructive fire at their brick church at Beaver, they moved their center of worship into Robert Gallagher's village, dragging the old foundation stones by oxen. It was a shock to those who for years had worshipped at the old site. Sister Mary Isadore wrote to her sister, Mary Gallagher, remarking

---

29 *Barnesville Enterprise*, February 13, 1897.

that their grandmother, Mary Ann Brinton Gallagher, "must feel lonely since the church has been moved to Temperanceville."[30] The Beaver graveyard endured, but only memories remained of the second Catholic Church building in the valley. Now, farm families walked the miles to Temperanceville for mass.

Temperanceville boasted a hotel (full since the oil and gas boom hit the valley in 1901), a blacksmith and carpenter shops, and "Charles Slevin was thinking of going into the picture business."[31] There was a special air

The altar at St. Mary's, Temperanceville, Ohio.

Courtesy Pearl Gallagher Reischman

of community in the close-knit families that comprised the village and its environs. It was distinctly different from the German-ness of nearby Calais and Miltonsburg.

The mass bell sounded and Father Trogus approached the altar. His parishioners were extremely proud of the ornate Gothic-style altarpiece. It had been purchased from the German congregation at St. Mary's in Fulda when they remodeled their church. James D. Gallagher stepped out of the old stone house of the Gallaghers and entered the church. He slid into his familiar pew and once again, as he had for nearly thirty years,

---

30 Letter in possession of Ruth Fox. The second church (1855-1891) was to the east of the original log church. Schlegel.

31 "Temperanceville," Bruce Yarnall, *Belmont County History*, (Walsworth Press, Inc., Salem, West Virginia, 1988) p. 29.

Sr. Mary Agnes and Sarah Gallagher Malone
Courtesy Pearl Gallagher Reischman

glanced around at familiar faces: his sister, Sarah Louise Gallagher Malone, Robert Gallagher–son of Christopher, cousins Ignatius and Rose Montag Gallagher. The progeny of pioneers Edmund, Anna, and Lydia Gallagher filled St. Mary's daily,[32] but others had begun a migration to larger towns.

Tobacco was "king of the hill" in the valley. Enormous amounts were raised and cured in drying sheds, which dotted the landscape, their vertical slats pushed out to provide cross-ventilation. The Poultons manufactured cigars in the village; in Barnesville, Anna Gallagher Heed's husband, Jacob, had a cigar factory. Their sons made Heed Brothers Cigar Plant famous with an invention that revolutionized the industry. Eighty people–a third of them women–worked to turn out thousands of Snow Flake Stogies each week.[33]

Parishioners of St. Mary Catholic Church, Temperanceville, Ohio, circa 1929.
Courtesy Pearl Gallagher Reischman

---

32 Gallagher Genealogies, Pearl Reischman.
33 Ibid.

Anna Heed's cousins took the trade to Columbus. Eugene Gallagher and brother Frank founded the Eugene Gallagher & Brother cigar factory. Their brother, Augustine, moved to St. Louis and became the president of the Modern Miller company. Ignatius remained on the Batesville farm and married Rose Montag, sister of Father George Montag.

Their father, Nicholas Gallagher, had lived his life on that farm, but spent his final illness in Columbus; he was buried from Sacred Heart Church and interred in Mount Calvary Cemetery. His second wife, Charlotte Foster, and his children, Mrs. J. F. McNulty, Anna, and her brothers, gave thanks for his life of faith, and for the conversion of their mother, Margaret Douglas, who was baptized before her death in 1843.[34]

Sundays after mass in Temperanceville, it was the custom to visit the graves of loved ones. Father Trogus walked with his parishioners to the Beaver cemetery and led them in prayer. They stood amid the tombstones of Gallaghers, O'Brians, DeLongs, Butlers, Slevins, Kerrigans, and Lowes. The original clans through generations of intermarriages had created strong family ties—and strong ties to St. Mary's parish.

Pearl Gallagher Reischman

View from Temperanceville Hill

Riding his horse up Temperanceville Hill towards Barnesville on Sunday afternoon, Father Trogus pondered the difference between the two communities. He was to visit with Father William Robbin that afternoon, and the two priests found that they always fell into the same

---

34 Reischman, Obituaries. The priest wrote "*Deo gratias*" beside this entry. St. Mary's Baptismal Records.

conversation—it was as if they inhabited different worlds.

Barnesville was, by far, the most vibrant town. The railroad tied the community to Ohio River traffic a scant twenty miles to the east. The town boasted a number of small factories: Barnesville Glass Company, Watt Mining Carwheel company, Atkinson's Woolen Mill, Hanlon Brothers Printing, and the cigar factories. All of these attracted its share of foreign workers to Barnesville. By 1916, a small portion of the population was immigrant. Many of them worked in the town's key industry: cultivation of strawberries.

An entrepreneur had experimented with commercially growing the berries in 1860; by 1888, farmers were harvesting a thousand bushels a day, and shipping eight hundred bushels to restaurants in Chicago.[35] Hundreds of acres were devoted to berry cultivation and this attracted farm labor. Some of the workers were Roman Catholics and they found themselves in a hostile climate.

Barnesville's original immigrants had been Scotch-Irish, with surrounding farms settled by Quakers from North Carolina, Pennsylvania, and Maryland. Other scattered Protestant denominations settled into the rolling hills of Belmont County. All of them harbored a traditional hostility towards Catholicism. The few Catholics they met were Irish immigrants working on the National Road or the railroads, or the Catholics from Temperanceville who tended to "stay over the hill."

The Know Nothing phenomenon of 1854 accelerated the prejudice: Catholics were associated with immigration, crime, and alcohol. However, Robert Gallagher, who platted the village of Temperanceville in 1842, was a strong Temperance man. Total Abstinence was an important movement in the Catholic Church at the time. Father John W. Brummer of Batesville, who oversaw the few Catholics in Barnesville, wrote to Archbishop John Purcell on May 24, 1855 about the conditions he found in the town:

> Concerning the widow with six children I sent to Cincinnati, I beg to state that it was in my view the best I could advise her to do in order to save her children from evident spiritual distruction [sic]. You have there your good schools with Catholic example and its salutary influence on young minds & probably also less difficulties for their temporal support than in this small fanatical place, where she lived. I have grown up in Cincinnati & am here long enough to know that cincinati [sic] is by 99

---

35 Henry Howe, *Historical Collections of Ohio*, V. I (C. J. Krenbiel & Co., Cincinnati, Ohio, 1904) pp. 324-5.

degrees more safe for a widow with a house full of children that must be instructed & raised for heaven than out in these degraded, bigoted & vicious little towns in the country filled with hatred of Catholics & other methods of distruction [sic] and impurities. What, I beg to ask, would become of a Catholic & perhaps careless widow with six already sadly neglected children, & poor & alone in such a place as Barnesville?[36]

Inhospitable as it might be, the railroads and the glassworks and the farms brought Catholic workers to Barnesville. Irishman Michael Welsh began working in 1861 as a laborer on the Baltimore & Ohio Railroad. His six sons–Michael H., John R., Charles T., William A., Martin E., and Joseph G.–would grow up to become engineers on that same line. The seventh son, James P., was a telegraph operator. The priest from Temperanceville sometimes said a home mass at the house of Michael Barrett on South Broadway. The few Catholics bought a lot on South Hill in 1871 and began the foundation for a church, but the work languished. After years of struggle, Father George Montag and his parishioners managed to raise their church. It was dedicated on September 29, 1889.

> *The Catholic Columbian* of October 5, 1889 had this to say: 'Father Montag's pretty little Church at Barnesville was dedicated by Bishop Watterson last Sunday. There must have been twelve hundred or fifteen hundred present. Of these the church would hold but 300. In order to reach the crowd, the Bishop preached the dedicatory sermon from the front steps of the edifice. The High Mass was sung by Father Montag, who with Rev. J. Tuohey after the Mass assisted the Bishop in the administration of the Sacrament of Confirmation to a class of fourteen. Of these two are adult converts. Exercises of the day began at 9:30 in the morning and did not close until 3 o'clock in the afternoon.'[37]

A decade later, the church was destroyed by a lightning-induced fire. Newly-arrived Father Dan Coffey, the first resident pastor, found his church a heap of burned timbers, broken glass, and scattered bricks. Walking through the untended cemetery next to the pile of rubble, Coffey sought the determination to begin again. He found little help from the diocese. In 1899, it was so heavily in debt that Archbishop Elder of Cincinnati wrote to Rome to the Sacred Congregation for the Propagation of the Faith to propose that the thirty-year-old Columbus Diocese be

---

36 Quoted in John H. Forbes and Rev. Bede Hansen, "History of the Church of the Assumption," *CRS*, XV, #8, August 1990. Quote courtesy of the University of Notre Dame Archives, Archdiocese of Cincinnati Archives Collection. *Barnesville Enterprise*, June 25, 1961.
37 Forbes and Hansen, *CRS*, XV #8, August 1990. Quotation courtesy of *Catholic Times*.

suppressed and reattached to Cincinnati. Among those owed money was Mrs. Mary Ann Gallagher, to whom the diocese owed $454 and $463.18 of interest. No payment had been possible for twelve years.[38]

However, with the arrival of Bishop Henry Moeller in August of 1900, a hardheaded German regime resulted in the apportionment of the debt throughout the diocese, and a resulting manageable situation.[39] In Barnesville, Father Coffey purchased two lots on Broadway Street in May of 1901, and bought the old Presbyterian Church; this was cut in two and moved down the street and reestablished as Assumption parish.

The first festive occasion in the new church was the wedding of Michael Gallagher and Matilda DeLong. The buoyant Irish priest, the happy bride and groom, the best man, William Gallagher, and the Maid of Honor, Josephine Creighton, then moved to a dinner party at the home of the groom's parents, Robert and Bridget Creighton Gallagher.

In 1902, Father Coffey gave first communion to twenty-five children. Catholicism had established a toehold in Barnesville. Parish life revolved around weddings, first communions, and funerals–one of the saddest being that of Tillie DeLong Gallagher, dead in July 1905, the victim of tuberculosis. She was laid to rest on the South Hill, as her husband Michael held the hands of two toddlers.[40]

Shortly after the 5 a.m. mass on Christmas Day, 1914, the church was again destroyed by fire. Originating in the furnace room, it roared through the wooden structure, threatening the feed mill and cider mill across the street. Volunteer firemen could not save the church. Even in a period of extreme anti-Catholic rhetoric, the fire appeared to be accidental. Barnesville's small faith community sacrificed and scrimped and, on June 2, 1915, Bishop James Hartley laid the cornerstone for the new church. The first mass would be celebrated on Thanksgiving Day.[41]

Father Trogus and Father Robbin shared a hot meal and companionship, and marveled at their different circumstances. Barnesville was infused with anti-Catholic bigotry; Temperanceville remained a bastion of faith. It seemed clear that residence in the larger town led to intermarriage and an occasional "falling away" from the church.

In the family of Christopher and Mary DeLong Gallagher, their

---

38 *Catholic Times*, February 26, 1993. "The Diocesan Debt in 1899," *CRS* XVII #8, August 1992.
39 Forbes and Hansen, *CRS* XV #8, August 1990.
40 Assumption Parish Scrapbook, Pearl Reischman. Robert was the son of Christopher and Mary DeLong Gallagher.
41 Assumption Church Clipping Book.

daughter Ann married Jacob Heed, a brick-maker, cigar maker and a native of Loudon County, Virginia. He was also a strong Mason. He and his wife became members of Barnesville's Methodist Church. All of Ann's other siblings retained the ancient faith, but her sister Elizabeth Meyer's daughter Minnie, who was living in Barnesville with her Aunt Ann, married M. O. Fowler (manager of the White Front Restaurant) in the Methodist parsonage in 1895. At her death, her obituary mentioned that she was "a near relative [cousin] of Bishop Nicholas Gallagher, eminent in the Catholic Church."[42]

More serious were defections of members of the DeLong family. Converted to Catholicism in the first generation of residency in Ohio, the DeLongs were pillars of the Beaver church, but dissension occurred when James, Jr. began to participate in politics. James married Sarah Gallagher (daughter of Edmund) in St. Dominic's in Beaver in 1835. Sarah died young, leaving two boys, Edward and Thomas, who were taken in by Dr. George Gildea and his wife, Margaret. In 1849, James, Jr. remarried. His bride was Lucinda Anderson, daughter of William and Jane Frew Wilson Anderson. William was the United Presbyterian minister in Fairview in Guernsey County. He and his brother, John, were prominent Scotch-Irish clergymen. James and Lucinda's seven children were baptized in her church.

As James's political career flourished (he was Guernsey County's first Probate Court Judge, holding office from 1852-1858), he built alliances with Willson Shannon, Ohio's first native-born governor and a native of Belmont County. James named his son Willson Shannon DeLong; his daughter, Jane, married the governor's son, Willson Shannon, Jr. Through these political connections, James found political power. When the Republican Party began its drive to prominence, James broke with Shannon's Democrats, and became a spearhead of Republicans in Belmont County. He was rewarded with a consulate to Morocco in 1860. In his obituary, DeLong's family ignored his natal Catholicism and emphasized his Protestant Huguenot background.[43]

In the age of the American Protective Association and its "Rum, Romanism, and Rebellion" banner, such defection from Catholicism for a political career was not uncommon. James G. Blaine, perennial

---

42 Assumption Church Clipping Book. Obituaries. Raymond F. Stephens
43 William G. Wolfe, *Guernsey County, Ohio* (W. G. Wolfe, Cambridge, Ohio, 1943) p. 94. DeLong Genealogy.

presidential candidate, abandoned his Catholic birth, and his connections with the Catholic Gillespies of Brownsville, Pennsylvania and the Ewings of Lancaster, Ohio–all for political gain.

Of James DeLong's children, only Edward remained Catholic. Another son, Thomas, became a Methodist minister. Edward was raised and nurtured by Dr. G. W. Gildea and encouraged to study medicine. Dr. Edward DeLong married Mary Gallagher, daughter of Robert and Elizabeth, and remained Catholic. However, their sons, John–baptized in St. Mary's on August 25, 1877–and Frank became virulent anti-Catholic preachers.[44]

Father Trogus shared a clipping with Father Robbin.
> Now in 1914 an anti-Catholic Methodist preacher is holding out in Roscoe, Illinois and delivering such treatises as "Is the Roman Catholic Church American." He is the brother to the notorious Rev. Frank DeLong, Baptist preacher of Indiana whose history has been written by Fr. Noll of the *Sunday Visitor*, Huntington, Ind. Both are brothers of James DeLong of Temperanceville.
> —Eugene F. Owens, March 1914[45]

The two priests in Barnesville shook their heads. How could two communities be so different? And how in the world had Temperanceville, a Catholic community, come to be? How did people settle Belmont County, Ohio? And how did such a minority as Roman Catholics come to be in Ohio?

---

44 DeLong Genealogy.
45 *The Catholic Messenger*, Davenport, Iowa, April 2, 1914. John DeLong had challenged a priest in Beloit, Wisconsin to debate on Catholicism, but when the priest accepted, DeLong refused to honor his challenge. Ibid.

Chapter Two

The Catholic Church in Colonial America
English and Irish Immigrants

Thirty-eight-year-old Father John J. Carroll sat on the veranda of his mother's plantation at Rock Creek, Maryland (near present-day Washington, DC) and rested his eyes. The priest was weary from travel and from the catastrophic events of the past year. Persistent efforts by European monarchs had convinced Pope Clement XIV to suppress the Jesuit order. In 1773, the Jesuit educational institutions in Europe fell before a whirlwind of eager government seizures.[1] Carroll's alma mater, St. Omer in northern France, and Bruges, where he taught, were confiscated. In the face of suppression, the orphaned Jesuits fled a hostile Europe. John Carroll returned home to the family haven in the American colonies.

Carroll was a stranger in his own land—absent for twenty-six years. Sitting on the veranda, he had time to contemplate the story of Roman Catholics and their church as it existed in the English "new world" and in the "old world"—the Ireland of his father, Daniel Carroll, and the England of his mother, Eleanor Darnall. In England, they were "the recusants."

Bishop Carroll's birthplace
Catholic Record Society, Columbus, Ohio

The English Recusants

In England, the turmoil in church life—begun by Henry VIII's schism with Rome—only deepened during the long reign of his daughter, Elizabeth I.

---

1 The Jesuit order would be restored in 1814. The only state which did not suppress the order was White Russia.

Against the background of Protestant Reformation, the Catholic Counter-Reformation, and Europe's religious wars, "patriotism" in England became equated with Protestantism, especially after the failed invasion attempt of the Spanish Armada in 1588.

When Henry VIII ascended the throne, the Roman Catholic Church in England was in need of reform, but Henry's political need for a divorce led him into schism from Rome. His Anglican Church, however, retained almost all Catholic forms. Even so, by 1540 Henry had confiscated and redistributed all monastic lands in a bid to secure the support of the nobility. A secret Protestant movement grew within the church and seized control of its hierarchy during the brief reign of Edward VI. At the boy-king's death, Henry's eldest daughter, the ardently Roman Catholic Mary Tudor, reversed these policies and reinstated the Roman clergy, but she could not recover the lost property. These "Marianist priests" worked to save any fragment of the old church from the Protestantizers. Protestant martyrs now went to the scaffolds where Roman Catholic martyrs had once died.[2]

Henry VIII of England
Hans Holbein, 1540

Elizabeth I of England
Hans Holbein, 1560

During the long reign (1558-1603) of Mary's half-sister, Elizabeth I, a sea-change in religious history occurred. Recognizing a Spanish threat, Elizabeth and her ministers sought to further unify the country. Her ministers rammed Acts of Supremacy and Uniformity through Parliament (1559). Those who refused to conform–radical

---

2   Between July 22 and November 27, 1588, twenty-one priests, eleven laymen, and one woman were executed. By 1603, sixty-one would die. These English martyrs, including the butcher's wife, St. Margaret Clitheroe, were canonized by Pope John Paul II. Some 300 Protestants were martyred in Mary's reign. "England," *New Catholic Encyclopedia*, First Edition, V. V, p. 359. Antonia Fraser, *Faith and Treason: The Story of the Gunpowder Plot*, (Nan A. Talese, Doubleday: New York, 1996) p. 35.

Protestants such as Quakers and Roman Catholics—were considered enemies of the state. Elizabethan England became the scene of a bitter struggle by English Roman Catholics to survive. This situation bred an underground.

A portion of England's high nobility retained "the Old Faith." They were too rich and powerful to be challenged. As long as they and the Roman Catholic gentry did not threaten the civil order—or appear to do so—they were left alone, as were their dependents. Their numbers were tiny; one estimate puts 1,500 "recusants" in all of England. Arch-Conservative Lancashire's Anglican clergy were "sympathetic to the recusant priests," and in Yorkshire, recusancy had "a stronghold," but recusants in that county were estimated at not more than one-percent.[3]

The tiny, but prominent, Roman Catholic upper class created a "vast Catholic cousinage" through marriages. Marianist priests either lived in such families as "servants" or traveled from safe-house to safe-house through thirty-six counties. Twenty-four of these counties, and London, are known to have had houses with "priest holes" to harbor them. In 1596, as many as fifty of the priests were still functioning. These Marianist priests kept the faith alive in England.[4]

Two types of Roman Catholics emerged in the realm. "Church papists" attended the Church of England services, but refused communion. It was common for such families to have the head "conform," while the wife and children did not. Others, the "Recusants," refused to participate in the Anglican worship, although an act of uniformity in 1581 and the Act Against Popish Recusants in 1593 forced them to risk real financial punishment for the refusal. Both kinds of Catholics kept up the distinct cultural traditions associated with Roman Catholicism: fast and feast days, and pilgrimages. The revered pilgrimage to the Holy Well of St. Winifred of Flintshire continued uninterrupted throughout the religious struggle.[5]

English refugees on the continent added to the struggle. In France, Cardinal William Allen (former principal of St. Mary's Hall, Oxford) launched a reform of the English remnant of the church under the

---

3 Christopher Haig, *Reformation and Resistance in Tudor Lancashire* (Cambridge University Press: Cambridge, 1975) pp. 266-7. Hugh Averline in D. J. Steel and Edward R. Samuel, *Sources for Roman Catholic and Jewish Genealogy and Family History* (Phillimore Publishing: London and Chichester, 1974) p. 813. *"recusare"*–to refuse.
4 Patrick McGrath and Joy Rowe, "The Elizabethan Priests: Their Harbourers and Helpers," *Recusant History*, pp. 216-7, 209.
5 Steel, p. 807. Edward Norman, *Roman Catholicism in England from the Elizabethan Settlement to the Second Vatican Council* (Oxford University Press: London, 1985) p. 26.

Cardinal William Allen

guidelines of the Council of Trent. He founded the college at Douai in 1565. A hundred exiled Oxford faculty and students formed a college at Louvain. These two institutions joined the English colleges that functioned in Rome and in Valladolid, Seville, and Madrid in Spain. In all, by the end of the century, some forty English Roman Catholic colleges, monasteries, and convents would be functioning on the continent. These "seminary priests" would return to England as missionaries, stirring the political and religious situation in their homeland.[6]

The Elizabethan government reacted to this persistent and stubborn underground by enacting the Act of 1585, which declared that any priests ordained abroad who returned to England were guilty of high treason. Such men were ordered to leave the country within forty days, or forfeit their lives. Educating a child abroad was also forbidden. Some powerful families conformed at that time, but others, such as the Weld family of Lulworth, Dorsetshire, confounded authorities by their loyalty to Roman Catholicism. Seminary priests, mostly Jesuits and Franciscans, continued to slip into England.[7]

The "seminary priests," animated by the more stringent Catholicism of the Counter-Reformation, forced church papists and recusants *to choose*: people were required to live their Catholic faith with vigor–in dangerous political times. The practitioners of the Old Faith already had a sense "of belonging to a distinct and universal religious society"–but that society was also "in some large measure sustained through the example of martyrdom." The "early seminary priests did frighten officials into tracking recusants down...." Rather than be extinguished by persecution, recusancy expanded after 1578 through the example of martyrdom. About half of the missionary priests who arrived in England were arrested and about half of those were executed. In 1581, St. Edmund Campion was executed. His friend, Robert Parsons, escaped to the continent and became the driving force in the English missionary effort. Parsons founded St. Omer near Calais in 1593. It became the heart of the movement.[8]

---

6 Steel, p. 807. Some 5,000 English men and women entered religious life between 1598 and 1640. Caroline Hibbard, "Early Stuart Catholicism: Revision and Re-revision," *Journal of Modern History* 52 March 1980, V. I: pp. 10, 11, fn 28.
7 McGrath, p. 211. Steel, p. 815. Hibbard, p. 10, fn 18. Norman, p. 17.
8 Hibbard, p. 19. Norman, pp. 15, 21, 16. Christopher Haig, "The Fall of a Church or the Rise of a Sect?: Post Reform Catholicism in England," *The Historical Journal*, V. 21, #1, 1978, pp. 268-9.

Upon Elizabeth's death in 1603, the English throne passed to her second cousin, James of Scotland, son of the very Catholic Mary, Queen of Scots. English Roman Catholics expected a respite and "a massive increase in recusancy [occurred] in Lancashire and Yorkshire." In 1603, there were perhaps 35,000 recusants in the country. About 4% of Lancashire and .8% of Yorkshire were recusants. However, instead of leniency, James I–who expected to control a uniform state church–ordered all Jesuits and other priests out of the country and re-imposed the fines for recusancy.⁹

A woodcut depicting the conspirators of "The Gunpowder Plot."

On November 5, 1605, a rag-tag confederation of Catholic gentlemen attempted to blow up Parliament as the King convened it. This Gunpowder Plot brought a catastrophic reaction down on Catholics in England. A modern writer declares that the plotters "were terrorists and they were defeated. They were not good men...." But, because of their folly, their co-religionists paid dearly. No longer could a recusant practice law, serve as an officer in the military, act as an executor of a will, or be the guardian of a minor. A child educated abroad had to conform or surrender an estate to the next Protestant heir. Catholics could not receive university degrees. They could not vote. They were ordered to marry, baptize, and bury in the Anglican Church. They would be enemies of the state if they refused.¹⁰

---

9 Alexandra Walsham, *Church Papists: Catholicism, Conformity and Confessional Polemic in Early Modern England* (The Royal Historical Society: The Boydell Press, 1993) p. 76. Haig, *Reformation and Resistance*, p. 275. Fraser, pp. 81, 85.
10 Fraser, p. 283, 295. Steel, p. 815.

English and Irish Immigrants

George Calvert
First Lord Baltimore
*Courtesy
Maryland Department,
Enoch Pratt Free Library*

The year that Edmund Campion entered England on his ill-fated mission (1580), George Calvert was born to an old and substantial family in Yorkshire. As a young man, Calvert rose rapidly in government service, becoming the private secretary to Sir Robert Cecil, chief minister of James I in 1606. In 1624, Calvert consciously ended his ascent in English circles by publicly announcing his conversion to Roman Catholicism. Too forthright to play the role of a church papist, Calvert spent the rest of his life seeking a safe haven for his co-religionists. However, Charles I maintained a friendship with Calvert. He appointed him as the first Lord Baltimore and paid off a debt to Calvert by granting him a proprietary colony in the English American colonies. His son, Cecil, the second Lord Baltimore, assumed its settlement.[11]

A proprietor acted in place of the king; thus, Baltimore could override existing anti-Roman Catholic laws and allow the faith to be openly practiced in his colony of Maryland (named for the Queen, Henrietta Marie). With a capital located at St. Mary's settlement on the peninsula formed by the Potomac River and Chesapeake Bay, Maryland quickly flourished. Its economy was based on the cultivation of tobacco by African slaves and white indentured servants.

Lord Baltimore enlisted the services of the Jesuits for his colony. They were to come as "gentlemen adventurers" and establish plantations to pay their way. In 1634, Andrew White SJ (who had studied at Vallodolid and Seville and had been a missionary in England), John Altham SJ, and Brother Thomas Gervase sailed with the other colonists on the *Ark and the Dove* to America. They were the first non-French or Spanish priests to work in North America.[12]

Ministering to arriving English and Irish Roman Catholics—and Piscatoway Indians, whose language he learned and into which he translated sermons—Father White soon became known as "The Apostle of Maryland." Many of the English were aristocrats or gentry, tired of living

---

11 George Calvert was a member of the London Company in 1629 and sought to plant a Catholic settlement in Virginia. He would not take the test oath, involving the denial of transubstantiation. John Tracy Ellis, *Catholics in Colonial America* (Benedictine Studies: Helicon, Baltimore, 1965) pp. 321, 324.

12 James Hennessey, "Catholics in the English Colonies," *Encyclopedia of American Religious Experience* (Charles Scribner's Sons: New York, 1988) p. 347. Thomas T. McAvoy, *A History of the Catholic Church in the United States* (University of Notre Dame Press: Notre Dame, Indiana, 1969) p. 11.

the recusant life in England. In 1633, Cuthbert Fenwick of Langshawes, Northumberland–who bore the bloodlines of the recusant Fenwicks and Powers–arrived to serve as steward to Thomas Cornwallys, Baltimore's Roman Catholic governor. Fenwick was soon elected to the colonial assembly and granted St. Cuthbert's Manor in Resurrection Hundred in 1651. St. Cuthbert's became a center of Catholic lay and clerical society.

Baltimore and the Jesuits wrangled over the gift of a plantation–St. Inigoes ("the oldest Catholic foundation with permanent existence . . . within the limits of the thirteen original states."). Fenwick then became the trustee for the Jesuit lands in 1641. This system of trusteeship would continue until 1792.[13]

Cecil Calvert
Second Lord Baltimore
*Courtesy
Maryland Department,
Enoch Pratt Free Library*

Hoping to secure a positive reaction from Protestants in England and Maryland, Lord Baltimore made extraordinary efforts to provide religious freedom for all. However, Protestant immigration soon outstripped Catholic; indentured servants became independent settlers, and Catholics once more became a minority–but an able and aristocratic one, as in the motherland. In 1641, of the four hundred colonists in Maryland, only one hundred were Catholic.[14]

In that year, a church clerical crisis engulfed England and led to savage civil war. Charles I's French connections–his wife and her Catholic chaplains–were a part of the causes of the upheaval; rigidly Protestant Parliament grabbed for power. The king was beheaded; his children were exiled to France. Oliver Cromwell was named as Lord Protector with almost dictatorial powers. Actions against Jesuits and recusants became intense.

In 1647 in Maryland, Puritans sacked the property of the Jesuits and of Governor Cornwallys. Fathers Andrew White and Thomas Copley were taken in chains to England, but eventually were released on a technicality. Three other Jesuits fled to Virginia, but died within two years under unexplained circumstances. There were no priests in the "Catholic Colony." The Jesuits returned in 1648, but fled to Virginia in 1655 when

---

13 H. S. Spalding SJ., *Catholic Colonial Maryland, A Sketch* (Bruce Publishing Company: Milwaukee, Wisc., 1931) np, frontispiece. Edwin Warfield Beitzell, *The Jesuit Missions of St. Mary's County, Maryland*, Second Edition, (Privately published: Abell, Md., 1976) p. 18.
14 Hennessey, p. 349.

St. Inigoes Manor was sacked. The Puritan-dominated Assembly repealed Lord Baltimore's Toleration Act. This was mitigated slightly when Baltimore was reinstated in 1658. However, because so few priests were in Maryland during this and succeeding decades, Maryland colonists became used to making do with their prayer services and retaining a faith community without the sacraments. "Maryland Catholics trusted only one another."[15]

Over the next few decades, Catholics declined in number and became "identified with an upper social stratum." By 1677, Quakers led the denominational groups, with Catholics lagging in last place. The Catholic First Families created "a vast cousinage" as they had in England. Newtown Manor School, which had operated irregularly since 1655, stabilized in 1677. In 1681, the first alumni entered St. Omer, thus tying Maryland Catholics with the "tiny, but well-to-do English Catholic community." Robert Brooke became the first native Marylander to join the Jesuits. In all, some forty-nine Americans became seminarians and half would return home as priests. Thirty-three colonial women joined the European English convents. In these ways, the faith life flourished.[16]

Charles II was restored to the throne in 1660 and a more *laissez faire* climate permeated religious life in England. Anglican clergy usually entered birth records administered by Roman priests, if the proper fees were paid. Catholic marriages were generally recognized until the Marriage Act of 1753; then, two ceremonies were routinely conducted. Relative tranquility evaporated, however, with the wild adventures of Titus Oates. Oates had been a Catholic seminarian in Spain, but was expelled, as he had been from two Protestant colleges. In 1678, Oates wrote and preached of a vast Jesuit plot to overthrow the English government. The ensuing hysteria resulted in the execution of seventeen seminary priests and the incarceration until death of twenty-three others. Eleven of the forty Catholic peers were imprisoned; Lords Stafford and Petrie were executed. St. Oliver Plunkett, Archbishop of Armagh, Ireland, was executed at Tyburn. The Test Act of 1678 (which required denial of

Titus Oates

---

13. Beitzell, p. 24.
p. 350. Beitzell, p. 39.

Transubstantiation) removed Roman Catholics from the House of Lords (they had been expelled from Commons a century before). The Titus Oates episode sent ripples of fear to the Catholics in the colonies.[17] Worse was to come.

When Charles II died in 1685, his widowed brother, James–a very open Roman Catholic–was permitted to assume the throne. Barely two decades away from bloody civil war, Parliamentary forces had no taste for reopening religious wounds, and decided to tolerate the aged Roman Catholic king. But James remarried and, within a year, his French Catholic wife produced a son–a Roman Catholic heir to the English throne.

Amid innuendo and intrigue (a Jesuit was supposed to have fathered the child), James's enemies forced the Royal Family to flee, thus triggering three generations of "risings" in the name of "The Pretenders." James's adult and thoroughly Protestant daughter, Mary, and her husband, Dutch Stadholder William of Orange, became rulers of Britain as a result of a bargain struck between them and Parliamentary leaders during this "Glorious Revolution." Soon a fierce and persistent anti-Catholic policy was initiated, both in England and in its colonies–namely Ireland and North America.[18]

During the Stuart flight, a large number of Roman Catholic nobles and gentry left England. The new Williamite government vigorously enforced the penal laws against Catholics. The laws were devised to force recusants into financial ruin. Anti-Catholic legislation accelerated under William III, with Catholics barred from the legal profession and their land subjected to double taxation in 1692. The laws struck at the nobility by forbidding possession of a horse worth more than 5£. A reward of 100£ was offered for information leading to the conviction of a priest. Some of the remaining old Catholic families conformed.[19]

In Maryland, Jack Coode's charisma propelled him to leadership and he led seven hundred Protestant settlers in a rising against the government; priests were scattered. The colony became a Royal Colony with the Church of England established, but "all but Papists" tolerated. The imposition of the Test Act, which required denial of the key Catholic

---

17 Norman, pp. 32, 38-9. McAvoy, p. 19.
18 A by-product of the Orange ascension was the signing of the English Bill of Rights, the immediate forbearer of the American Bill of Rights signed a century later. Verbalized in this document were the "rights of Englishmen" which became the intellectual touchstone of American Rebels during the two decades which led to the American Revolution.
19 Norman, pp. 40-1. Roman Catholic-held lands were registered in 1716 to enable collection of this tax. Ibid. "England," *New Catholic Encyclopedia*, First Edition, V. V, p. 364.

dogma of Transubstantiation, effectively eliminated Catholics from public life. This was the beginning of a fifty-year campaign to drive the Catholic Church out of Maryland.

Still, the Catholic First Families held on. Charles Carroll the Settler, an Irish lawyer who had migrated to Maryland prior to the coup and served as the colony's attorney general, became a merchant, an importer, a money lender, and a planter. He founded one of the great colonial fortunes. He intermarried with the already broad "Catholic cousinage" of the families of the Brookes, Sewalls of Mattapany, Digges, Darnalls, Neales, Fenwicks of Maryland, and Brents of Virginia.[20]

Ireland

The Ireland that Carroll left behind was an unhappy place for Roman Catholics. English monarchs from Henry through William had been frustrated in their attempts to establish the Church of Ireland in the staunchly-Catholic (and anti-English) island. Elizabeth resorted to plantations of Protestants. This accelerated under James when the Ulster Scots colony in nine northern counties was planted. Additional plantations of French Huguenots and Quakers were scattered through the midland counties.

The Celtic-Irish and the Anglo-Norman English had been at odds since the twelfth century, when Henry II attempted to invade the country to give a patrimony to his youngest son, John "Lackland," later of Magna Carta infamy. The Normans carved out a "pale" (colony) radiating out of the fortress castle at Dublin. The nobility, who would later constitute the Anglo-Irish, established family seats. For centuries, the native Irish rulers kept up a spirited defense from the north, west, and south. England responded by issuing the Statutes of Kilkenney (1366), which outlawed the Irish language, dress, and music. Having been defeated by Scottish tribal identity under Robert the Bruce and William Wallace, the English clearly saw that their future in Ireland depended upon destroying the Irish identity. The plan did not work. This bitter Irish/English feud arose before there was a rupture over religion. The Protestantization policy of the Tudors was just another layer in the catalog of wrongs that the Irish harbored against their colonial master. In this way, "History had prepared

---

20 Hennessey, pp. 340, 350. Beitzell, p. 52.

the Irish to live among strangers and to deal with the problem of foreign rule."²¹

English authorities knew that land equaled power; they sought to deny Catholics the possession of land. In 1603, the year of Elizabeth's death, Catholics owned most of the land in Ireland. By 1709, they held 14%; by 1775, only 5%. The deciding factor in this disaster was the nine-month occupation of Ireland by Oliver Cromwell's forces after the English civil war. Cromwell cold-bloodedly carried out frightful massacres at Drogheda and Wexford. The terror thus unleashed fought the war for him. An exodus of dispossessed former landowners to Connaught (the west) began, propelled by the Act of Transportation of 1654; except for the western fringe of the island, by 1650, Ireland belonged to the English.²²

Oliver Cromwell

The occupying authority rigorously imposed the penal laws. In England, where Catholics were such a tiny minority, only crisis brought such enforcement. In Ireland, with its stubborn Catholic majority, the penal code was ruthlessly imposed. Catholics were forbidden to lease land for more than thirty-one years; they were forbidden to send their children abroad for education; the concept of *primogeniture*, which had created great Medieval estates among those observing English law, was abrogated: all land was to be divided among all children in a family *unless* the eldest son became a Protestant.²³

An Irish-based revolt against William and Mary met a tragic failure after the Battle of the Boyne in 1690. In June 1690, King William landed at Carrickfergus and the Irish fell back to the south of the River Boyne. On July 1, the royal army crossed the Boyne at Slane. After some fighting, the Irish retreated toward the South. King James departed for exile in France.

The Irish army fought on, but was defeated on July 12, 1691 at Aughrim. The commanders surrendered their force on honorable terms at Limerick on September 23. The Treaty of Limerick provided for favorable terms for the Irish: free exercise of religion, citizenship rights,

---

21 Patrick J. Blessing, "The Irish," *Harvard Encyclopedia of American Ethnic Groups* (Belknap Press: Harvard University, 1980) p. 524.
22 Ibid.
23 Ibid., p. 525. Donald M. Schlegel, *The Ancestors of the McDonalds of Somerset* (privately published, Columbus, Ohio, 1998) pp. 154-155.

and guarantees of life and liberty. However, when the army disbanded (some toward home, others to France), the Williamite government brushed the treaty away, and the worst penal times in the history of the island began. The laws, and a rapid influx of more Protestant Scots, were aimed at crushing the Irish spirit. Catholics were then deprived of all rights, barred from the military, the law, and every civic activity, and the concept of the Green versus Orange was introduced into Ireland. Irish Quakers were also severely persecuted. Those Irish who could leave the island did so—many of them to Maryland and Pennsylvania.[24]

In 1689, half a world away, the tiny minority of Roman Catholics in Maryland felt the gall of deprivation of what they considered ancient rights. Mimicking the Williamite Parliament in England, the Maryland Assembly issued several restrictive acts, including a twenty-shilling duty on every Irish Catholic servant imported into the colony. New York and North Carolina did this also. The duty was doubled in 1717. The Catholic leadership, including former attorney general—and recent immigrant—Charles Carroll, worked to mitigate the effects of the new laws and to succor a sub-surface Catholic life. Although he migrated before the '89 Rising, Carroll still keenly felt the centuries of slight. His feisty reactions to some colonial authorities is explained by his past.[25]

By the time of his death, Carroll's estate consisted of business enterprises and more than 60,000 acres of Maryland soil. He was the richest man in the colony. He and his second wife, Mary Darnall, had ten children. Their son, Charles Carroll of Annapolis, would marry his cousin, Elizabeth Brooke. Their only child, Charles Carroll of Carrollton, married his cousin, Mary Darnall. The First Families aided the Jesuit underground. Andrew White's successors were tireless in "making the circuit" to say mass privately in colonial homes.[26]

Maryland Catholics lived under the threatened enforcement of the 1704 Act to Prevent the Growth of Popery, which made it illegal to celebrate the mass, to proselytize, or to keep a school; it required Catholic children to take the oath of allegiance within six months of their majority or forfeit their inheritance to the nearest Protestant kin. This act targeted the 2,974 Roman Catholics in Maryland (1708) and authorities carefully monitored

---

24 Schlegel, pp. 154-155.
25 Beatriz Bentancourt Hardy, *Papists in a Protestant Age: The Catholic Gentry and Community in Colonial Maryland, 1689-1976* (University of Maryland: College Park, 1993) p. 69. Beitzell, p. 45.
26 By 1720, every priest in Maryland was a Jesuit. The circuits radiated out of Bohemia Manor. During this period, the Jesuits amassed 9,133 acres of farms by 1727, which were worked by slave labor—as were all the plantations. McAvoy, p. 23. John Tracy Ellis, *Catholics in Colonial America* (Benedictine Studies: Helicon, Baltimore, Md., 1965) p. 330.

their strongholds: they accounted for 31% of the settlers in St. Mary's County and 21% in Charles County. The fourteen Jesuit chapels were located in those counties.[27]

The Scottish Rising of 1715–called "the Fifteen"–on behalf of the Stuart Pretender, once again created a hostile climate in Maryland. Charles Carroll the Settler was in despair and thought seriously of leaving the British Empire for land in Spanish-held Arkansas. However, between 1720 and 1740, more peaceful relations resumed. In 1731, the Jesuits even dared to build St. Francis Xavier Church in Newtown in St. Mary's County. From this church, disguised on the exterior as a tobacco barn, the Jesuits kept their circuit and their illegal schools alive.[28]

To the north of Maryland was William Penn's Pennsylvania. Founded in 1681 as a haven for his fellow Quakers, its Assembly of property owners had guaranteed freedom of religion for all, but English authorities insisted that Catholics and Jews be barred from voting and holding office. After 1689, restrictions became more intense. There were complaints about "popish masses." That act had been forbidden in 1704. In 1733, Jesuit Josiah Greatin–who had traveled out from White Marsh plantation in Maryland since 1721–moved to Philadelphia and, in defiance, opened a tiny chapel near Fourth and Walnut Streets. St. Joseph's became the only openly Roman Catholic Church in the English-speaking world. Greatin worked at this "Roman Mass House" for twenty years, serving Germans, Irish, English, and, eventually, French Acadian Catholics.[29] In Maryland, the First Catholic Families went to great lengths to provide a Catholic sub-culture for their children.[30] The Jesuits opened a school at Bohemia

---

27 Hardy, pp. 109, 111. McAvoy, p. 22.
28 Hardy, pp. 157, 171, 175. Internet source.
29 Greatin was born in 1680 and ordained in 1719. Internet source. Beitzell, p. 61.
30 Intermarriage among a sampling of the First Catholic Families:
Henry Darnall of Woodward, Prince George County, was stepfather to Thomas Brooke and Robert Brooke, S.J.
William Boarman and Joshua Doyne were brothers-in-law.
Joshua Doyne was father-in-law to Ignatius Matthews of Charles County.
Ignatius Matthews was the father of William Matthews and Ignatius Matthews, S.J.
William Matthews and Mary Neale were the parents of Ignatius Matthews, William Matthews, S.J., Sister M. Aloysius, and Sister M. Eleanor.
Bishop Edward Fenwick was uncle to Father Dominic Young, O.P.
Father Dominic Young's niece, Henriette Young, married Hugh Boyle Ewing, son of U.S. Senator Thomas Ewing (Ohio).
Hugh Boyle Ewing, born in Lancaster, Ohio, was the son of Tom Ewing and Eleanor Gillespie of Brownsville, Pa.
Thomas Mudd married Julianna Gardiner. Their son, Thomas Nathan Mudd, and daughter, Mary Ann, were parents of two nuns at Carmel of Port Tobacco. Their son, Henry, was the great-grandfather of Dr. Samuel Mudd.
Tom and Eleanor Gillespie Ewing's son, Tom, Jr., defended Dr. Mudd at the Lincoln murder trial.
Luke Mudd's daughter, Mary, married Mordecai Lincoln, brother of Thomas Lincoln, father of Abraham Lincoln.

Manor in 1741. The plantation became the center of missionary activity to Delaware, Pennsylvania, and Maryland, with each priest traveling a territory that averaged 130 miles long and thirty-five miles wide. The priests journeyed from Catholic house to Catholic house, ministering the sacraments and keeping school–just as they had done for more than two centuries in England.[31]

Of primary concern to the Catholics was the education of their young. The Carroll path of education was one well-trodden by other Roman Catholic colonials of means. Young Jackie Carroll was first educated at Rock Creek Plantation by his mother, Eleanor Darnall, the product of a French convent school. He attended the illegal primary school of Bohemia Manor, run by the Jesuits on St. Francis Xavier plantation in Cecil County. From there, Jackie and his cousin, Charles, prepared for their voyage to St. Omer–the Jesuit College in France where Lord Baltimore educated his sons.[32]

Of Maryland's Catholic population, 6% of the third generation was educated in Europe; 51% of the fourth generation was sent there. All of the boys went to St. Omer or Bruges. At Bruges, Leonard Neale, S.J. supervised the education of his brothers, Charles and Francis, and visited his sister, Ann, a Poor Clare nun in a nearby convent. In these classically-based schools, the "Maryland Catholic gentry [became] one of the best educated groups in all the American colonies." While this shadow culture continued, English civil authorities kept an eye on the minority, but was convinced that it would wither away.[33]

English recusancy did not disappear, but struggled after the restrictive legislature imposed on it in the wake of the final Rising for the Young Pretender (1745). In Maryland, Dr. Charles Carroll converted to the Church of England in 1738 and carried out a public vendetta from the Assembly against his family. Charles Carroll of Annapolis was losing heart and, in 1752, made a voyage to France to seek a grant of land along the Mississippi River. In the end, however, Dr. Carroll's actions only strengthened the Catholic circle in Maryland. It enjoyed much vitality between 1760 and 1776. In 1700, there had been fourteen chapels serving 3,000 Catholics. By 1740, there were thirty-four chapels and 8,000 Catholics. By 1760, there would be fifty chapels.[34]

---

31 McAvoy, p. 31.
32 Hardy, p. 132. McAvoy, p. 31. Hennessey, p. 2. Internet source.
33 Hardy, p. 315. There were seventeen Marylanders at St. Omer's in 1754 and twenty-five in 1762. Ibid.
34 Hennessey, p. 35. Hardy, pp. 191, 251, 321. Ellis, p. 355.

However, the Catholic location in Maryland shifted. Charles Carroll the Settler had been a sponsor of an expedition sent out in 1714 to measure the boundary between Pennsylvania and Maryland. Although the line was not established, the territory around the Cumberland Gap became better known. Thus, after the 1689 catastrophic legislation, many Roman Catholic families settled in that area, "upon the borderland of Pennsylvania."[35]

In Pennsylvania, the busy Port of Philadelphia became the chief avenue of immigration into America, and it received a steady flow from Ireland. In 1725, some 6,000 "Irish" disembarked there. Many of these people were Scotch-Irish–the "wild Irish"–who would soon relocate to the Pennsylvania frontier, but some were undoubtedly Catholics. Irish Catholics were found occasionally on the frontier in the first half of the eighteenth century.[36]

Most of the ships dropping anchor in Philadelphia, however, came from German ports. Thus the majority of Catholics in the colony were Germans. In 1741 in Berks County, Germans established a colony at Goshenhoppen; another was established by Catholic Rhinelanders and Palantines at Conewago in Adams County. They were joined by Marylanders led by John Digges. Lord Baltimore had granted him ten-thousand acres on the Maryland/Pennsylvania borderland. He arrived with Jesuits who were supported by an inheritance from Father Gilbert Talbot, S.J., thirteenth Earl of Shrewsbury.[37]

Conewago Chapel
Courtesy Diocese of Harrisburg, Parish History Archives. Used with permission.

In another generation, some of these people pushed westward. By 1748, "the Forks"–the peninsula formed by the Monongahela and Allegheny Rivers to form the Ohio River–became a well-known goal for

---

35 Hardy, p. 169 fn. Thomas J. Stanton, *A Century of Growth: The History of the Church in Western Maryland I*. (John Murphy Company: Baltimore, 1900) p. 6.
36 Records for Irish and Scotch Irish before the American Revolution are sparse. British authorities did not consider them immigrants, as they were merely relocating <u>within</u> British territories. German records are far more complete. A. A. Lambing, *A History of the Catholic Church in the Diocese of Pittsburgh and Allegheny* (Benziger Bros.: New York, 1880) p. 26.
37 Ibid. p. 21. Hennessey, p. 351.

both Irish and Germans on the path to the west.

The Irish who landed at Philadelphia were fleeing economic hardship—some of it engineered by English authorities intent upon protecting English goods and trade; some of it was, however, the result of assaults by nature. The basis of Irish wealth had been beef and butter in the countryside, and linen and cotton in the towns. The harvests failed from 1699-1703; droughts ruined the crops in 1710 and from 1714-1717. Wet weather in 1721 and 1723 reduced harvests; poor crops were gathered from 1725-1730. Famine and epidemic took heavy tolls. Freebooters and other bandits roamed the countryside, robbing and murdering. In 1737, a plague of insects ravished crops. It was a killing frost that claimed the entire potato crop in 1740. Some 400,000 Irish died. Crop failures and famines occurred in 1728-29, 1740-41, 1744-45, and 1756-57. The trading world sank into a depression that lasted from 1740 until 1780. Scotch-Irish Protestants flooded out of Ulster on flax ships returning to America. This was especially true when the linen trade collapsed and created a banking crisis in the 1770's.[38]

Roman Catholic peasants had, for generations—even centuries—left Ireland to work as migrant labor as far away as the Polish silver mines and the New Foundland fisheries. They left Ireland when they could. Established emigrant networks existed between Galway and Seville in Spain, and Waterford and Bordeaux in France. Many Irishmen ended up in continental armies. Cromwell had made that exodus involuntary: Irish were sold into servitude or "transported" to penal colonies. In the aftermath of the 1689 disaster, so many Irish sold themselves into indentured servitude that the colonies passed import duties to try to restrict the practice. The influx of poor Irish continued until the American Revolution. Thus, two classes of Irish emerged in eighteenth century America: the debtor and the substantial.[39]

Most of the poor Irish were too broke and sick to venture past the American coast settlements. However, Irish history had taught Irishmen to live under hostile circumstances, and some of them set out for the American frontier.

In the 1740's, soldiers and settlers explored the Allegheny Mountain passes and the "river roads" which led to the Forks. Their pressure was a factor which pulled England and France into war. During the conflict,

---

38 McAvoy, p. 202. Schlegel, *Ancestors....* pp. 156-157. Blessing, p. 525.
39 Blessing, p. 525.

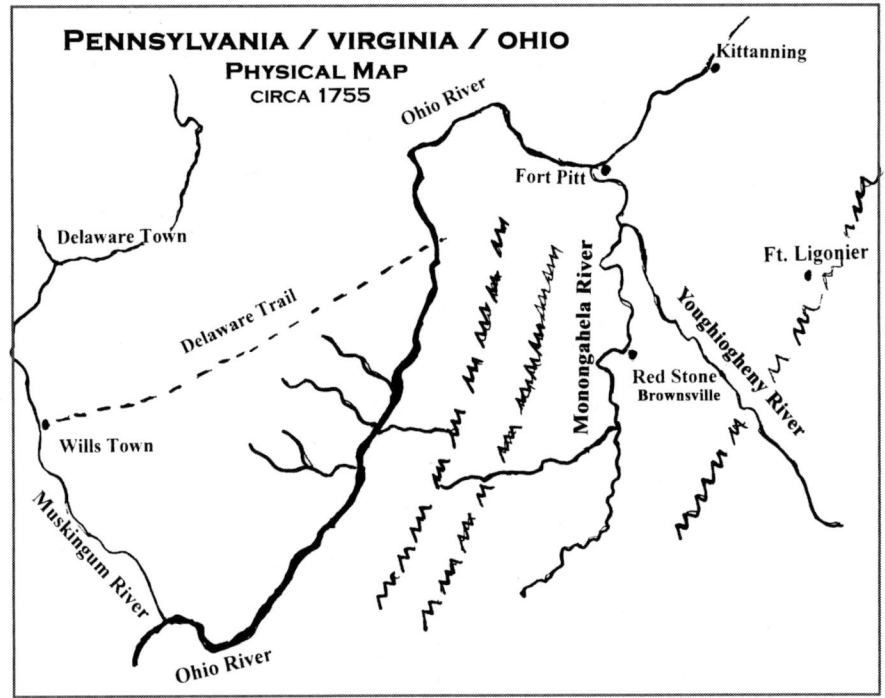

Virginia Lieutenant Colonel George Washington built a fort where the Red Stone Creek emptied into the Monongahela River. Red Stone Old Fort, fifty-three miles by river from the Forks, was a strategic site during the war and a "jumping off" point for immigrants bound for Kentucky. People poled their way north on the Monongahela to Pittsburgh and then floated south on the Ohio River to the Virginia colony of Kentucky.[40]

During the French and Indian War, Braddock's men carved out a rough military road along the existing warpath of the Delawares (Nemaolin's Path) which snaked through Maryland's Cumberland Gap to the site of Uniontown, Pennsylvania. This road gave immigrants access to the Youghiogheny River and Fort Pitt. Uniontown and Brownsville (Red Stone Old Fort) became key stops on the way west.[41]

A sprinkling of Roman Catholics ventured west,[42] but anti-Catholic prejudice flourished during the French and Indian war. (There was great pressure put on Philadelphia officials to close St. Joseph's.) Maryland

---

40 Lambing, p. 21.
41 Ibid.
42 As early as 1751, Felix Hughes wrote to the Jesuits *in Philadelphia* asking for a priest for Carmichael Settlement in present-day Greene County. Hughes's tie with the church was in Philadelphia, not Maryland. Lambing, pp. 21, 24, 36.

Catholics were double taxed. Because settlers suspected that Catholics favored the French (Catholic) cause, Pennsylvania authorities made a survey of the colony's Roman Catholics in 1758.[43] The German priests cited in the inventory and the Jesuits in Maryland would labor on to care for their people under difficult circumstances, but their lives, like all others, would change radically with the outbreak of the American Revolution.

---

43 Beitzell, p. 45. Lambing, p. 24: A list of All the Roman Catholics in Pennsylvania, 1757 (that is, of all such as receive the sacrament, beginning from twelve years of age or thereabouts)

	Men	Women
Under the care of Robert Harding:		
In and about Philadelphia, being all Irish or English	72	78
In Chester county	18	22
Under the care of Theodore Schneider:		
In and about Philadelphia, being all Germans	107	121
Philadelphia County, but up country	15	10
Berks County	62	55
Northampton County	68	62
Northampton County Irish	17	12
Bucks County	14	11
Chester County	13	9
Chester County Irish	9	6
Under the care of Father Farmer:		
In Lancaster County, Germans	108	94
In Lancaster County, Irish	22	27
In Berks County, Germans	41	39
In Berks County, Irish	5	3
In Chester County, Irish	23	17
In Chester County, Germans	3	-
In Cumberland County, Irish	6	6
Under the care of Matthias Manners		
In York County, Germans	54	62
In York County, Irish	<u>35</u>	<u>38</u>
	<u>692</u>	<u>673</u>
Total sum		1365

April 29, 1757

Chapter Three

"Hair-buying" on the Pennsylvania/Virginia Frontier
"The Indian Wars"

During the decade of the 1740's, the frontiersmen and surveyors pushed into the Ohio River region (western Pennsylvania, Ohio, Tennessee, and Kentucky). The unfolding knowledge of geography made it clear that Ohio's watershed was the key to controlling the North American continent. Great Britain and France–rivals for world empires–claimed the region.

During the eighteenth century, the two competitors fought a series of wars for domination of Europe and far-flung colonies. In North America, the French pushed into the region with a strategy that would tie Canada with French holdings in the Mississippi Valley. They built alliances with the native tribes, particularly the Shawnee, exchanging weapons for furs. The British countered by cultivating ties with the Iroquois. Wary of each other's designs, the French and British began building forts in the disputed region, the French anchoring their claims with Fort Duquesne at the confluence where the Monongahela and Allegheny Rivers form the Ohio. This colonial chess-match grew dangerous in 1754.

The colony of Pennsylvania claimed the western river region, but the Quaker majority in the Commonwealth's Assembly refused to approve military funds for its defense. Pennsylvania's administrators appealed to Virginia for help in "showing the flag" to counter French moves. Governor Dinwiddie sent a twenty-one-year-old militia lieutenant colonel named George Washington into the wilderness in search of the French stronghold. Virginia thus asserted a claim to the western region; Washington's mission was to order the French commander to vacate the disputed territory.

Words escalated into shots; an out-manned Washington desperately threw together Fort Necessity. With no aid coming from Pennsylvania or

Maryland, the young colonel surrendered his command.[1] This minor skirmish on the Pennsylvania frontier was the opening salvo in what would be a global war. The American phase was called the French and Indian War; the larger, more serious war–the Seven Years War–was waged in Europe, India, and the Caribbean. The outcomes transformed European politics and left Britain as the dominant military power in the world.

In America, the results of the French and Indian War led directly to the American Revolution. During the frontier war, British "redcoats" and American "buckskins" were combined under the command of General Edward Braddock. In the ensuing decade, as feelings mounted for revolution and independence, the disdain of the colonials shown by Braddock and his officers would be another source of the irritation. The colonials drew on these feelings, as momentum built to sever ties between England and her American colonies.

In 1755, Braddock's regulars and the American militia hacked out a rough military road from Fort Cumberland, Maryland Colony, to Pennsylvania's Fort Duquesne, the key French strategic point in the West. Poised for battle, Braddock's command was unwilling to heed colonial warnings about a new style of war. Braddock's army was soundly defeated by the French and Indian force that poured out of the woods around Duquesne. That spring of 1755, the frontier was dominated by the French.

THE OHIO COUNTRY 1753–1755

---

1   Sylvester K. Stevens, *Pennsylvania: Birthplace of a Nation*, (Random House: New York, 1964) p. 52.

The ease of Braddock's defeat energized the native tribes. Delawares at Kittanning allied with Shawnee. Left undefended, American settlers faced the wrath of the Indians. A bloodbath threatened.

In Philadelphia's Assembly Hall, the pacifist Quaker majority refused to provide militia protection for the frontier. When tales of tribal atrocity reached the capital during elections in 1756, the Quakers lost fourteen of their seats. Then, under the deft (if shadowy) hand of Benjamin Franklin, the Assembly passed the Defense Act of 1755 and a new policy emerged. Between 1756–1763, some two hundred defensive sites, including a few real forts, were built on the western frontier. Frontier Rangers were recruited to defend their homes. Thus, Colonel John Armstrong's Rangers marched out of rude compounds and into the Kittanning Valley. They utterly destroyed the Delaware capital. Then in 1758, Swiss-born Colonel Henry Bouquet–arguably the best soldier in pre-Revolutionary War America–brought intelligence and planning to the British frontier strategy. Bouquet's men widened a bridle path, as General John Forbes's men followed, carving out a military road from Bedford to the Forks (Forbes Road). With a well-provisioned army, Bouquet struck. Fort Duquesne soon fell and was renamed Fort Pitt (1758).[2]

The following year at the Plains of Abraham in Quebec, the British Army crushed the French. In 1763, the global Seven Years War ended with the Treaty of Paris. The North American prize–the lands west of the Alleghenies and east of the Mississippi River–fell under the paper control of the British.

Hovering over a map, William Pitt and his ministers drew a line from the Great Lakes southward along the crest of the Allegheny Mountains. With this Proclamation Line of 1763, the sovereign state of Great Britain declared the land west of the line to be free from white settlement. Imperial policy mandated that the native tribes, and their fur trade, should be the exclusive domain of licensed British traders. "Buckskin" colonials had other ideas. After another Indian war, the buckskin desire to "wester" would be even more intense.

In 1763, although deprived of French arms, the Ottawa Chief Pontiac raised a multi-tribal alliance and overwhelmed frontier forts. Only the heroic efforts of Bouquet's men at Bushy Run enabled the British to recover Fort Pitt and establish a period of peace on the frontier. Bouquet knew, however, that Indian raids would continue from across the Ohio

---

2   Stevens, pp. 54-5.

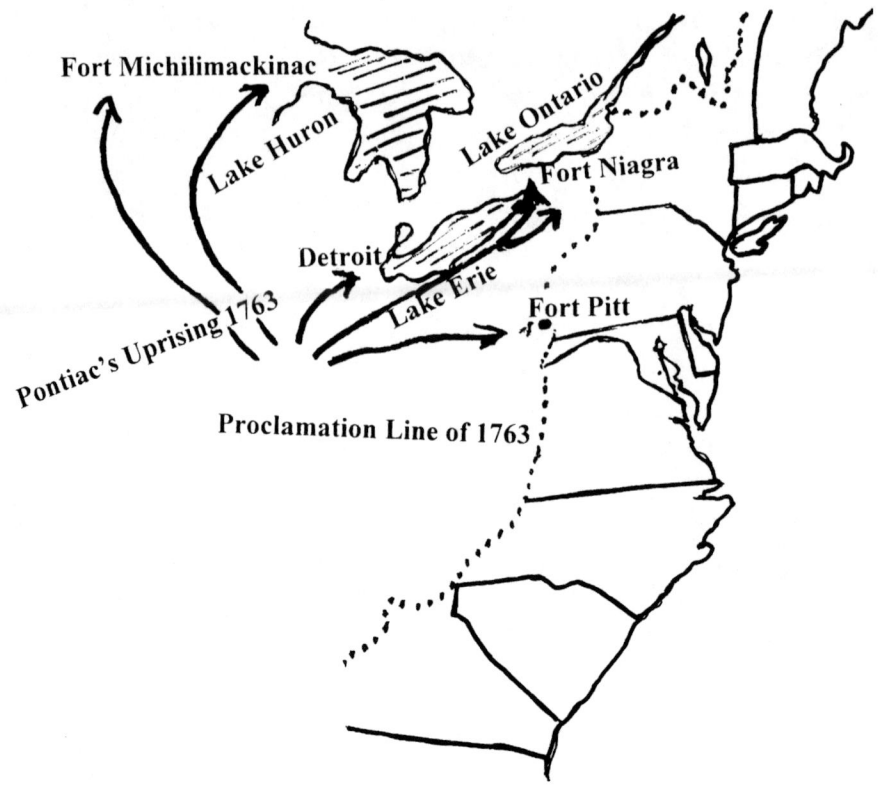

THE AMERICAN FRONTIER 1763

River. His initial expedition into that area—as far as the headwaters of the Muskingum River (Coshocton County, Ohio)—was as much a scouting mission as an effort to rescue white captives.³

Pontiac's War aside, the enforcement of the Proclamation Line was highly unpopular. The British authorities were seen as arrogant and selfish. The slow, but inevitable schism between Britain and America widened. Within a decade, the rift would be unbreachable; the American Revolution would be underway.

Chief Pontiac

The frontier settlements along the Alleghenies' crest were home to migrating Germans—half of Pennsylvania's population in 1740—and the Scotch-Irish. The latter were not anxious to obey "city law." For years, the Carolinian and Pennsylvanian leadership encouraged Scotch-

---

3 Stevens, pp. 56-7.

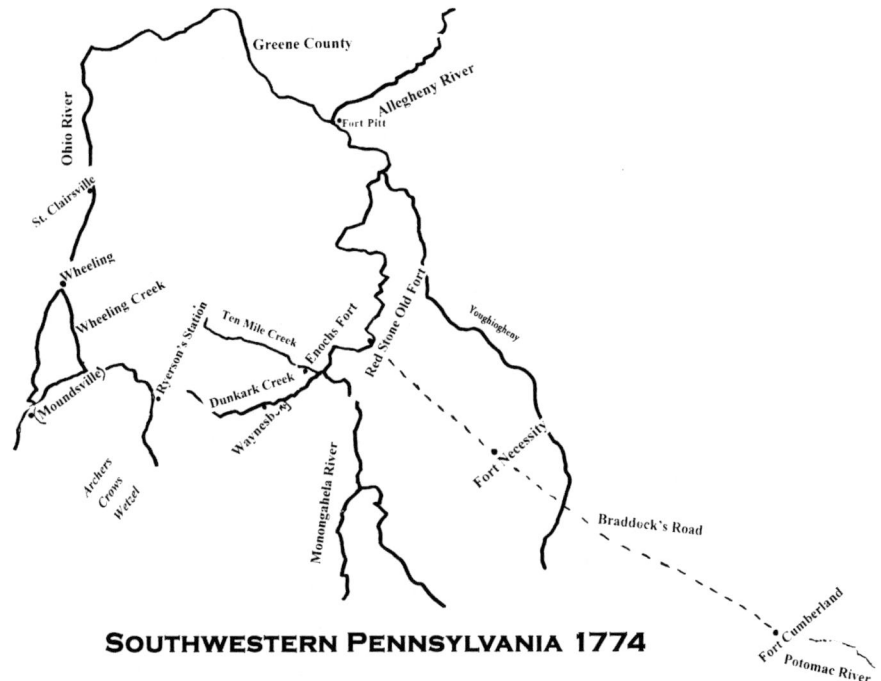

SOUTHWESTERN PENNSYLVANIA 1774

Irish settlements on their frontiers as an expendable buffer against hostile indigenous tribes. It was a small loss if such "wild Irish" were killed. In turn, they became used to "squatting" wherever and whenever they chose, staking out "tomahawk rights" to the land.[4] These were the people who moved westward to turn Fort Duquesne into Fort Pitt, and to carve out settlements in what would become Pennsylvania's Allegheny, Westmoreland, Butler, Armstrong, and Greene counties.

They were greeted by vast hardwood forests and rich river valleys criss-crossed by Indian paths. Chimney smoke began to punctuate the skies around Fort Pitt. But the most remote part of the Pennsylvania frontier–southern Washington County (later to be named Greene County) did not see a white settler until 1750. At that time, a group of fifty moved along Braddock's Road to Old Red Stone Fort and then down the rivers into the area, probably landing at Rice's Landing and pushing on via creeks to Fort Jackson. Further penetration was slow, but frontier "word-of-mouth" encouraged more settlement.[5]

In the 1770's, some families ventured out of Maryland's

---

4 Stevens, p. 64. Tomahawk rights meant a claim delineated by tomahawk chops on the trees.
5 Samuel P. Bates, *History of Greene County, Pa.* (Nelson, Rishforth & Co.: Chicago, Il, 1881) p. 240. Only in 1796 would the population merit the designation of a county government.

Conocheague Valley west of Hagerstown, and began the long trek west on Braddock's Road. It would be the path of hundreds of thousands of pioneers: west on Braddock's Road to Cumberland to Jacobs Creek (near present-day Connellsville) and across the Allegheny River (at present-day Freeport). Others would drop off at Brownsville, the terminus of the Cumberland Trail at the head of navigation of the Monongahela River, and then pole north on the river to Pittsburgh. The Irish Gillespie family kept a tavern at Brownsville, and ran a clearing house for Catholic information. James Archer (later described as a "'roving hunter with the Indians'") cleared land in Greene County in 1772.[6] His brother, Joseph, was squatting on a plantation in Cumberland Township (later Franklin Township) in 1774. They were the first of their family who, "'East of the mountains [were] poor ridge romans, [sic]'" and began settlement in the area. Soon, their Irish-born father, Patrick, joined them.[7]

Chief Logan

For a decade after the Treaty of Paris (1763), the red and white peoples of western Pennsylvania lived in general peace. Then, in April 1774, Mingo Chief Logan's family of thirteen was massacred "in the most dishonorable manner" by Daniel Greathouse and his band of drunken men, as the family camped at Yellow Creek, sixteen miles north of present-day Steubenville, Ohio. Settlers west of the Monongahela fled eastward as Logan took revenge. The acts of reprisal and retaliation escalated into Lord Dunmore's War. Once again, Virginia's governor sent relief into the region. This time, however, the Pennsylvania government began to pay attention to its western frontier.[8]

Greene County settlers retreated into tiny log compounds that were generously called forts: Fort Enochs (near Graysville), Enochs' Fort

---

6 George Archer, *Patrick Archer and His Descendants*, (George W. Archer: McLean, Va., 1999) p. 8. George Archer believes that the Archers were in Frederick County at least by 1759; Patrick Archer was sued for debt by William Cambel in Frederick County, Maryland on November 26, 1759, Liber F/894. Patrick Archer was listed as one of twenty debtors living in the county (1767). An Archer in-law named Wells moved west from the Conocheague Valley at the same time that the Archers moved into Greene County.

7 George W. Archer has spent three decades researching his Archer roots. He has generously shared his meticulously researched and closely reasoned material with me. I use it gratefully. It supercedes all other available source material on the topic. Archer successfully tracked down William Rhodes's Diary and transcribed it with the permission of Rhodes's great-great-granddaughter. Rhodes ran a trading post at Fort Jackson (Waynesburg) and mentions the Archers. Archer, pp. 5-6, 9-10.

8 Stevens, p. 93. In 1770, Greene County was divided into three Virginia counties: Yohogania, Ohio, and Monongalia; Archer, p. 33.

66   ST. PATRICK'S PEOPLE

(Clarksville), and Ryerston Station, which sat astride "the great Indian war-path leading across the Ohio River to the Monongahela, at the confluence of the north and south forks of Drunkard Branch of Wheeling Creek." There, "the authorities of Virginia had a fort built" to be commanded by Captain James Seals.[9]

Virginia-based British soldiers (called "Longknives" by the tribes) pushed into the Ohio region on rafts built by settlers and Frontier Rangers. They worked their way up the Muskingum River to the Shawnee village of Wakatomica. Ferocious fighting also took place at the mouths of the Great Kanawha and Ohio Rivers in Kentucky.[10]

This vicious tit-for-tat border war merged with the American Revolution when gunfire erupted on Concord Green in distant Massachusetts. In the East, where America's population was concentrated, a third of that population favored independence, a third sided with the British, and a third cared not a fig. As George Washington's men starved at Valley Forge, as Benjamin Franklin wheedled a vital French Alliance, as

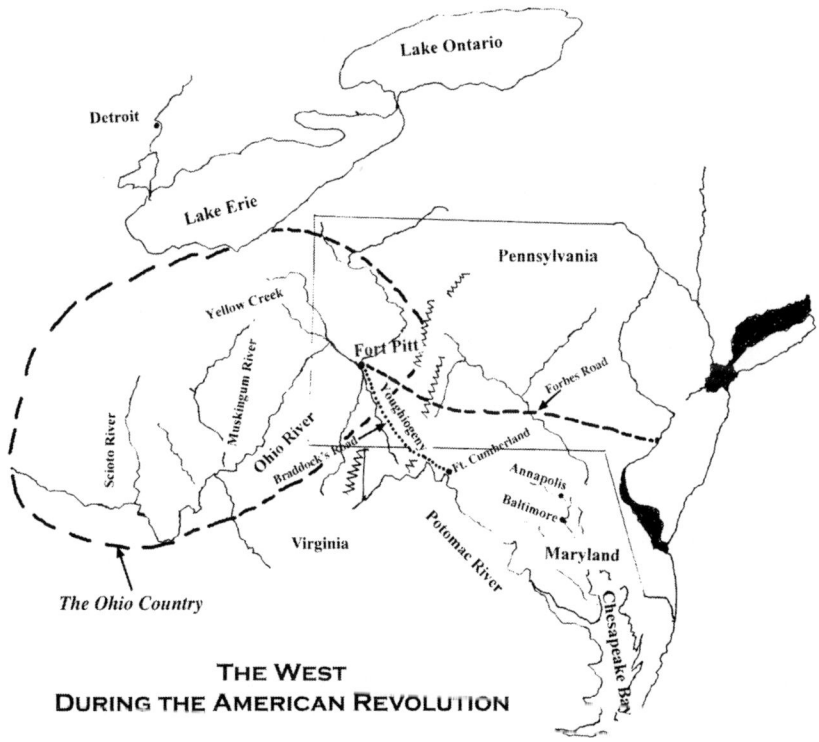

**THE WEST
DURING THE AMERICAN REVOLUTION**

---

9   Bates, pp. 536-7.
10 Ibid., p. 241.

"The Indian Wars"

the British Parliament dillied and dallied, and the American-French forces finally triumphed, the West lay unprotected and on its own.

There, British agents sought tribal allies and encouraged "hair-buyers." In 1777–the "year of the bloody sevens"–the western frontier was aflame. Families clustered together in rude compounds while Frontier Rangers defended them. Enoch Enochs, born in Hampshire County, Virginia in 1750, was elected as captain of the militia at Enochs' Fort in 1775, 1776, and 1777.[11] James Archer enlisted in Captain David Owens's company. Owens migrated to Kentucky and, although he was a Catholic– a member of a distrusted minority–Archer was elected as captain. In 1776, Archer's men built a fort at the mouth of Fish Creek, a tributary of the Ohio River, which rose in Greene County and flowed west.[12]

The Irish Archers were rather unique among their comrades, who described them as "'Roman Irish.'" They were a Roman Catholic family, apparently one of but a few in the region.[13] During the French and Indian War, out of fear that Catholics in America would side with their co-religionists (the French) the Pennsylvania Militia Act of 1757 forbade Catholics to own arms, and imposed on them a twenty-shilling tax, the same tax that was placed on conscientious objectors. Obviously, with Archer's election, the rule was not enforced on the frontier during the Revolutionary War years.[14]

The "grande design" of warfare sometimes touched the West. Frontiersmen from Greene County helped launch the boats for expeditions by George Rogers Clark to capture Kaskaskia, Cahokia, and Vincennes in Illinois Country in 1776.[15] But generally, recruitment for local defense was the order of the day. In 1782, James Archer was elected captain of the 1st Battalion 5th Company, Washington County Pennsylvania Militia; his brothers, Joseph, Michael, and Simon, served under him. In 1784, James was elected as captain of the 2nd Battalion under the command of Col. Henry Enochs. In 1786, James was the captain of the 3rd Company, 4th Battalion under Lt. Col. William Crawford. All these units were made

---

11 L.H. Watkins, *Noble County History* (Chicago, Il., 1887) p. 440; Enoch genealogy from "Family Research in Monroe County" by Catherine Foreaker Fedorchak, Monroe County Public Library; hereafter cited as Fedorchak.
12 Howard Lecky, *Tenmile County*, Vol. 1, p. 42. Payroll land warrant #55090, Pennsylvania Archives; Archer, p. 41.
13 Archer, p. 6; J. Hennessey, p. 350; McAvoy, p. 29; *A Church in the United States* (University of Notre Dame: Indiana, 1969) p. 29.
14 George Archer believes there was an enclave of Catholics in the northeast corner of Greene County. I think it may include the German Kirche (Church) family.
15 Smith, p. 5.

Archer Genealogy

Patrick Archer
& Unknown

    Capt. James Archer Sr.
    & 1) Sophia McCleland

        James Archer Jr.
        & Rebecca Enochs

        Nancy Archer
        & Elisha Enochs

        Susan Archer
        & John Preples

        Jane Archer
        & Henry Church

        Joseph Archer
        & Phoebe Enochs

        Polly Archer
        & John Moore

        Elizabeth Archer
        & George Harris

        Michael Archer
        & Rhoda Grandon

        Jacob Archer
        & Sarah Grandon

        Sarah Archer
        & George Church

        Simon Archer
        & Rhoda Enochs

        Nathan Archer
        & Rebecca Mooris

        Rachel Archer
        & George Hupp

    Capt. James Archer Sr.
    & 2) Jane Linicome

    Joseph Archer
    & Margaret Church

    Michael Archer
    & Elizabeth Wells

    Simon Archer
    & Nancy Church

    Jacob Archer
    & Nancy Church

Capt. Enoch Enochs
& Rebecca Morris

    Rhoda Enochs
    & Simon Archer

    Lydia Enochs
    & Nathan Linicome

    Nathan Enochs
    & Rebecca Morris

    Rachel Enochs
    & Frederic Crow

    Elisha Enochs
    & Nancy Archer

    Phoebe Enochs
    & Joseph Archer

    Hannah Enochs
    & Henry Grandon

    Rebecca Enochs
    & James Archer

    Henry Enochs

    Enoch Enochs Jr.

    Amy Enochs
    & Mathew Gray

Jacob Crow
& Unknown

    Frederic Crow
    & Rachel Enochs

    Christian Crow
    & John McBride

    Martin Crow
    & Elizabeth Cackler

    Michael Crow
    & Sara Lucas

    John Crow

    Katherine Crow

    Elizabeth Crow

    Suzanna Crow

up of Frontier Rangers poised for defense against British and Indian raids.[16]

The Frontier Rangers were protecting their own. The Archer clan represented the inter-connections of frontier families. Patrick Archer and his wife were natives of Ireland. Patrick was the father of James I (Senior), Joseph, Michael, Simon, Elizabeth, Polly, Nancy, and Jacob. This first generation in America married into the Wells, Fee, and Kirche (Church) families. Joseph married Margaret Church, Simon married Nancy Church, and Jacob married Nancy Church. [**Note:** It is not known if these were two women, or one. Margaret and Nancy were the daughters of George and Jane Church.] Michael married Elizabeth Wells and Elizabeth married William Wells. Polly Archer and Nancy Archer married George Fee. [**Note:** It is not known if there were two George Fees.]

James Archer I (Senior) married Sophia, and then Jane Lincicome. His daughter, Sarah, married George Church; her sister, Jane, married Henry Church; both men were sons of George and Jane Church. James Archer, Jr. married Rebecca Enochs, daughter of Enoch Enochs. Other Archer daughters and sons married into the Enoch Enochs family: Nancy married Elisha, Joseph married Phoebe, and Simon married Rhoda Enochs. Rachel Enochs married George Hupp.

James Archer Senior's other children married into the family of Bernard Grandon: Michael Archer married Rhoda Grandon and Jacob married Sarah Grandon. Mary Archer married John Moore, Elizabeth married George Harris, and Nathan Archer married Rebecca Morris. These interrelated families mixed with Crows and other settlers in frontier Greene county.

The Archer clan fell victim to one raid when hostiles fell upon a cabin and massacred a number of people. James's daughter, ten-year-old Jane, was scalped and left for dead. She hid and survived into adulthood.[17]

In 1781, three sons of Jacob Crow, John, Frederick, and Martin, were attacked at their fishing camp along Fish Creek. John died of wounds, Martin's ear was shot away, and Frederick was wounded. According to

---

16 Smith, p. 6; Archer, pp. 52-3; 54fn.
17 This story is hopelessly garbled after two centuries of oral tradition and several tellings in print. In George Archer's best judgment, the above sparse account is all that can be said with any certainty. Lecky names the child as "Jennie." She may have been Sara (who supposedly married George Church [Kirche] or Jane (who married Henry Church). The account might even be a version of the Crow massacre (see below). None of this story, as of now, can be verified with any certainty. Lecky, p. 370; Archer, pp. 21-23. George Archer has spent years piecing together fragments concerning James Archer's wives. He finds no evidence of a connection between James's wife, Sophia, and the Robert McClelland family. He also deduces that James's second (or third) wife, Jane Lincicome, was the widow of Joseph Lincicome. Their son, Nathan, lived with James Archer and his wife, Jane, during the Indian Wars

oral tradition, the two treated themselves with poultices made of chewed sassafras leaves, then staggered home.[18]

Five years later, Michael Archer, son of Patrick and husband of Elizabeth Wells, was killed by hostiles. The uncertainty of frontier life during the wars was reflected in the fact that, as a youth, Nathan Lincicome lived off and on with his mother, Jane, and her husband, James Archer I, presumably after she had been widowed and remarried.[19]

The course of the Revolution absorbed all the energies of the Continental Congress, and the affairs on the frontier were largely ignored. However, settlers in southwestern Pennsylvania, who were subject to taxation and military calls by both Pennsylvania and Virginia, agitated for a settlement to the border issue. The Greene County people thought of themselves as Virginians and, historically, only Virginia had provided them with any military protection; "in reality, the only government the early settlers of Greene County knew in the early 1770's was Virginian." Twice, residents petitioned the Continental Congress. James, Simon, Michael, Joseph, and Patrick Archer signed these petitions. Congress commissioned the Mason and Dixon survey line, but the permanent line was not agreed to until 1786. It remained a festering issue.[20]

The American Revolution ended in Independence in 1783, but the British were slow to withdraw their interests from the Great Lakes region. Still, as settlers worked their claims, a world away, the new committees of the American government faced the first great national issue: what to do with the frontier? Ceded by Britain in the Treaty of Paris (1783), the vast lands of the Ohio River's watershed were scarcely known, only roughly mapped, and incredibly rich. Congress faced a question utterly new in political history: Was the American West to be America's colony?

The Congressional committee, which drafted the Northwest Ordinance of 1787, created one of the most important of all American laws. It mandated that the territory was to be surveyed and the land sold to pay the national debt. The states with claims to the region ceded it to the Federal Government. Anti-slavery sentiment—which could not survive

---

18 Bates, pp. 541-543.
19 A deed verifies the relationship. Archer, pp. 18-19.
20 Smith, pp. 6, 7; Between 1774-1780, 2,000 residents west of the Laurel Hill petitioned the Congress. Petition No. 8 from Sundry Inhabitants of Yohogania and Monongalia to be Laid before (Virginia) Assembly, 1782. Cited in Archer, p. 40.
Samuel Doak Porter, *A Genealogy of the Porter Family of Maryland, West Virginia, and Michigan*, Kerrville, Tx., 1971, p. 5. Two members of the Mason Dixon survey team were John and Michael Porter, who lived 12 miles north of Fort Cumberland on the east side of the Great Savage Mountain. They would be part of another Roman Catholic migration into Ohio (Knox County).

the Constitutional fight–surfaced in the ordinance. The entire region was to be free of slavery and, when a population of 60,000 was achieved, each state–up to five–would be welcomed into the Union as an equal partner.

In Pennsylvania's "frontier"–the southern part of Washington County (Greene County)–civilian life returned to a semblance of order. James Archer, Sr. was elected supervisor of Franklin Township (1787) and an associate judge for Washington County in 1790. In that year, he and other farmers endured a "'most dreadful famine. Corn mostly frostbitten.'" In face of such disappointment and with new lands opening, the Archers and their neighbors began to eye new lands in "the West."[21]

Settlers pushed into what was, to them, western Virginia–the panhandle of (West) Virginia, which bordered Greene County. Surveyor parties moved across the Ohio River into the Ohio Territory. Lew Wetzel, already legendary as an Indian scout and fighter, led the way. Wetzel had a cabin on Wheeling Creek in Greene County, but roamed through Ohio and Kentucky at will. With Wetzel was his young neighbor, Martin Crow. Crow grew up hunting meat for surveyors and learning "woodsy ways" from Wetzel. On one expedition into Ohio, according to family tradition, the buckskin pair scouted a beautiful valley as a future home for the Crows of Greene County.[22]

While frontier settlers pushed into new land, speculators in the east planned organized settlements. Soon, armed with military warrants, individuals and groups began to move down the Ohio River in search of their assigned land. Marietta, the keystone New England Settlement, was platted in 1787. William Rhodes, writing from his store in Fort Jackson (Greene County), stated that

> in the year 1788 or 1787, the New England settlers at the Mouth of the Muskingum relieved the people from forting hereabouts; hunting and range became scarce and the Archers left here in pursuit of both.[23]

The "forting" at Marietta was Fort Harmar, but its commander had only three hundred "bluecoats" to police the entire Ohio River. And the "redcoats" did not go quietly. Chaffed by the humiliation of a loss to colonial upstarts and convinced that America would fail and then be re-annexed to the Empire, the British encouraged and paid for another Indian war.

---

21 Archer, pp. 32, 38 quoting Rhodes.
22 Bates, p. 480.
23 Quoted in Archer, p. 6.

Fort Harmar at the confluence of the Muskingum and Ohio Rivers.

Henry Howe

German-born Jacob Crow built his cabin five miles below Ryerston Station in 1769. After building the cabin to assert tomahawk rights, Crow and his sons set about felling trees, planting corn and tobacco, and hunting meat for the table. In May 1791, youngsters scampered over the fields in search of dandelion greens, while their mother churned butter and thought of all they had accomplished over the winter months. Suddenly, Indians–led "by a heartless renegade white man by the name of Spicer"–fell upon the cabin. Elizabeth, Suzanna, and Katherine were tomahawked. Ten-year-old Christina hid in a shed. Katherine would linger in agony for three days before dying.[24]

Such scattered Indian raids led to a full-scale frontier war in 1794. Men of the increasingly inter-related families in Greene County marched out once again in search of Indian camps, to destroy stockpiles of food and arms. Elisha Enochs and Nathan Lincicome mustered into Captain Paul's company at Enoch's Fort.[25] Captain James Seal's unit at Ryerston Station included Elisha's brothers, Henry and Enoch, Jr., and James Archer, Sr., James Archer, Jr., and Simon Archer.[26]

Enoch Enochs, Sr. and his wife, Rebecca Morris, surveyed their

---

24 Bates, p. 540; Smith, p. 4; Martin Crow's daughter, Susan Crow Smith, was called "the daughter of the Indian fighter" in her 1917 obituary. Fedorchak, p. 14.
25 In an 1854 sworn affidavit sealed with his mark and entered in Monroe County, Ohio, James Archer, Jr. attested that Elisha Enochs and Nathan Lincicome served in these units. Fedorchak, p. 95.
26 Another sworn affidavit filed on October 31, 1850. Ibid., p. 95.

family compound as men said goodbye. Elisha Enochs left his wife, Nancy Archer; Amy Enochs kissed Matthew Tray; Lydia Enochs said goodbye to Nathan Lincicome; Rachel Enochs parted from Frederick Crow.[27] However, this would be the final campaign of the Frontier Rangers and the American Army for control of the Ohio Country.

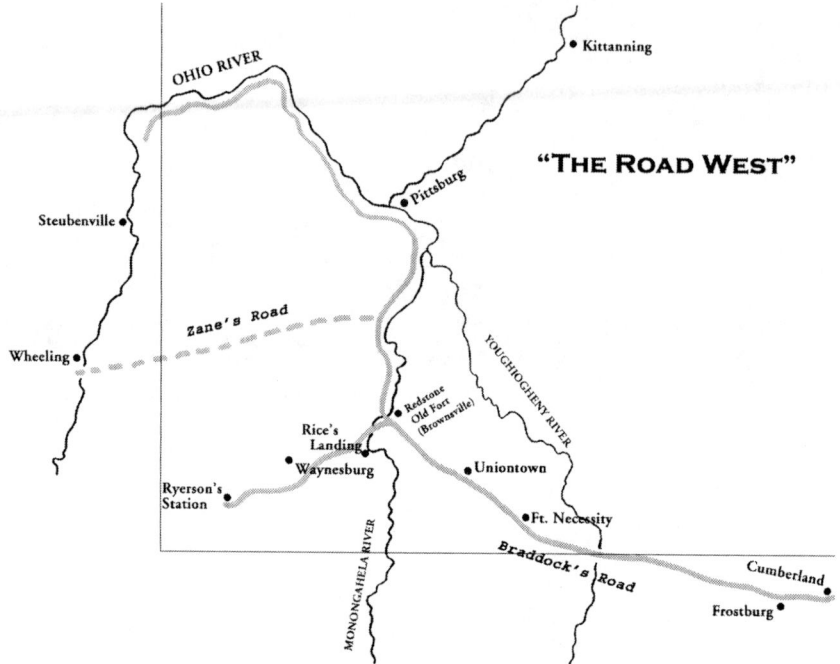

The successful Revolutionary War general, "Mad Anthony" Wayne, relished the chance to clear out the Indian "problem." His great victory in northwest Ohio at Fallen Timbers on August 20, 1794 not only freed western Pennsylvania from future attacks, but it also opened up Ohio for "westering." Many on the frontier had "itchy feet" and wondered what lay beyond the next hill. Martin Crow still frequently accompanied Lew Wetzel on his adventures. In 1792, they were near modern-day St. Clairsville in Belmont County.[28] Although Wetzel grew tired of crowds and moved into the Mississippi Valley by 1795, men like Martin Crow knew how to guide parties into Ohio. Martin's family group pushed on to the edge of the Ohio River.

The Archers began to sell land. James, Sr. and Sophia sold a portion of White Oak Bottom to his brother, Joseph, in February 1793. In

---

27 Genealogies.
28 Howe, pp. 307-8; Family tradition places Crow with Wetzel many times. Fedorchak.

December of that year, they sold another portion to William Rhodes.²⁹ The family began moving up the Fish Creek from Pennsylvania, into the Virginia panhandle (Marshall County, WV), and to the mouth of Graves Creek. James Archer, Sr. and Nathan Lincicome filed for land in today's Marshall County (WV) in 1796. James, Jr. and his brother, Joseph, filed for land in 1798, along with Enoch Enochs and Barnet Grandon. On April 6, 1803, James, Jr. recorded a survey for thirty-seven acres on both sides of the Fish Creek. In a span of thirty years, the Archer family had moved from Frederick, Maryland to Greene County, Pennsylvania, and then to Marshall County, (West) Virginia.³⁰

In 1797, an overland route into Ohio was blazed by the Zane brothers of Fort Henry (Wheeling). Elisha Enochs may have taken this route; he recorded land in Belmont County, Ohio in 1801. Susan Archer's marriage to John Preble was recorded in Belmont County on December 3, 1804. A James Archer (Jr.?) was paid one dollar for a wolf scalp in Belmont County on November 3, 1805. This is circumstantial evidence that the Archers were again "westering,"³¹ at least exploring the Ohio side of the river.

Others from Greene County and Ohio County paddled their way down the Graves, Fish, and Wheeling creeks into the Ohio River and down to Marietta, where they re-provisioned, then took the Little Muskingum and Duck creeks into the area that had been scouted a decade before by Wetzel and Crow. Simon Archer was recorded in the 1802 Washington County census. Joseph Archer bought and sold family holdings in Greene County, and his family pushed on into Ohio, perhaps as early as 1808.³² Girdling trees, building cabins, and planting corn and tobacco, the Archers joined in the sweat of other settlers of the East Fork of Duck Creek: Enochses, Morrises, Davises, Lincicomes, Grandons, and Crows. In their new home, the Archers were once again unique. Of their group, the Archers for certain, and the Grandons, the Churches, and the

---

29 Archer, p. 30. Patrick Archer witnessed this document. It is the last trace of him in available records.
30 Archer, pp. 19, 58; Ohio County Land Book 1785-1813, p. 253, cited in Archer. James, Sr. remained on these tax rolls until 1807; Joseph until 1812. George Archer takes this as good evidence that they were in Ohio County and not in Ohio. Archer, p. 42. Ohio County was divided north and south. Today's Ohio County in West Virginia is the top panhandle of the state. The above settlement was in Marshall County, WV.
31 Belmont County Marriage Book 1803-1806, p. 17; by JP David Ruble. Archer, p. 47.
32 George Archer arrives at the 1808 from the fact that settlers were permitted a five-year tax holiday on new lands. James began paying taxes on his Guernsey County claim in 1814. James, Jr. recorded land in Guernsey County on July 10, 1816 (Ohio Deed Book, Vol. 1, C, p. 117). Two children of Joseph were married in Guernsey County in 1811 and 1812. Archer, p. 265. Archer has found no paper trail for the Archers between 1808 and 1814.

Lincicomes may have been Catholics. Through intermarriage, they would create their own Catholic colony in eastern Ohio. Archer Settlement and nearby Beaver Settlement tell a story seldom told in Ohio history: the story of Irish Catholics on the Ohio frontier.

Chapter Four

Native and Emigres: The American Church in an Age of Revolution
Missions in Kentucky, Pennsylvania, and The West

At the same time that George Washington pushed his way through the Pennsylvanian wilderness on behalf of the Virginian investors in the Ohio Company in 1753, Jack Carroll of Rock Creek Plantation in Maryland graduated from St. Omer and entered the novitiate of the English Jesuits at Watten. His cousin, Charles Carroll of Carrollton, began to prepare for the law.[1] Both of these young Americans would be caught up in the political dissent which followed the English victory over the French in 1763.

Once the French threat was removed, the British government (with its Proclamation Line of 1763) looked on its newly-won American West as a place to develop an empire based on Indian fur trade. The "buckskins" west of the Allegheny–and eastern investors–were outraged. as the decade progressed (1763-1773), Britain tried to force the Americans to pay for their own defense and to contain them to the seaboard. Escalating anger at these English policies arose with each action: the Stamp Tax; the Tea Tax. A number of British colonials, who were becoming American in their psyche, reacted: the Boston Tea Party; Committees of Correspondence. The angry British closed the port of Boston. American "minute men" gathered to face down the "redcoats" or "lobsterbacks." With skirmishes at Lexington and at Concord, a Revolution was underway.

When this crisis came, Maryland Catholics' position had improved. By Assembly action in 1775, all free men with income of 40£ were admitted to vote "'without religious distinction.'" This law–and Virginia's Act on Religious Freedom, written by Thomas Jefferson–were reflective of the Enlightenment Philosophy which forged the minds of the Revolution's

---

1 Hennessey, p. 4.

leaders.[2] In Maryland where he had previously been deprived of a public life, Charles Carroll of Carrollton penned eloquent newspaper articles on the issues dividing Americans from Englishmen. After 1775, Carroll played an important part in the Revolution, becoming the only Roman Catholic to sign the Declaration of Independence. Charles also drew his cousin, Father John Carroll, into Revolutionary circles.

Charles Carroll of Carrollton, 1834 by Thomas Sully, oil on canvas.
Courtesy Maryland Commission Artistic Property of the Maryland State Archives, MSASC 1545-1114

Father Carroll's experience in the stifling atmosphere of France had convinced him of the necessity of laws to promote religious freedom. Coupled with his childhood experiences in bigoted Maryland, Carroll became a fervent advocate for freedom of conscience. The priest's views made him acceptable in Enlightenment circles. Carroll's fluency in languages (Latin, Italian, and French) made him an important go-between. When the Continental Congress sent a delegation to Canada, consisting of Benjamin Franklin, Samuel Chase,

---

2 Wm. H. Sadlier, "Our Catholic Roots," Internet. The situation for Catholics in England also improved. A new policy was rooted in the government's need to recruit Catholic Scottish Highlanders for the American war. The first Catholic Relief Act of 1778 repealed a great portion of the statutes enacted in 1699. Catholics were again able to purchase and inherit land. The new atmosphere affected the approximately 80,000 Roman Catholics in England in 1770. The Catholic elite still produced leaders for the church; for example, Father James Talbot, (the brother of the Earl of Shrewsbury) was the last priest indicted in England for saying mass (1771). "John Talbot," *Catholic Encyclopedia*, V. XIII, p. 918. Norman, p. 51. "England," *Catholic Encyclopedia*, V. V, p. 365.

Things were less positive in Ireland. The Catholic Relief Act still made property rights conditional upon taking the test oath. Resentment grew. The Catholic Association, founded in 1759, campaigned non-aggressively for a relaxation of land laws, for the right to establish schools (granted in the 1790's), and for the right to practice law (granted in 1792). The gradual relaxation of the Irish penal code was played out against the English need for a peaceful Ireland, as the Empire waged war with France and the Stuart Pretenders, Charles and Charles Edward. Against the backdrop of the 1745 Rising, a new English government in Ireland stopped the priest-hunting and permitted Catholic chapels to open. In the 1750's, other laws were increasingly ignored. Fears of Irish action during the American Revolution led to further relaxation of laws. During the French Revolution, Catholics were given the vote on the same restricted basis as Protestants (a property qualification), but barred from Parliament. Schlegel, *Ancestors*, p. 160.

But a population explosion complicated Irish politics. The population doubled between 1700-1800. By 1780, the potato was a staple. One acre of land with that crop could feed a family of six. But the 1780's also saw an economic depression which led to rural discontent in Ulster, Cork, and Kerry. At issue was the tithe to the Church of England and a potato tax.

For many, Ireland seemed unfixable. A trickle of European-educated Irish elites made their way to America where their Irish experience fed their anti-English attitudes as war developed. Norman, p. 51. Hennessey, p. 354. R.F. Foster, *Modern Ireland*, (Penguin Putnam, 1990) pp. 208, 210-11, 219, 224.

and Charles Carroll, aiming to seek French aid, John Carroll was invited along. Over the ensuing months, the priest became a confidant of the aged Revolutionary leader, Benjamin Franklin. When the dust of war settled, a papal diplomat approached Franklin (the only American well-known in Europe), seeking information about the distant American Catholic Church. Franklin recommended John Carroll for a leadership role.

Carroll was a relatively young man and, clearly, the leader among the aging group of exiled Jesuits. In November 1773, he called a meeting of the twenty-three Jesuits in Maryland and Pennsylvania. The few who were able assembled at Whitemarsh, a Jesuit farm in Maryland. A decade later, six Jesuits met with Carroll and hammered out a constitution for the Select Body of Clergy, an organization which would administer property and evaluate the credentials of immigrant priests. The group also petitioned Rome to appoint a superior of the American mission.[3]

The new United States began its political life under the Articles of Confederation. Each state determined its religious life. All but Maryland, Pennsylvania, Virginia, and Delaware legally restricted the practice of Catholicism. The twenty-three priests in the new country were painfully aware of restrictions and hostility. In 1784, when Benjamin Franklin recorded in his diary that "'the Pope . . . on my recommendation, appointed Mr. John Carroll Superior of the Catholic clergy in America,'" he knew that his friend had a Herculean task.[4]

Soon, Carroll was elected the Bishop of Baltimore, a see that covered the entirety of American territory. Carroll chose to be consecrated in England. He reunited with his friends, Mr. and Mrs. Thomas Weld, whom he had met on an earlier trip. The Welds's ancestral Lulworth Castle in Doretshire stood as a monument to unbowed recusancy. When Weld built a small chapel in the castle in 1786, it was apparently the first Catholic church that had been built in England since the Reformation.[5] There, on the Feast of the Assumption of the Virgin Mary–August 15, 1790–the Right Reverend Charles Walmsley, Senior Vicar-Apostolic of England, consecrated John J. Carroll as the first Bishop of Baltimore. Young Thomas Weld–a future English cardinal–participated in the ceremony. The new bishop's coat of arms featured the thirteen American stars surrounding

---

3 Sadlier. "John Carroll," *Catholic Encyclopedia*, V. III, p. 152.
4 Quoted in Hennessey, p. 2.
5 McAvoy, p. 62.

the Virgin and Child.[6]

Bishop Carroll's immediate concern was for the seaboard Catholics, but he was acutely conscious of the vastness of the American West and the salvation of the few souls it might hold. During his lifetime, the West was slowly mapped. He began to receive calls–which he could not fill–for priests. Felix Hughes of Greene County, Pennsylvania, wrote to priests in Philadelphia in 1751, asking for a priest. Later, Hughes would visit Carroll in Baltimore. There was a steady trickle of such requests.[7]

Carroll had no one to send. In 1785, he made his first report to Rome of the situation of the American church. He reported 15,800 Catholics[8] and nineteen priests in Maryland, 7,000 Catholics and five priests in Pennsylvania, 1,500 Catholics in New York, and two hundred Catholics in Virginia. Of his twenty-three priests, five were over seventy years of age. The American population was 2.5 million; the Catholic population was less than one percent. Carroll appealed to Rome for missionaries.[9]

One of the first would be a native-born convert. Father John Thayer came from a Unitarian tradition. After graduating from Yale, he served as a chaplain in the Revolutionary War. During a visit to Italy, he came into contact with Jesuits. He converted to Catholicism in 1783, studied at Saint Sulpice, and was ordained in 1787. Carroll sent him to Boston, then to Scott County, Kentucky, where his views of slavery were unwelcome. Thayer died in Ireland and willed his estate toward the establishment of an Ursuline convent in Boston.[10]

Carroll's flock was increasingly scattered. In Pennsylvania in July of 1785, the venerable Father Ferdinand Farmer received a letter from Western Pennsylvania informing him of seventy-three people who were in need of a priest.[11] Carroll observed that the Maryland missions were in good shape, but they were beginning to see an attrition as people moved to Kentucky. The economic debris of the Revolutionary War and the lingering anti-

---

6 Ellis, p. 454. Hennessey frontispiece. The English hierarchy was restored in 1850. Frazier, p. 292.
7 Mary Ramona Mattingly, *The Catholic Church on the Kentucky Frontier, 1785-1812* (The Catholic University: Washington, DC, 1936) p. 25.
8 Including 3,000 slaves.
9 Ellis, p. 431. Carroll also heard of a German Carmelite working in the west. Ibid. Sadlier. Donald Schlegel, *CRS*, V. XX #4, April 1995.
10 "John Thayer," *Catholic Encyclopedia*, V. XIV p. 3. Mattingly, p. 49-50, n48. This is the convent that rioters burned in 1834.
11 Ellis, p. 441.

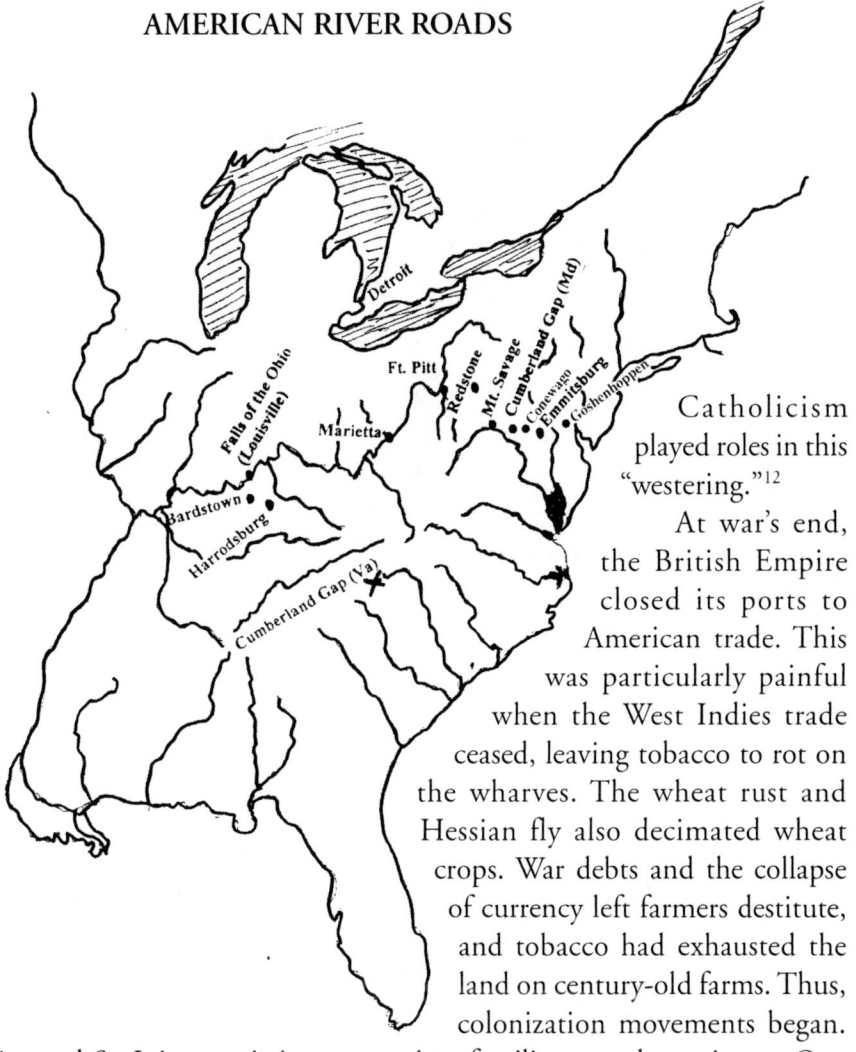

Catholicism played roles in this "westering."[12]

At war's end, the British Empire closed its ports to American trade. This was particularly painful when the West Indies trade ceased, leaving tobacco to rot on the wharves. The wheat rust and Hessian fly also decimated wheat crops. War debts and the collapse of currency left farmers destitute, and tobacco had exhausted the land on century-old farms. Thus, colonization movements began. Around St. Inigoes mission, some sixty families agreed to migrate. One group was led by Joseph Fenwick and his brothers, great-grandsons of the immigrant, Cuthbert Fenwick. They added up their economic plight and the impact of "the remnants of colonial penal legislation" which hampered their religious life, and they began to move in 1785.[13]

---

12 Ellis, p. 434; Although Maryland, Pennsylvania, and Virginia granted full toleration to Catholics with Independence, it was not always so in practice. Colonial laws only slowly gave way to new state laws. Vermont dropped legal restrictions in 1786; South Carolina in 1790. Delaware gave the vote to every free male at the turn of the century. Georgia then abolished its test for office holders. In 1818, Connecticut abolished her established religion, Congregationalism. In 1822, New York removed an oath that barred office-holding by Catholics and Jews, as did Massachusetts. McAvoy, p. 50.

13 Beitzell, p. 97. Mattingly, pp. 4, 6, 8. Ellis, p. 439. In 1803, some twenty-five of these families moved on to Perry County, Missouri, and settled on land purchased by Joseph Fenwick. Timothy J. O'Rourke, *The Catholic Church on the Frontier: the Missouri and Texas Settlements of Maryland Catholics* (Brifney Press: Parsons, Kansas, 1973).

The St. Inigoes migrants journeyed some six hundred miles to Pottinger's Creek in Nelson County, Kentucky. They traveled up the rough roads to Pennsylvania and Braddock's Road, then to Pittsburgh and down the river to Limestone. Fearing Indian attack, they left the river there and cut their way overland.[14]

A few immigrant priests began to arrive. In 1785, an Irish Franciscan Capuchin friar arrived in New York City. Charles Maurice Wheland had been a chaplain for the French navy during the war. After serving in eighteen engagements, he was captured by the English and imprisoned at Jamaica until war's end. Carroll sent him with a group of Maryland immigrants into Kentucky in 1787. He left the colony in 1790 in a dispute over salary. Wheland traveled down the Ohio and Mississippi to New Orleans, and then by ship to New York.[15] The Irish priest, William de Rohan, would build Holy Cross Church on Pottinger's Creek in 1792. He arrived with immigrants from Tennessee and North Carolina, via Daniel Boone's Wilderness Road, and spent two years in Nelson County.[16]

From the beginning, Bishop Carroll faced the problem of ethnic parishes, a problem in a country which would become a melting pot. Pennsylvania's German Catholics had been served from St. Mary's Church in Philadelphia. Most of the parish was English-speaking, but the elderly priest, the ex-Jesuit Father Ferdinand Farmer (aka Steinmeyer), was German. When Farmer died in 1787, a non-German succeeded him, to the dismay of the Germans in the parish. Then, two German Franciscans–brothers John and Peter Helbron–disembarked from a ship at Philadelphia in October 1787. They immediately began to attract a German congregation, even though they had not been recognized and accredited by Bishop Carroll.

The brothers had come to America in response to an advertisement placed in a German newspaper by desperate German Catholics. Peter Helbron entered the Franciscan Order from the life of a Prussian army officer. He was an expert horseman and a man of "'culture and refinement.'" Carroll diffused the crisis in Philadelphia by naming Helbron as the pastor of a new German parish, Holy Trinity, in 1789.[17] John Baptist Helbron returned to Germany on a "begging trip," but was caught up in the French

---

14 Mattingly, pp. 18-19.
15 Sadlier. Lambing, p. 35.
16 Ellis, p. 440. Mattingly, pp. 41-42.
17 Sadlier. Omer U. Kline, O.S.B. *The Sportsman's Hall Parish Later Named Saint Vincent 1790-1846* (St. Vincent Arch-Abbey Press: Latrobe, Pennsylvania, 1990), p. 23.

Revolution. The Capuchin was guillotined in Bayonne, France on November 25, 1793, at the age of forty-seven.[18]

In 1788, six families from the German colony of Goshenhoppen made a two hundred and fifty mile trip to Greensburg in Westmoreland County. As others from their former home arrived down the well-beaten road, they brought with them the promise that a priest would visit them. Peter Helbron made at least one journey to them. In 1789, the Dutch priest, Theo Browers, of the Minorite Order of St. Francis (O.S.F.), landed in Philadelphia from the West Indies. Peter Helbron welcomed him and urged him to remain in Philadelphia, but Browers had heard of the Westmoreland colony and decided to adopt that area as his mission field. He journeyed west and wintered over 1789-90 with members of his new congregation.[19]

The Rotterdam-born priest was another cultivated man. Born in 1738 and ordained in 1762, he had taught at seminaries in Holland and Belgium until 1776, when he was sent as the superior of a missionary band to Curaçao, where he remained until he went to Philadelphia. Browers had means at his disposal. He purchased 165 acres of land called O'Neill's Victory for £106 from a seller in Philadelphia. The farm proved to be too distant from the rest of the colony, so Browers spent £475 for a hunting lodge called Sportsman's Hall, located seven miles east of Greensburg. Eventually, Sportsman's Hall would become "another Conewago"–the "Cradle of the church in Western Pennsylvania" and, after 1835, the site of St. Vincent Abbey. However, before that could happen, it had to endure a sorry spectacle.[20]

Theo Browers died in 1790, leaving his property to "the Roman Catholic priest who shall succeed me . . . ." Unfortunately, the next two priests were un-credentialed renegades. John Baptist Cause, an Alsatian Franciscan, appropriated the property, then absconded to buy a traveling show, "Panorama of Jerusalem," and enjoy the "carnival" life. The German Franciscan, Francis Fromm, at first ingratiated himself to the congregation, and then absconded with money, throwing the tiny community into more turmoil. So scandalous was it, that German settlers dropped off the trail at Shade Valley, Sinking Valley, or Frankstown, rather than settle around Sportsman's Hall.[21]

---
18 Kline, p. 24.
19 The Christian Ruffner family. Kline, p. 4. Lambing, p. 363.
20 Internet. Kline, pp. 2-4.
21 Internet. Schlegel, p. 567.

It took decades for Carroll to secure the property.[22] The entire affair of Sportsman's Hall scandalized the Catholic and non-Catholic communities in Westmoreland County. Even though it remained difficult to verify documents of priests immigrating from Europe, Carroll had no choice but to seek out immigrant clergy to serve his increasingly pressing needs.

The French Revolution began to spin out of control. Religious in French territories began to filter out of Revolutionary control. In the English-speaking convents in the Lowlands, American and English nuns began to pack. Some dreamt of establishing a community in the new United States. At the Antwerp Carmelite convent, and at Hoogstraeten in Holland, American-born religious donned secular clothing and made their way to port cities. On May 1, 1790, four Carmelite nuns of the Maryland Matthews family sailed with Father Charles Neale, S.J. (who was returning to America after an absence of thirty years) and Father Robert Plunkett, escaping from European turmoil to an unknown situation in America.[23]

Plunkett left the party in New York, but the others went on to Baltimore and then to Father Neale's family home, Chandler's Hope, overlooking the seaport of Port Tobacco. Since Bishop Carroll was in England for his investiture, the nuns informally organized themselves into the convent of Carmel of the Sacred Hearts of Jesus, Mary, and Joseph. Soon, they would become the first Discalced Carmelite convent–indeed, the first house of women religious–in the United States.[24]

News from France was more and more frightening. In 1792, Bishop Carroll had to announce to his few priests that 3,000 of their brothers had been executed in France. By 1797, some 5,500 French clergy and 5,950 laity were refugees in England; Parliament unexpectedly voted them a subsidy.[25]

As the Reign of Terror traumatized France, refugee priests made

---

22 Schlegel, p. 570. Internet. Hennessey, pp. 36-71. Kline, pp. 11, 27. Cause apparently reconciled with Carroll before his death. Ibid. Fromm died un-reconciled in 1798 during a yellow fever epidemic in Philadelphia.
  The suit over ownership of Browers's property established the authority of a Roman Catholic bishop in American civil courts. Kline, pp. 21, 27.
23 *Carmel of Port Tobacco Almanac* (LaPlata, Maryland, 1990). The nuns were the relatives of Father Ignatius Matthews, S.J. The flight from revolution led to the reestablishment of Catholic colleges in England: Douai to Old Hall, Ware, Herefordshire, Jesuits at Stonyhurst (a Weld house) in Lancashire and Benedictines at Amperforth in Devonshire. Dominicans established a school in Devon. "England," *New Catholic Encyclopedia*, First Edition, V. V, p. 365.
24 Steel, p. 821.
25 Ibid.

their way to America. A body of such refugees arrived in Philadelphia in 1792 and another landed from the French West Indies in 1793. Most of them were dedicated to their vows. Notable among them was French Sulpician, Benedict Joseph Flaget.[26]

The Sulpicians intended to establish an American seminary, and their work at St. Mary's in Emmitsburg would "form the character of the American priest." The Sulpicians were reformed according to the precepts of the Council of Trent, dedicated to church discipline and to the paramount importance of the sacraments in Catholic life.[27]

Faced with such desperate need, Carroll could not spare priests for the seminary; he sent Flaget west to the old French settlements at Vincennes and Cahokia. In 1792, Flaget arrived in Pittsburgh, but the Ohio River was low and he remained in the Presbyterian bastion for six months, tending to the very few Catholics there. When he boarded a flat boat for the trip to Vincennes, the American general, George Rogers Clark, provided escort.[28] Soon after Flaget left Pittsburgh, two of his companions arrived from the flight out of France. Stephen Badin, who completed his studies and was ordained by Bishop Carroll–becoming the first priest ordained in English-America–and Father Michael Bernard Barriere, walked into Pittsburgh at the end of the long journey from Baltimore. They were two more of the foreign priests that Carroll relied upon to serve his people.[29]

In Ireland, a long saga of restiveness against British rule burst into a savage Jacobin-style bloodbath which colored immigration patterns to America. In America and in Ireland, the Irish felt a fellowship with American causes. When Americans argued that their "constitutional rights–the ancient rights of Englishmen" were being subverted, the Irish argued for the "restoration of lost rights."[30] During the American Revolution, Roman Catholic Irish fought in the American army and navy–notably, John Barry of County Wexford, the "Father of the American Navy."[31] The transformation of American politics radicalized elements in Ireland. Independence became the goal of the United Irishmen.

The most radical of the agitators was Theobald Wolfe Tone. He was energized by Tom Paine's *Rights of Man*, which went through seven Irish

---

26 Internet.
27 McAvoy, p. 71.
28 Mattingly, p. 210.
29 Badin was ordained on March 25, 1793 by Bishop Carroll. Hennessey, p. 36. Schlegel, *CRS*, V. XX #4, April 1995.
30 Foster, p. 241.
31 Blessing, p. 527.

editions between 1791-92. Paine's ideas had been important in formulating the American philosophy, but were too radical for practice. Paine then became an agitator in France, even becoming an officer in the Revolutionary Guards. Wolfe Tone immersed himself in this philosophy and steeled himself to become as ruthless and as dedicated a revolutionary as his contemporary in France–Robespierre. Tone, however, would not come to power.[32]

Wolfe Tone

Tone sought American support in 1792 and then cut a deal with Napoleon to aid his cause by invading Ireland. Tone's personality persuaded the French to provide support; otherwise, there would have been no Rising in 1798, "The Year of the French." The resulting actions produced "the most violent and tragic event in Irish history between the Jacobite wars and the Great Famine." The United Irishmen (Protestant and Catholic) were not ready; the French invasion in County Mayo was half-hearted; overall direction failed. The peasants—who thought that liberty meant the end of tithes and taxes—rose up in a Jacquerie-style revolt, killing all who were "above." The government replied with a savage campaign to disarm them, turning parts of Kildare and Wicklow into wastelands.[33]

During the three-month Rising, over 30,000 people died. Peasants on killing binges roamed through Clare, Galway, Wexford, and Wicklow. The imprisoned Wolfe Tone was denied a soldier's death, and committed suicide. The loss of property was on a scale unknown since Cromwell's time; Ireland's economy was in shambles. During the Mayo winter, "the peasants, who had lost all they possessed, huddled together in the caves and bog-holes as famine followed in the wake of the revolution." Ireland's political independence was a dream which disintegrated into a nightmare. On January 1, 1801, Ireland was annexed to England by Act of Union.[34]

During the Rising, Irishmen were impressed into the British military and people were transported to penal colonies. After the rising, a wave of emigration ensued, averaging 50,000 a year. The immigrants to America after 1799 carried this nightmare in their memories. These were largely the "shanty Irish"—or the "Pre-Famine Fled." Between 1800 and 1802, six-thousand such people entered Philadelphia's port. In 1816, the port

---

32 Foster, pp. 265, 734.
33 Thomas Pakenham, *The Year of Liberty*, Prentice Hall, Inc. (Englewood Cliffs, N.J., 1969) pp. 13, 36, 353. Foster, pp. 175, 225.
34 Ibid., p. 293.

saw 6,000, and 9,000 the following year. In 1818, the number was 20,000. The Irish numbered 6,000 in the city in 1800. They were seven-percent of the population, but accounted for 36% of the arrests. These people were the displaced poor of the Rising of '98.

The Irish knew about the opening of new lands in America's West from newspaper reports. They continued their migration. From 1783-1803, about 3,000 Scotch-Irish migrated to America each year; from 1803-1807, the number was 1,100 per year. During the European Embargo (1807-1810) and the War of 1812 (1812-1814), migration halted, but then burst out again when the sea lanes were free. In 1816, it was a flood, and Irish escaped from poor markets for harvests and crippling new taxes levied to pay for the Napoleonic wars.[35]

In Ireland, one more attempt at insurrection was led by Robert Emmet, who had been expelled from Trinity College in '98, along with other radicals. But Emmet's Rising of 1803 amounted to little more than a scuffle. Real reform in Ireland would come only through legal agitation. That was the special province of Daniel O'Connell of County Clare. His life's work–and the cooperation of Irish-born Prime Minister, the Duke of Wellington–would produce the Catholic Emancipation Act of 1829.[36] The gradual equalization of roles in Ireland commenced.

In England, the threat of double taxation had been successful, and many of the old Catholic nobility went over to the Church of England. In 1660, thirty Roman Catholic families held peerages. By 1829, only five remained Catholic. Still, an estimated quarter of a million Roman Catholics resided in England in 1811, many of them Irish and French. Since they were no longer feared, the penal laws were relaxed. by 1815, the First Peer of the Realm, the Duke of Norfolk, was again a Catholic. Two years later, Catholics could receive military commissions. In 1814, the Jesuits were restored worldwide, and the entire underground church surfaced. A historic period was at an end.[37]

In the infant United States, Bishop John Carroll sought to steer his tiny church through the shoals of "foreign-ness," and to serve an increasingly scattered people. He relied almost entirely on foreign priests. One of these was Father Patrick Lonergan, Order of Friars Minor of St. Francis (Franciscan), a native of County Waterford, Ireland, who arrived in America sometime before 1796, perhaps with a wave of French exiles. Lonergan's letters to Carroll reveal a visit to Conewago and time spent in

---

35 Blessing, p. 528. Schlegel, *Ancestors*, pp. 175-176.
36 Foster, p. 354.
37 Steel, p. 840.

Northumberland County where he crossed verbal swords with the "'North of Ireland gentry'" of that place. A letter dated January 1797 spoke of the purchase of a large farm twenty miles from Milltown, which Lonergan intended to cede to his sister (a Franciscan nun) for the establishment of a convent. However, the efforts among the few Irish Catholics in Northumberland failed, and Lonergan moved west.[38]

Lonergan tried, but failed, to oust the renegade, Francis Fromm, from Sportsman's Hall. Lonergan then went on to the Irish Catholics in Fayette County at Jacob's Creek on the Youghiogheny River. From there, he and some families from Sportsman's Hall moved on to Greene County, where he purchased five lots in Waynesburg, with the intention to build a church. In the meantime, he offered mass and "instructed his small and scattered flock in private houses."[39] "Discouraged and impoverished, Rev. Patrick Lonergan left Waynesburg in the autumn of 1801." He made the tortuous trip from Pittsburgh to New Orleans, where he died in 1804. Greene County Catholics then fell under the care of Peter Helbron who had succeeded in securing control of Sportsman's Hall.

In November 1799, Bishop Carroll sent sixty-six-year-old Peter Helbron into the turmoil of Browers's legacy. The kind priest's quiet diplomatic skills brought stability to the community. Helbron had a parish of seventy-five communicants, and a circuit that covered seven Pennsylvania counties: Westmoreland, Fayette, Washington, Greene, Allegheny, Butler, and Armstrong. Helbron wrote his bishop that he rode "'as far as the lake. [Erie]'" In his quest to search out un-churched Catholics, Helbron had only the aid of Father Demetrius Gallitzin, who visited Helbron from his log church at McGuire's Settlement (Loretto) in Cambria County (1799). (Both spoke German.) In his "labored English syntax: [Helbron wrote] he was 'the only help to me...and I to him.'" Father Helbron kept a baptismal register that covered 1799 to 1815. Unfortunately, no mention of the few Catholics in Greene County is inscribed.[40]

---

38 An article in the *Pittsburgh Catholic*, November 1, 1923, cites work done by Msgr. Martin Hughes which disputes the published claims that Lonergan established a failed colony in West Alexandria, Washington County. The author argues that the story really reveals the saga of the Northumberland endeavor.

39 Ibid. Kline, p. 20.

40 Kline, pp. 27, 29, 30, 32. Helbron ventured to the Kittanning area in 1803, saying mass at "Buffalo Creeke" (Sugar Creek, twelve miles northwest of Kittanning). Lambing, pp. 412-3. This is equidistant in miles and difficulty from Noble/Monroe County, Ohio. "It is impossible to trace the religious history of these pioneers and to learn by whom they were ministered to." Lambing, p. 227. *Pittsburgh Catholic*, November 1, 1923. Helbron's register begins only in 1800, but he was in the area before that. The register does not reflect the entire circuit, but rather only a handful of places: Unity Township, Derry Township, Greensburg in Westmoreland County, Hannatown near Kittanning, the River Yock (Jacob's Creek) in Fayette county, and Donegal Settlement at Sugar Creek in northern Armstrong County. Edmund Adams and Barbara Brady O'Keefe, *Catholic Trails West: The Founding Catholic Families of Pennsylvania*, Vol. II (Gateway Press, Inc., Baltimore, 1989) passim.

Another native-born American priest began his work in 1804. Edward Fenwick, son of Ignatius Fenwick, a colonel on Washington's staff and descendent of Cuthbert Fenwick, was born into one of Maryland's first Catholic families. His mother was Sara Taney of the aristocratic Irish Catholic family. Fenwick was born on the family estate overlooking the Patuxent River in St. Mary's County. Educated in secret schools, he sailed for Europe and, at sixteen, entered Bornham, the Belgium school founded in 1658 by the exiled English Dominicans under the leadership of Philip Thomas Howard, later Cardinal of Norfolk.

Father Edward Fenwick
Catholic Record Society, Columbus, OH

Father Edward Fenwick was ordained in 1793 and, like other talented American expatriates, taught in Dominican schools in Europe. Fenwick taught in England. In 1804, he returned home to America.

Bishop Carroll sent Fenwick to serve the Fenwick colony in Kentucky, and to determine if the area could sustain a Dominican foundation. Traveling with his brother-in-law, the layman, Nicholas Young, the pair went to Pittsburgh, then floated down the Ohio for thirteen days before reaching Louisville. Once established in a log cabin in the Marylander colony, Fenwick determined to use his family inheritance to establish St. Rose of Lima Priory near Springfield (Washington County), Kentucky. In 1806, he and three other friars began building the convent in the Kentucky hills.[41]

---

41 Mattingly, pp. 79, 81. Anthony Lisska, *CRS*, Vol. XXV, #10, p. 8.
                    Priests in America (Author's Note)
    1785   23 in America: 19 in Maryland, 5 in Pennsylvania; 5 of these were over age 70
    1785   Maryland migration to Kentucky
    1785   Ch Maurice Wheland arrived in Kentucky (but Farmer died in '87)
    1787   Thayer ordained; to Scott County, Kentucky
    1789   John and Peter Helbron to Philadelphia from Prussia
                    Theo Browers to Westmoreland County: Sportsman's Hall
    1792   Irishman William de Rohan to Kentucky
                    French émigré priests to America
    1793   French émigré priests from West Indies to America
                    Flaget, Badin, and Barriere walk to Pittsburgh from Baltimore
    1796   Patrick Lonergan to Sportsman's Hall, then to Waynesburg
    1799   Helbron to Sportsman's Hall
    1810   7 priests in Kentucky

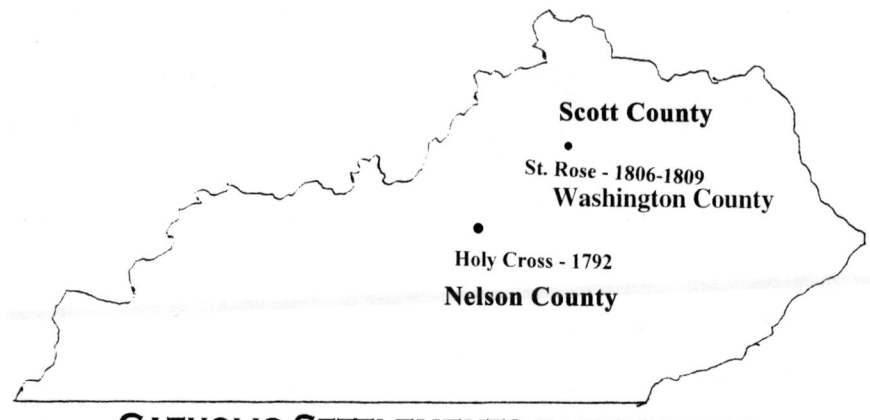

CATHOLIC SETTLEMENTS IN KENTUCKY

Soon after Carroll sent Fenwick to Kentucky, he sent another young priest into the wilds of Michigan Territory. French Sulpician, Gabriel Richard, had been secretly ordained at Issy, Paris in 1791, in defiance of the Revolutionary government. Gabriel was another of the French émigré priests struggling to learn English and taking out American citizenship. He made the long journey from Baltimore to Pittsburgh, to St. Louis, and then up into Michigan Territory where he served a parish of some 10,000 French and Indians. When the village of Detroit burned on June 11, 1805, Father Richard's leadership thrust him into a position of great respect; he became the voice of Catholicism in the far northwest.[42]

In 1808, Pope Pius VII acknowledged the magnitude of the expansiveness of the American mission field by creating four new American dioceses. This was sorely needed. In 1799, Stephen Badin had written to Carroll of the great need for a bishop: "'many Catholics, even far grown in years, have never received the Sacrament of Confirmation.'" One of the new dioceses was based at Bardstown and covered Kentucky, Tennessee and the Old Northwest Territory: the emerging states of Ohio, Michigan, Indiana, and Wisconsin. John Carroll recalled Benedict Joseph Flaget from Cuba, where he had been sent to establish a college, and

Benedict Joseph Flaget
Catholic Record Society, Columbus, OH

---

[42] Louis Horton, "Portrait of an Ecumenist: Father Gabriel Richard," *The Catholic Digest*, March 1969, pp. 57-60. "Gabriel Richard," *Catholic Encyclopedia*, V. XII, p. 484.

consecrated him as Bishop of Bardstown on November 4, 1809. The new bishop wrote

> I found myself in the middle of a bishopric that was two or three times the size of France, and contained five huge states and two immense territories . . . .

Bishop Flaget and Edward Fenwick set out, searching for the Catholics of the west.[43]

---

43 *CRS*, Vol. XXV, #10.

CATHOLIC ENCLAVES IN OHIO • 1790–1820
Catholic Record Society • Diocese of Columbus

Chapter Five

On The Verge of "Nothingness"
The Ohio Mission Field: 1790–1825

When the native tribes were defeated at the Battle of Fallen Timbers in 1794, white immigrants pushed into the Ohio Territory. Moravian missionaries who had earlier accompanied Christian Indians from the Kittanning area of Pennsylvania estimated that, by 1794, there were already three-thousand immigrants along the "river roads" into the territory. However, the heavily-wooded terrain of the south and east hindered penetration. At that point, the United States Government sought a winter mail route to Kentucky, in case the Ohio River froze. Congress authorized Ebenezer Zane, of Wheeling (Fort Henry), to blaze a trail to serve that purpose. The Zane's Trace was completed in 1796. Travelers called it a "tunnel through the trees," but the rough mule trail brought immigrants inland into Ohio. A string of support settlements sprouted up along the Trace: St. Clairsville, Old Washington, Cambridge, Zanesville, Somerset, Lancaster, Chillicothe, and Aberdeen. So many immigrants flooded into the territory that it qualified for statehood in 1802, and became a state with the requisite 60,000 citizens in 1803. Among those people were a few hundred scattered Roman Catholics.

On the southern border, Gallipolis, an ill-fated French colony without a priest, had disintegrated. Elsewhere, singularly and in family groups, Catholics staked out claims in the new land. In 1796, Daniel Shehy (Sheehy) and John Young began to survey land in the Mahoning River Valley. Shehy was born to a prosperous and politically-active family in County Tipperary (1749?). In a violent episode in the 1760's, his relatives Father Nicholas Sheehy of Clogheen and Edmund Sheehy—were arrested and executed by English authorities. For twenty years, Father Sheehy's head decayed on a pike above the gates of Clomel Jail—as a message to other rebels.

Daniel Shehy was classically trained in the usual Irish émigré manner, and was destined for priesthood. However, he joined an underground Irish independence movement, probably "the White Boys," and when the authorities cracked down, Shehy fled to America. During the American Revolution, he enlisted and served under Captain Laurence Keen in the Eleventh Pennsylvania Line. Along the way, he met John Young and they went west. Shehy was a man of substance. In 1797, he purchased a thousand acres from Young's claim and "proved up" a homestead, which became the village of Youngstown. He married Jane McLain of Ligonier, Pennsylvania, in that same year. Even though they had no contact with a priest for decades, the Shehys considered themselves Catholics. Only in 1817 would Father Edward Fenwick find them. The Shehy story is but one of dozens of such stories of the scattered Catholics in Ohio.[1]

In 1799, Hugh Boyle, an educated Irishman who left the homeland in the wake of the failed '98 Rising, settled in Lancaster, on Zane's Trace. There he became the respected Clerk of Courts in what was Ohio's legal center. Boyle, who was born in County Donegal, married Eleanor Gillespie of Brownsville, Pennsylvania. Thus, they were part of a network of Catholics spaced out along the "road west."[2]

In 1803, the Dittoe-Finck party worked their way down the Trace. Jacob and Peter Dittoe, their brother-in-law, John Finck (Fink), and their families left the German colony of Conewago in Adams County, Pennsylvania and pushed west in 1803. The Dittoes were sons of a German-Alsatian immigrant. Jacob was born in 1760 on the Maryland/Pennsylvania border. Both he and Peter were part of the Conewago Chapel congregation in 1790. Following the baptism of Jacob and Catherine's son, Henry, in 1803 (the sponsors were John and Mary Finck), the clan began "westering."[3]

They traveled the familiar path down Braddock's Road and on to Brownsville, then up the Monongahela to the private road carved by the Zanes out of the wooded terrain. The crafty Zane brothers thus diverted travel from Pittsburgh to their emerging town of Wheeling and onto the Zane's Trace. At Brownsville, the Catholic community would have informed the Dittoes and Fincks of the tiny Catholic community in

---

1   Donald Schlegel, *CRS*, XIII, #1, January 1988. A footnote cites John Mitchel's *History of Ireland* (D&J Sadlier, N.Y., 1868) pp. 99-105. No family legend is known regarding contact with Sportsman's Hall priests. Geographically, that would have been entirely possible.
2   Their daughter would marry Thomas Ewing, the U.S. Senator from Ohio. Their granddaughter was the wife of General William T. Sherman. Genealogies by Lorle Porter.
3   Donald Schlegel, *CRC*, Vol. XX, #4, April 1995.

Lancaster. As the Germans were anxious to retain their faith, their choice of land near Lancaster may have been dictated by the presence nearby of other Catholic families with marriageable children.[4]

Hopeful that a priest would come to them, the families began carving out their homesteads two miles off the Trace in "Middletown," halfway between Lancaster and Zanesville–"14 miles from Lancaster toward Baltimore."[5]

Jacob Dittoe zealously sought to make his family's presence known to Bishop John Carroll. On January 5, 1803, he wrote

> There are of our profession in this place that I am acquainted with, about 30 souls, two families of my acquaintance that will be here this ensuing spring, adding the probable migration from the neighbor land of Conawago [sic] under similar expectations with me (when I saw them) leaves little doubt with me but a considerable congregation may be here in a little time.

Dittoe knew that that an ordination was to occur in the spring (another clue to the Catholic grapevine) and that some of the priests would be sent to Kentucky.

> If so, this place will be on their way. . . .

Dittoe asked that the priests seek him out also.

> Mr. [Hugh] Boyle of the said town who with his family are of the same church.

In February 1807, Bishop Carroll was informed by two laymen in Chillicothe of

> betwixt 30 and 40 which came from the Eastern Shore and were in that Zane's Trace town.[6]

On a cold February 1, 1808, Dittoe poured out his heart to the bishop in Baltimore:

> Everyday's acquaintance in this country brings to my knowledge some of the [Catholic] profession tossed about through this country by the vicissitudes of fortune, deprived [sic] of the advantages of church communion, and extremely anxious for an establishment . . . of a church . . .

In the interim, Dittoe asked if Catholics could be married before a Catholic lawyer in Zanesville.[7]

---

4   *CRS*, #13, January 1988.
5   John H. Lamott, *A History of the Archdiocese of Cincinnati* (F. Pustet Co.: New York, 1921) p. 24.
6   Ibid., pp. 22-23.
7   Lamott, p. 23.

Bishop John Carroll
*Courtesy Notre Dame Archives
Notre Dame University, Indiana*

Father Edward Fenwick met with John Carroll in Baltimore (Maryland) in the spring of 1808. The bishop sent the priest on a mission in search of lost souls in what was then the western wilderness of the vast diocese which was the United States.[8]

Returning east in September of 1808, Fenwick stumbled onto the Dittoe farm. While listening to the forest sounds, he heard the reverberations of an axe. He followed the sound to the cabin. The mass that followed brought great joy to the hearts of the immigrants and to Edward Fenwick, who had come to "'the end of his search, the fulfillment of a commission he had received from the Bishop of Baltimore . . . .'"

In 1810, Dittoe wrote to "finnic" that "'there are some young Catholics in this place that do wish to join in marriage that are waiting upon [your] coming, as it is a point of some importance.'" Requests like this were common. In 1811, there were seven priests in Kentucky and they served some six-thousand Catholics in that state. Trappist monks from Amsterdam established a monastery in Kentucky under the leadership of Urbain Guillett. Traveling with the Trappists was Father Charles Nerinckx, a Belgian priest who fled the Revolution in 1797. The Trappists would move on to Illinois in 1809, but Nerinckx became an important missionary in his adopted Kentucky. By 1812, the Sisters of Loretto and the Sisters of Charity of Nazareth would also be established there. The western church was taking shape in Kentucky, and Ohio would become its mission field.

In 1811, Fenwick and his party worked their way west on Braddock's Road and on to Pittsburgh. There they joined the party of Bishop Benedict Joseph Flaget, who was traveling west to his new see of Bardstown for the first time. They boarded a flatboat for the journey down the Ohio. It is possible that Fenwick and Bishop Flaget then left the flatboat and accompanied Fenwick's nephew, Nicholas Dominic Young, as he drove

---

8   Mattingly, p. 208.

the remuda of horses down the Zane's Trace.⁹ At Middletown (Somerset), Fenwick and John Finck did not recognize one another after an absence of three years. Once again, contact had been made with the German colony in Perry County.¹⁰

En route to a council in Baltimore, Bishop Joseph Flaget and Father Stephen Badin crossed the Ohio River at Maysville on October 7, 1812, and rode up the Trace. Along the way, Badin shouted that they were Catholic priests. In Chillicothe, they found a few Catholics "'who were ashamed to confess their faith and were accustomed to frequent Protestant services.'" In Lancaster, on October 9, they baptized five children. On October 10, they were visiting the Dittoes and the Fincks. Jacob Dittoe showed them the land that he intended to donate for a church; the two clerics urged him to build it for community worship until Flaget could send them a priest. They were instructed to say the mass prayers together, to pray the rosary, and to say the litanies.

The bishop was haunted by his lack of priests.

> not a day passes that we do not find great numbers of these strayed sheep, who, because they do not see their real shepherd, become Baptists, Methodists, etc., or at least nothingists.¹¹

Catholics continued to filter into Ohio. In 1811, "Long Jim" Gallagher and his brother, Patrick, boarded a stage in Baltimore bound for Somerset, Ohio, to inquire about buying land in the Catholic enclave. While spending the night at a tavern on Poultny Ridge in Guernsey County

---

9   McAvoy, p. 79. Mattingly, p. 79. The Trappists established a convent at Monks Mount, Illinois. It broke up in 1813. Mattingly, pp. 67-8. The above is based on Donald Schlegel's reasoning. He bases his hypothesis on a close study of the prime source written by John Martin Henni.
    Early missionaries to the west included John Martin Henni, a Swiss who spoke English, German, and French. With Henni was his friend, Martin Kundig, who would be ordained by Fenwick in 1829. James J. Hartley, *History of the Diocese of Columbus*, V. I & II (Diocese of Columbus: Ohio, 1918), pp. 114, 438-9.
    Henni wrote a "Glimpse of the Ohio Valley," which is an important primary source for the early church in Ohio. He has an account of a meeting between Fenwick, Bishop Flaget, and Finck that appears to be the initial meeting between a priest and the Dittoe-Finck community. But the Henni account does not fit the published lives of the two priests. Schlegel believes that Henni has been misread. Based on internal evidence, including a paucity of information about the flatboat trip between Pittsburgh and Limestone, Schlegel believes Fenwick and Flaget left the boat at Wheeling and re-boarded it at Limestone, thus placing them on the Zane's Trace in 1811. Schlegel posits that Flaget could have been at Somerset in 1811 when he and Stephen Badin made their trip. When he traveled to Kentucky to assume the bishopric in 1808, all accounts place him on the Ohio River. Henni's account could be a jumbling of the two expeditions: Fenwick's in 1808 and Flaget/Badin's in 1811-12. *CRS*, Vol. XXVI, #10, October 2001.
10 Anthony J. Lisska, "Bishop Fenwick's Apostolate to the North Americans," *CRS*, Vol. XVII, November 2000. "Bishop Fenwick, The Apostle of Ohio," *The Catholic Times*, March 3, 1968. Donald Schlegel, *CRS*, Vol. XX, #4.
11 Ibid., p. 5. Mattingly, p. 106.

(site of "Lost Town"), the brothers heard about a sale of Western Reserve Land. They bought 200 acres of "proved up" land; it had a rude cabin by a spring. The Irishmen returned to Baltimore, where they dug ditches in order to meet the payments.[12]

Sometime between 1808 and 1814, the Pennsylvania Archers joined their in-laws, the Enochs, and other Greene county settlers in the Duck Creek Valley.

Ten miles north of the Enochs/Archer settlement, another group of Pennsylvanians began the process of "tomahawk improvements" (securing a homestead). The Ward, DeLong, and Jefferis families had "picked up sticks" and left the Commonwealth of Pennsylvania in another episode of the "westering" that their families had done for half a century.

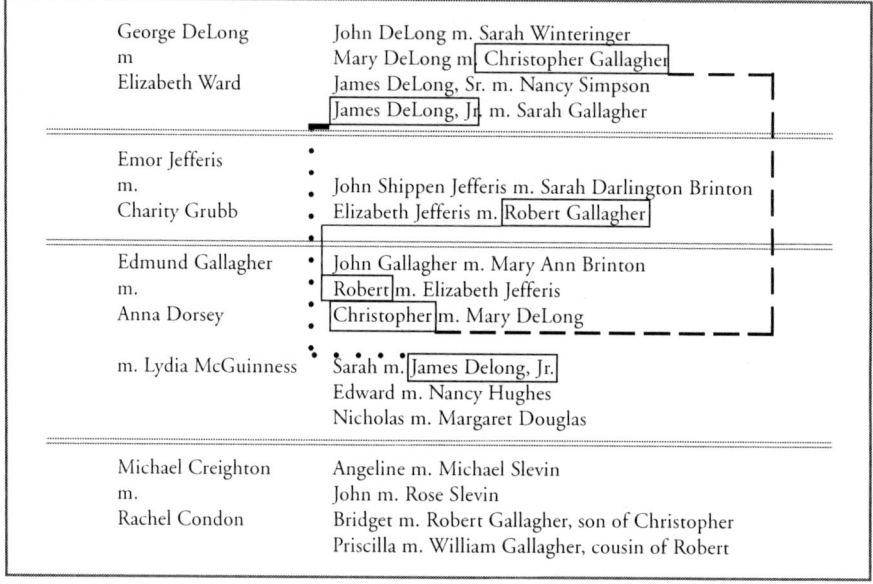

Connecting lines indicate the same individuals.

John and Mary Ward[13] built their cabin in Fannell Township, Cumberland County, in 1756. By the end of the decade, John was in possession of land warrant #131. Cumberland County at that time was the Pennsylvania frontier. John and his sons, William and Edward, hunted for food, chopped down trees, and kept their ears cocked for the gobble of a wild turkey—a possible sign of Indian presence. These experienced buckskin frontiersmen fit the frontier hand to glove: they knew "woodsy

---

12 Marie Gildea, Gallagher Family Memories, an oral history conducted by Kathy Kreppner Graham.
13 The Wards were "perhaps" from Ireland.

ways." Edward's wife, Morning Dove, was possibly a Native American.[14] Frontier families normally intermarried and, in 1769, Elizabeth Jane Ward connected the Wards to the DeLongs, a family of French Huguenot descent, by marrying George DeLong (1745-1860).

During the American Revolution, George DeLong served as a Ranger of the Frontier in a battalion of Cumberland County Militia, under Captain Thomas Ashley. George served during 1778; his brother-in-law, William Ward, remained in the outfit from 1777 until 1781.

In the first American census of 1790, George and Elizabeth Ward DeLong lived with ten children in Mifflin County, north of Cumberland County. William Ward, however, continued "westering." In March of 1800, he purchased land on North Fork of Big Grave Creek (Marshall County, West Virginia). This move brought the Wards into close proximity with the Archers.

In 1803, Edward Ward came west. He purchased land in Ohio County, (West) Virginia in 1805. By that time, their brother-in-law and sister, George and Elizabeth DeLong, had crossed the Ohio River into the new western state of Ohio.[15]

The DeLongs pushed down the Zane's Trace into Belmont County and paced out land at the forks of Wills Creek (near Batesville). Their cabin was reputedly the first raised between Wheeling and Zanesville, other than that of Ezra Graham and George Beymer at Wills Creek ford (Cambridge). The DeLongs were in the vanguard of a wave of immigration into the new state. Earlier, in 1799, David Newell, a "man of Scotch extraction," left Westmoreland County, Pennsylvania, and laid out a village on the Zane's Trace, which he named for his cousin, Arthur St. Clair, the governor of the Northwest Territory. This village became a market town for Quakers who lived around its fringes and in the rest of the region bordering the Ohio River. In 1799, southern Quakers had sent a scouting expedition into the Northwest Territory in search of a land without slavery. The next year, their migration began with the first worship meeting convened at the location of present-day Colerain in Belmont County. By 1814, enough of the faith were settled to constitute the Ohio Yearly Meeting at Mount Pleasant. By 1826, more than 8,000 Quakers were

---

14 Fedorchak. Cumberland County records are non-existent; they were burned by Confederates during the Civil War. Edward Ward, a descendent, agrees that she was an Indian. Judging from the name and the time of the marriage, this seems plausible.
15 Fedorchak. August 27, 1818: Joseph and Edward Ward (who were literate) and George DeLong (who signed with a mark) sold William's land in Elizabethtown, Ohio County. Deed Book 9, p. 274.

living in Belmont, Jefferson, eastern Guernsey, and southern Harrison counties. The DeLongs joined the non-Quaker immigrants who settled near or in St. Clairsville and Barnesville. In 1804, George DeLong served on the first murder trial jury convened in Belmont County.[16] St. Clairsville began to flourish.

South of St. Clairsville, the family cabins spread out over the Leatherwood Creek basin: John Francis DeLong (1770-1840) and his wife, Sarah Winteringer; James DeLong, Sr. (1774-1830) and Nancy Simpson; Issac DeLong (1779-1842) and his wife, Nancy; Edward DeLong and Rachel Baker; George DeLong, Jr. and Mary; Joseph DeLong and Elizabeth; David DeLong and Jean Law; Mary and Fleming Davidson; Ann and Sam Leith; and, Elizabeth and David Hight.

The Wards joined the settlement when, on March 17, 1807, James DeLong and his uncle, Edward Ward, bought adjoining farms. These small settlements in the Duck Creek and Leatherwood Creek valleys were typical of settlement patterns over the entire state.[17]

Although now a state, Ohio was primitive and its population far-flung; no town of 400 existed. Communication and tax collections were difficult. County government was far more important than the shaky state government. Into this frontier mentality came a great shock which galvanized Ohioans into one–the threat of invasion by the British during the War of 1812. British forts remained manned on American soil in Michigan Territory. Ohioans responded when war erupted.

In Autumn of 1812, Detroit was forced to surrender to the British. Father Gabriel Richard, who cherished his naturalized American citizenship, became an important leader of the defeated Americans. Governor Return Johnathan Meigs of Ohio called for five-thousand volunteers. Men from the settlements "rallied round the flag." Seven sons of George DeLong served: John Frances DeLong was a colonel of the First Regiment of Ohio militia, which mustered 738 men from Belmont and Fairfield counties. These included his brothers, James, George, Joseph, David, Edward, and their sister Angelina's husband, Robert Finley. The troops marched through Lancaster, Franklinton (Columbus), and Delaware toward the northwest and the Great Swamp–an enormous barrier which covered eighteen future Ohio counties, and was crossed only by a knee-deep mud-clogged Indian trail. En route, they received word of

---

[16] J. A. Caldwell, *History of Belmont and Jefferson Counties, 1880*, p. 224. Material supplied by Bruce Yarnall, a historian of Quaker life.

[17] Fedorchak. In the 1820 census, George resided between James and "Widow Ward."

Commodore Perry's victory on Lake Erie. When the men arrived at the camp at Lower Sandusky, they replaced troops already sent ahead for the final Battle of the Thames in Canada. The successful conclusion of the War of 1812 opened up all the Northwest Territory for settlement. Road improvements—so badly needed for troop movements—became a national priority.[18]

When peace returned, Edward Fenwick wrote a report to Pope Pius VII on April 10, 1815.

> I found 50 Catholic families in the State of Ohio. I heard there are many others scattered in various parts of the same state, but those who have migrated into those regions have never seen a priest (since they left their former homes.) Hence many of those I met have forgotten their religion and they are bringing up their children in complete ignorance.[19]

The absence of priests was a constant worry. Thus, Bishop Carroll rejoiced when, in the fall of 1816, he was able to send newly-ordained priests to St. Rose in Kentucky. In 1818, Fenwick was able to "'give his uninterrupted service to the scattered Catholics of Ohio.'" Traveling down Zane's Trace with him in the winter of 1818 was his nephew, Dominic Young, who was ordained on December 18, 1817. Both priests and the Dittoes and Fincks, and an Irish family named McFadden, rejoiced when the little log church of St. Joseph in Somerset was dedicated on December 6, 1818. Fenwick opened the baptismal record and wrote:

St. Joseph, Somerset, Ohio
Courtesy St. Joseph Catholic Church

> In the year 1817 and 1818 I baptized in different parts of the Ohio state 162 persons both young and old whose names and sponsors cannot now be recollected, as I was then an Itinerant missioner and such persons were generally discovered and brought to me accidently [sic]–R. N. [Reverend Nicholas]
>
> Young, during his journey to Maryland and back to Ohio in this year of 1818, baptized about 20 in similar circumstances.[20]

---

18 *CRS*, Vol. XIII, #8, August 1988. Raymond F. Stevens, Family Genealogy.
19 Lamott, p. 28. He also reported twenty-five families in Tennessee. McAvoy, p. 87.
20 *CRS*, #1, January 1975. Nicholas Dominic Young was born on June 11, 1793 in Maryland. He was educated at St. Thomas Aquinas College, St. Rose, Kentucky, and ordained by Bishop Flaget. He died at St. Joseph, Somerset, on November 28, 1878. The journey to Baltimore took the priests through Mount Savage, Maryland. Occasionally, one of the Ohio/Kentucky priests recorded a sacrament in those records. Schlegel, *Ancestors*, p. 88.

As the only Catholic church in Ohio, St. Joseph became a magnet for migration. Germans and Irish moved into Perry County in great numbers. Philip Ward and his wife, Catherine, left County Monaghan for Philadelphia in 1816. Their daughter, Mary, married Michael McKenney, a printer, in 1819 in Philadelphia's Irish church, St. Augustine. His sister, Susan Ward McDonald, and her sons, Felix, Philip, James, and Patrick, began the long journey across the ocean to Philadelphia. By 1821, Felix and James were in Somerset; the family soon joined them (Susan and Patrick had been living in Pittsburgh in 1820.)

Other connected family members made the trip from Dublin and Londonderry. James McDonnell from Monaghan sailed to New York aboard the *Ontario*, disembarking on August 7, 1816 after 47 days. Philip Ward's family landed in Philadelphia on August 17 from the *Charlotte*. Philip McDonald disembarked at Baltimore on September 3, 1816, from the *Nancy*. Philip married Bridget Logan in Chambersburg, Pennsylvania in 1821. In 1825, they joined his family in Somerset.

By 1827, so many Catholics were clustered around St. Joseph that a second parish, Holy Trinity, was opened in Somerset.[21]

Fenwick had a busy time with these two parishes, but he made his circuit around the state. Some of the baptisms he recorded at St. Joseph were those of Irish immigrants in Belmont and Monroe counties.

Another Irish family traveled down the New State Road (which paralleled the Zane's Trace) in 1813: James Creighton (McCraren) of Clontibret Parish, County Monaghan, and his mother, Bridget (1758-1842) with his siblings, Francis, Andrew, Christopher, John, Mary, and Michael, had arrived on American shores aboard the *Roe Buck* from Newry, Ireland on September 21, 1805. Now James, Francis, John, Christopher, Michael, and their mother pushed west.

James Creighton married Bridget Hughes of County Armagh in St. Joseph

---

21 Schlegel, *Ancestors*, pp. 176, 188, 189, 254-5.

Creighton Genealogy

Unknown
& Bridget Creighton
  1758-1852, Co. Monaghan
├─ **James Creighton**
│   & Bridget Hughes
│   ├─ **Edward Creighton**
│   │   Creighton University
│   │   & Lucretia Wareham
│   └─ **John Creighton**
├─ **Francis Creighton**
├─ **Andrew Creighton**
├─ **Christopher Creighton**
│   & Mary McKiggan
│   (Methodist)
│   └─ **Michael Creighton**
│   & 1) ?? Delong
│   **Michael Creighton**
│   & 2) ?? Haren
│   **Michael Creighton**
│   & 3) Sarah Slevin
├─ **John Creighton**
│   & Anna Mary Barrighman
│   ├─ **Sr (nun) Creighton**
│   │   Florrisant MO
│   ├─ **Mary Creighton**
│   │   & Unknown McCabe
│   └─ **Sarah Creighton**
│   & Frank Hughes
├─ **Mary Creighton**
│   & Michael Brady
└─ **Michael Creighton**
     & Mary Rachel Condon
     ├─ **John Creighton**
     │   & Rose Slevin
     ├─ **Bridget Creighton**
     │   & Robert Gallagher
     │   occ. Christopher
     ├─ **Priscilla Creighton**
     │   & William Gallagher
     ├─ **Angeline Creighton**
     │   & Michael Slevin
     │   Hannah Gallagher Slevin
     └─ **Michael Creighton Jr.**
          & 1) Amanda Frye
        Michael Creighton Jr.
          & 2) Ann Slevin

Church (Philadelphia) in 1811. Two years later, they staked out a farm in Belmont County. A few miles away, on Wills Creek, Francis built his cabin. The Creightons were typical of frontier Catholics, in that the long absence of priests caused great difficulties. Typically, when they married, it was in a ceremony conducted by a Methodist circuit-rider; thus had Christopher married Mary McKiggan in 1809. He joined the Methodist church of his wife. But Michael and Mary Rachel Condon, who married in 1821, raised their children Catholic, as did John and his wife, Anna Mary Barrighman Creighton. Methodist arrangements usually ceased once the Somerset priests were on their circuits.[22]

The Irish Slevin clan migrated from County Tyrone and settled onto farms in the Leatherwood Valley; they would intermarry with the Gallaghers and Creightons.[23]

Edmund Gallagher was born on November 11, 1772 in County Meath, Ireland. A stonemason, he was a skilled craftsman in his native land. When the country was in turmoil following the failed Rising of 1798, he and others with some means were able to escape.[24]

Gallagher arrived in America on June 16, 1798. He settled around Easton in Chester County, Pennsylvania. Just to the west of the port city of Philadelphia, this area became a "first stop" for many immigrants. King of Prussia was a German colony.[25] Gallagher married Anna Dorsey and their children were baptized in St. Joseph Church in Philadelphia. John (1801), Christopher (1802), Rosanna (1804), and Robert (1806), were all entered into the baptismal book. For £210, Gallagher bought seven acres near the town of Berwyn (Grassley) in Easton Township in 1804. Gallagher filed for citizenship on April 14, 1802, and it was recorded in

---

22 Ruth Fox, Creighton Genealogy. Typescript. Donald Schlegel, "The Creighton or McCraren Family, Catholic Pioneers in Ohio and Omaha," *CRS*, Vol. XIX, #10, October 1994; #11, November 1994. (genealogy chart)

23 Edward (1813-1897) married Hannah Gallagher, daughter of John and Mary Gallagher. Her cousin, Sarah, daughter of Christopher and Mary Gallagher, married Edward's brother Michael in St. Mary's, Temperanceville in 1849. Sarah's brother, Thomas, married Mary Slevin.
   Ann and Rose Slevin married into the Creightons, and Edward Joseph Slevin married Mary Ann Butler. John Slevin married Mariah Fordyce, daughter of pioneer Lemuel Fordyce. Both Mariah and her brother Lemuel converted to Catholicism. Ruth Fox and Pearl Reischman, Creighton and Slevin research.

24 Tradition relates that Edmund Gallagher served under Robert Emmet and Lord Fitzgerald during the rising and was, perhaps, an aide at the Battle of Dunboyne and Tara in County Meath in May of 1798. This story is first known in print in the *History of Mount St. Mary's Seminary*, Michael J. Kelly and James M. Kirwin (Keating & Co.: Cincinnati, Ohio, 1894) p. 273. Father Kirwin was a close colleague of Bishop Nicholas Gallagher. He may well have heard the story from the bishop, who was Edmund Gallagher's grandson. Otherwise, it cannot be verified. Suspicion arises about the story, as Robert Emmet did not participate in the 1798 Rising, but in a minor one in 1803.

25 A colony of Gaelic speakers settled near Bardstown, Kentucky at about this time. Mattingly, p. 61. Gallagher material from Pearl Gallagher Reischman.

Deed Docket Book 2, page 265, in 1806.[26]

> Edmund Gallagher's Application for U. S. Citizenship in 1802
> 252
> **Edmund Gallagher**: A native of the United Kingdom of Great Britain and Ireland. Presents his Petition setting forth that he was residing within the limits, and under the Jurisdiction of the United States, between the 16th day of June 1798 and the 14th day of April 1802 and has resided within the same for five years & upwards last past, one year thereof last past within the Commonwealth of Pennsylvania, That he wishes to become a citizen of the United States, and has never borne any hereditary titles or order of nobility of the Kingdom from whence he came or elsewhere. We therefore humbly Pray that on his making the proofs, and taking the Oath, prescribed he may be admitted to become a citizen of the United States of America, Satisfaction proof being made in open court that the facts contained in the Petition above set forth are true, and it further appearing to the State faction of this Court, that during the same time he has behaved as a man of good moral character, attached to the Principals of the Constitution of the United States, and well disposed to the good order of happings [sic]of the same. And the said, Edmund Gallagher, on his solemn Oath in open court, declaring that he will support the Constitution of the United States, that he doth renounce and relinquish any title or order of nobility to which he is or hereafter maybe entitled and that he doth absolutely and entirely renounce and abjure all allegiance to any foreign Prince Potentate, state and Sovereignty whatever, and particularly to the King of the United Kingdom of Great Britain and Ireland, to whom he was heretofore a subject, he is thereupon admitted a Citizen of the United States of America.

Sometime after the purchase of their land, Anna Gallagher died. It is feasible that she succumbed after the birth of two more children, Bridget Ann (1808) and William (1809). Gallagher fathered four more children: Sarah (1812), Edmund (1815), Thomas (1816), and Nicholas (1820). When he sold the land in April 1818, his wife was Lydia McGinnis. They sold their property for $700 and began "westering"–toward Ohio on the Braddock Road.[27]

---

26 The Irish character of the area is deduced by names of landowners: McClenahan, McGoogin, Markley, O'Neal, McIlree. Plat Book. Deed Book H, #404. Berwyn, a Welsh settlement since 1704, was later known as Grassley. It is on U.S. Route 30 (the Lancaster Pike).Gallagher bought lots 3 and 4 of Square 10. Chester Book 43, Vol. 119, p. 151. Anna was illiterate. She signed her documents with a mark.

27 The three year gap between the birth of William and Sarah might be a clue to Anna's death and the McGinnis marriage. Nicholas was born when the family moved to Ohio; we can be certain that he was the child of the second marriage. Deed recorded November 21, 1818, Book Q 1, p. 197. Chester County. Lydia McGinnis was born in New Hampshire in 1780 and died in Ohio on July 10, 1857. Pearl Gallagher Reischman.

It is probable that the Gallaghers made a stop for re-provisioning in Brownsville; the National Road had been completed to that point by their move. Brownsville was a hustling pike town. Its other advantage was Neil Gillespie's tavern, which was the Catholic center in the region. Priests from Sportsman's Hall said mass at the tavern, and it served as a clearing house of information about places where a Catholic might settle with comfort. The Gillespies were intermarried with the Boyles of Lancaster (Ohio) and were keys in the "Catholic grapevine." The Gallaghers chose to settle in Guernsey County, perhaps because of the presence nearby of other Catholics (the Archers).

On December 17, 1818, Edmund Gallagher purchased a quarter section of land in Guernsey County, paying $316.24 for 158 acres. He and his adult sons began to establish their farms in Beaver Township.[28] The Gallaghers, McConnagheys, DeLongs, and Jefferises began to knit themselves into a large extended family, connected by religion.[29]

The lure of the rich Ohio land was all it took to attract immigrants, but in the case of one family, it was also the occasion for a "fresh start." The Jefferis-Brinton family came from long-standing Quaker roots. When John Shippen Jefferis (1793-1872) began proving up his Ohio land, he was the fifth generation of his family to have done so in America.[30]

Robert Jefferis (1656-?) left Pewsey Parish, Whiltshire, England for America in 1681. He and Jane Chandler Jefferis settled with other Quakers in Chester County, Pennsylvania. Their son, James Jefferis, and his wife, Elizabeth Tull, built near Chadds Ford. Their son, Emmor (1732-1802) and his wife, Elizabeth Taylor, continued to live on this farm, as did Emmor, Jr. and his wife, Charity Grubb. Their son, John Shippen Jefferis, married Sarah Darlington Brinton in 1813.

Sarah was also from Quaker stock, but her parents–William Brinton and Deborah Darlington–were supposedly married in 1779 "by a priest." This act caused William to be disowned. Whatever turmoil this caused in the family is unknown, but John Shippen Jefferis and Sarah Darlington

---

28 Beaver Township was created from segments of Seneca and Oxford Townships on June 3, 1816. This area became part of Ohio's last county, Noble County, in 1851. By 1830 (the oldest tax record available), Gallagher had added another 142 acres of section 10 to his holdings. Reischman.
29 Christopher Gallagher married Mary DeLong before Father Nicholas Young on November 25, 1825. John Gallagher married Mary Ann Brinton before Father Young on May 31, 1828. Robert Gallagher married Elizabeth Jefferis before Father Richard Miles in 1830. Sarah Gallagher married James DeLong, Jr. before Father James Butler in 1833. St. Mary's records.
30 John Shippen Jefferis's land patent for 65 acres in Section 33 of Somerset Township (Twp. 7, Range 6) was recorded April 16, 1833. Irene M. Ochsenbein and Catherine F. Fedorchak, *Belmont County, Ohio Before 1830*, n.p. 1977, p. 3.

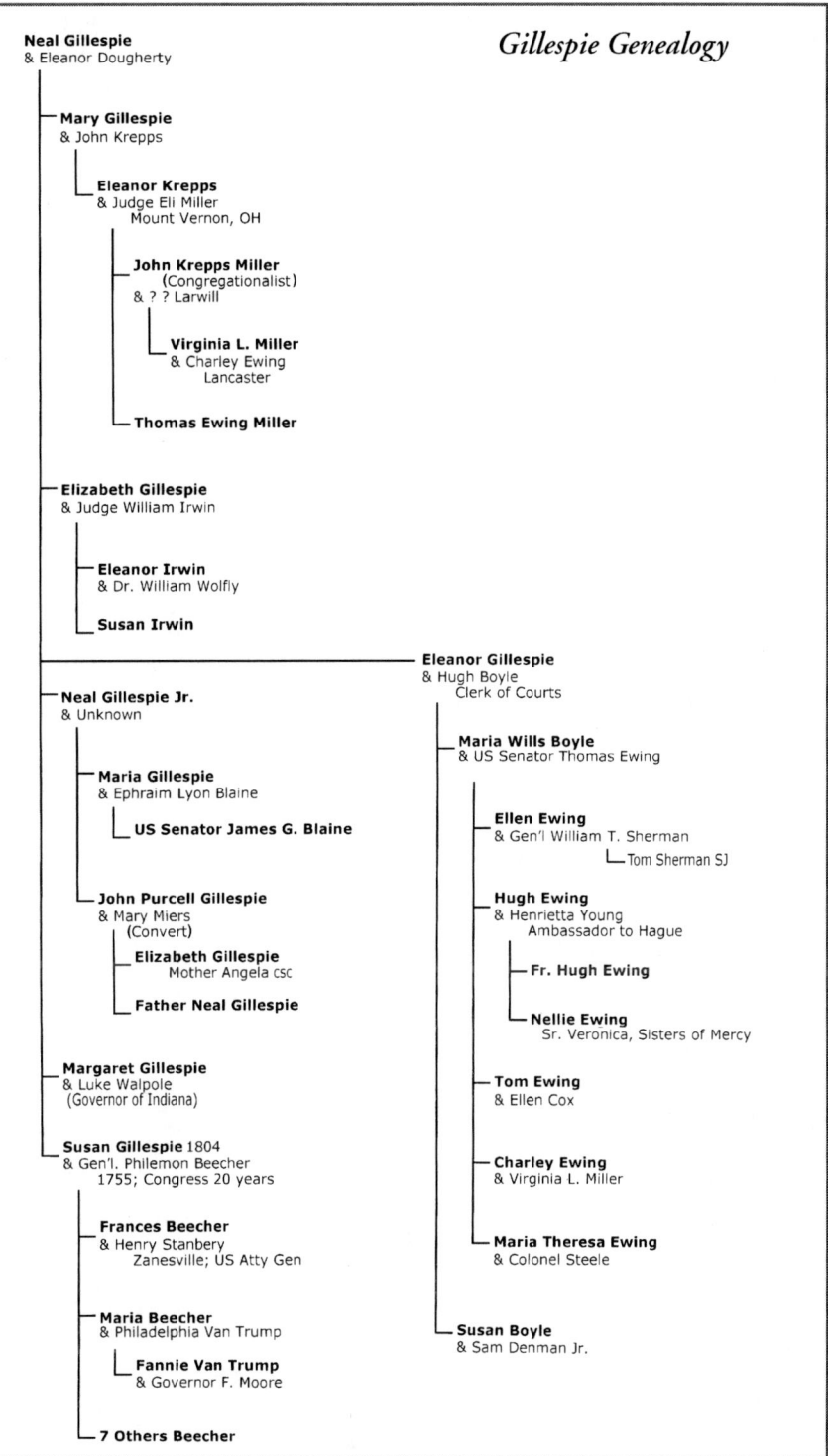

Brinton migrated early in their marriage to Ohio. All but one of their children were born there. In Belmont County, whether by the influence of her mother's probable religion, or by the situation in the environs, John and Sarah became members of the Catholic Church.³¹

Catholic Conversions

First Generation 1820		Second Generation	Third Generation
John & Sarah Jefferis	12 children		
	John H	John J	
	Thomas	Joseph	
	Pius	Simeon	
	Ambrose	Charles	
	William	Edward	
	Nathan	Frances m. Bunting 1905 Protestant	b. Baily Mills Protestant Cemetery
George & Elizabeth DeLong	11 children		
	Col. John Frances DeLong		
	Sarah Winteringer	*first communion 1845	
		Dr. John * 1845	
	James, Sr. Convert 1830 John Frances, Sponsor		
		James, Jr. 1) m. Sarah Gallagher 2) m. Lucinda Anderson	Dr. Edward m. Mary Gallagher Thomas, Prot. John, Prot. Frank, Prot.
	Issac to Perry County 1840 agent Catholic Times		
	Edward to Perry County		
		James baptized 1818	All children Protestant
	George	Joseph baptized 1820	
	Joseph (sponsor in 1822)		
	David	John baptized in 1820	

Farmers from these scattered homesteads made their way to villages for trade. St. Clairsville emerged as a drovers' post on the way to Wheeling. Throughout the county, social life revolved around harvest festivals and other "socials" and "singings," which followed communal labor. Thus, the DeLongs and Wards came into the world of the Archers and the Gallaghers. According to family tradition, George DeLong, Sr. was "the first to convert."³² This was probably in 1817 or 1818. By late 1818 and

---

31 Abraham Darlington Genealogy. Eugene L. Jefferis, Jr., typescript genealogy, 1986. A Temperanceville story has Sarah's Quaker bonnet and shawl hanging in the Catholic Church as a symbol of her conversion. Bruce Yarnall, a scholar of Quaker life, has researched the Hinshaw Genealogies (*The Encyclopedia of American Quaker Genealogy*) without success in establishing this story. The Quakers, meticulous record-keepers, would have recorded such an event as "marrying out of the meeting." Yarnall did not find Darlingtons or Brintons bearing the same first names as the emigrants to Ohio. It is clear, however, that Brinton, Darlington, and Jefferis have Quaker connections.

32 A story says that, as a boy, John Frances became lost in the forest and wandered until he and his sister found a cabin. A Catholic priest living there sent them home, but they became lost again and ended up back at the priest's cabin. This influenced the parents to convert. This would have been in Mifflin County, Pennsylvania. [Author note: I cannot place a priest there during this time period.]

early 1819, his grandchildren were being baptized by the Dominicans of Somerset, and the parents listed as Catholics. Father Fenwick recorded the baptism of Joseph DeLong, son of Edward, on December 27, 1818, and of Mary, daughter of Joseph DeLong, on January 10, 1819.[33] The circuit of the Dominicans–covering all of Ohio–was underway.

Fathers Edward Fenwick, Nicholas Young, Thomas Martin (an Irish Dominican), and Vincent DeRymacher (a Flem), established their convent in a rude cabin beside St. Joseph's log church. They began the circuit: visiting Zanesville, twenty miles distant, once a month, and other missions once or twice a year. Fenwick's baptismal records in 1819 placed him in Somerset, Mount Vernon, Wooster, Canton, and New Lisbon in the spring, and in Stark and Guernsey counties in the fall and winter. As the priests placed dots on their maps and organized their trips, they emulated Stephen Badin's practice of inserting advertisements in any existing newspapers, announcing the date of their arrival. Once, DeRymacher rode for twenty-five hours straight to meet his appointment.[34]

Father Stephen Badin
Catholic Record Society, Columbus, Oh

The priests continued to hear of distant Catholics. In 1814, Fenwick asked Jacob Dittoe to inquire about Catholics settled on the Owl Creek in Knox County. The priest had heard about them from relatives of theirs in Kentucky. Familiar Marylander names of Arnold, Mattingly, "Logisdons" (Logsdons), McKenzie, and White were being served in Kentucky by the Italian missionary, Father Nicholas Zocchi. The Dominican "grapevine" sent Fenwick in search of the Ohioans who had left Arnold's Settlement (Mount Savage) west of Frostburg, Maryland, to settle the Ohio wilderness.[35]

John Mattingly was apparently the first Catholic to settle around Cumberland, squatting there at the end of the French and Indian War. Soon thereafter, Patrick Burns, Peter Dugan, and Gabriel McKenzie were building log cabins west of Fort Cumberland. Archibald Arnold's tavern on Turkey Foot Road grew into a cluster of cabins called Arnold's

---

33 St. Joseph Baptismal Records, *CRS* #1, January 1975. [See Records, next page.]
34 Mattingly, p. 100.
35 Stanton, p. 82. Richard T. Koch and Phyllis I. Davidson, *Western Maryland Catholics 1819-1851* (Clearfield Company, Inc.: Baltimore, Maryland, 1988) p. 46. Logsdons and Durbins were in Madison County, Kentucky by 1800. Mattingly, p. 63.

Baptism in the Beaver Valley and Vicinity: 1819–1833

Note: Names were transcribed exactly as found in the records. In most cases, the variations were for the same families.

Recorded at St. Joseph's near Somerset (From Volume I of the Bulletin)

July 25, 1819	Jane, wife of Hue McCaughy
July 27, 1819	John and Ann, children of Hue and Jane McCaughy
February 3, 1820	Hannah Archer, of Jacob and Sarah
same	Eliseus Archer, of Michael and Rudy [Rhodes]
same	Robert A. Archer, of Simon and Rudy [Rhodes]
same	Roseanna Crossin, of Manuel and Mary
February 23, 1820	Mary Timoney, of Denis and Ann
same	Mary, daughter of Hue and Jane McConnaughy
February 28, 1820	William Waterhouse, of William and Eleanor
February 29, 1820	Daniel, son of Hue and Jane McConnaughy
same	James, son of George and Rachel
April 7, 1820	Jane , of Edward and Rachel
August 18, 1820	John Gallagher, of Peter and Bridget
Oct/Nov 1820	"12 children in Stark and Guernsey counties"
November 29, 1820	Adah Archer, of George and Rebecca
same	Ann Archer, of Henry and Mary
same	Elizabeth Carrol, of George and Ann
same	Henry Archer, of James and Ann
same	Joseph Archer, of Henry and Mary
same	Joseph Archer, of Michael and Cynthia
same	Mary and Margaret Carrol, of George and Ann
same	Michael and Margaret Archer, of George and Rebecca
same	Michael Archer, of Michael and Cynthia
same	Margaret Archer, of James and Ann
same	Sarah Archer, of James and Ann
November 30, 1820	Simon Lincicome, of David and Mary
—— 1825	Joseph Creton, son of James Creton and Bridget Hughes; spons. James Sherlock and Frances Collin
—— 1825	Elenora Temple, daughter of William and Bridget (Egan); spons. James Creton and Bridget Hughes

Recorded at Zanesville, St. John (Transcription)

January 11, 1829	Hugh McConncoughy, son of Hugh McConncoughy and Jane Maxwell; spons. John and Rosana Gallagher. Richard P. Miles, O.P.
December 11, 1829	Daniel, son of William Windell and Effa ; spons.: John and Elizabeth Jeffries. RPM
same	Sara, daughter of John and Elizabeth Jones; spons.: John and Catherine McDaniel. RPM
December 12, 1829	Elizabeth Ann, daughter of Peter Ward and Elizabeth Timony; spons.: Bridget Ann Gallagher
same	John Augustine, son of Christopher Gallagher and Mary ; spons.: Robert Gallagher and Effa Windell
same	Mary A., daughter of Michael Brady and Mary Creton; spons.: Christoph. and Bridget Gallagher. RPM
December 13, 1829	Catherine Ann, daughter of William Temple and Bridget Egan; spons.: Rosa Gallagher
December 14, 1829	Priscilla and John, children of Michael Creaton and Rachel Conden. RPM
May 15, 1830	James , convert; spons.: John
May 16, 1830	Martha, daughter of John Steward and Sarah Lewis; spons.: Rosana Gallagher
same	William, son of John Gallagher and Mary Ann Brenton; spons.: Bridget Gallagher
same	Sara, daughter of Farrel (?) Jones and Anna ; spons.: Anna Morgan
same	Mary, daughter of John McConnaughy and Elizabeth West
same	Enoch, son of William and Anna Morgan; spons.: Effa Wendal and John . RPM
May 19, 1830	Lucinda, daughter of Nathan Archer and Rebecca Morris; spons.: Rody Archer

Zanesville, St. John (continued)

May 19, 1830	Roda, daughter of Simon Archer and Roda Enocky; spons.: Rebecca Archer	
same	Samuel, son of Michael Archer and Roda Grander (?); spons.: John	
May 20, 1830	Jonathan and Isaac , converts; spons.: John . RPM	
February 22, 1831	Mary, Walter, and Martha, children of Michael Burns and Martha McWilliams; spons.: Michael McNamara and Mary Smith (Wheeling)	
same	Michael and Abraham, sons of Michael and Sara Seams; spons.: Michael and Martha Burns. RPM	
May 12, 1831	Benjamin, son of Thomas Dillehey and Susana Martin; spons.: Anna Low (Leatherwood)	
same	Lucinda, daughter of Henry Low and Anna Dillehey; spons.: Henrietta Dillehey (Leatherwood)	
same	Margaret, daughter of Peter Timony and Elizabeth Ward; spons.: James and Anna Gallagher (Leatherwood). RPM	
May 14, 1831	Isaac, son of George Morgan and Anna ; spons.: Anna Jones (Beaver)	
same	Christina, daughter of Peter Meahan and Elizabeth Morrison; spons. Moyiia (?) Rinehart (Beaver). RPM	
September 18, 1831	Jane, daughter of William Temple and Bridget Egan; spons. Mary Temple	
same	William, son of William Windal and Effa ; spons. Mary Gallagher	
same	Mary, daughter of John and Elizabeth Jones; spons. Effa Windal	
same	Charity, daughter of John Jeffries & Sara Brenton; spons. John & Catherine McDaniel	
same	Mary, daughter of John McDaniel and Sara Maring; spons. Bridget Gallagher. RPM	

Copyright 1988, Catholic Record Society, Diocese of Columbus, Columbus, Ohio.

Settlement. There, en route to Kentucky in 1793, Stephen Badin said mass. From 1795 to 1799, Prince Father Demetrius Augustine Gallitzin, who was based in Emmitsburg, visited Mount Savage. Gallitzin was born in The Hague, Holland in 1770 to a Russian Prince diplomat and a Prussian Countess. He was disowned after his conversion to Catholicism. In 1792, Gallitzin arrived in America, armed with letters of introduction to George Washington and Charles and John Carroll. After studying in Baltimore, he was

Mattingly Genealogy

Henry Mattingly
& Honora Durbin
Allegheny Co. Cumberland, MD

└ **Samuel Mattingly**
    Conewago Chapel
    & Elinor Durbin
    (Ohio immigrants)

└ **William Mattingly**
    (Ohio immigrants)
    & Sarah Mathis

  └ **John Mattingly**
      & Ann Majors

Prince Father Demetrius Gallitzin
Catholic Record Society, Columbus, Ohio

The Ohio Mission Field: 1790-1825

ordained in 1795. On one visit to Arnold's Settlement in 1799, he witnessed the marriage of Gabriel Porter and Rebecca Frost.[36]

In 1805, an expedition from Mount Savage set off along the immigrant trail, passing through Brownsville, then up the Monongahela, down the Zane's Trace, and up the rivers north until they settled on Owl Creek in the Walhonding Valley of Ohio's Knox County. Carving out homesteads in the nine-mile stretch between Danville and Howard, these members of "the mountain community ten miles west of Frostburg" were sons and daughters of the two-century-old Catholic colony in Maryland. George Sapp, Jr. built a saw and gristmill at Sapp's Settlement. He was virtually the only non-Catholic in the colony; his wife, Catherine Arnold, and their children, were of the old faith.

The settlers built a good life in the rich farm country, but they longed for their old log cabin church, St. Ignatius, which they had helped build in 1792. They pined for the periodic visits of a priest. In Pennsylvania, they had been on Prince Gallitzin's circuit. In Ohio, they waited in vain for fifteen years. When Fenwick located them, their faith community finally had access to the sacraments. On October 24, 1818, Father Fenwick performed the colony's first baptism: Fanny, the daughter of George and Catherine Sapp.[37]

In 1812, William Mattingly led his group of Irish and Anglo-Catholic Marylanders from the same area of Allegheny County, Maryland, on the same well-trodden path. They crossed the Ohio River at Bridgeport and worked their way cross-country to Newcomerstown, and then down the Muskingum River, settling north of Zanesville.[38]

Others joined the existing communities. Hugh McConnaghy was born in Ireland in 1778. In America, he married Delaware native, Jane Maxwell. After settling in Belmont County in 1819, Hugh finally had access to a priest. His son, John, was baptized at sixteen by the priest at St. John's in Zanesville. Jane converted. Another son, Hugh, was baptized in 1829, with John and Rosanna Gallagher as sponsors.[39]

While Germans from Prince Gallitzin's community at Loretto (McGuire Settlement in Cambria County) began to filter into southeast Ohio at Deavertown, south of Zanesville, and into Monroe County at

---

36 Stanton, pp. 12, 81.
37 Koch, pp. 1-3. Connections remained between the Mount Savage and Knox County people. In 1830, Jonathan Sapp of Knox County and Mary Durbin of Mount Savage were married at St. Ignatius. Father Michael Young, O.P. of St. Joseph, Somerset, spent three months at Mount Savage in 1821.
38 Mattingly genealogy. *CRS*, XIII, #7, 1988.
39 *CRS*, XIII, #8, August 1988. St. John's records.

the invitation of settlers who were seeking marriageable youth, a trickle of Irish continued to put down roots in the area, too. In 1820, Bartholomew Longstreth and his wife, Margaret, sold two acres to Father Nicholas Young, for use as a church and cemetery; this was to be St. Barnabas. To the east, on Meigs Creek, John Duffy of County Tipperary, set up his homestead a mile north of Unionville. Nearby were Honora Duffy O'Neill and her husband, John, of County Cork. David Dougherty and Sarah Maloy Dougherty migrated with his brother, Patrick, and Rose McTeague Dougherty, from Letterkenny, County Donegal to Monroe County in 1817. They settled around Crane's Nest, just ahead of a flood of Alsatian Germans who would, in time, turn the area into "Little Switzerland." In Guernsey County, Patrick Sherlock of County Tipperary and his wife, Ann Clary of County Laois, purchased 160 acres. They became a part of the Beaver community.[40]

It remains a wonder that such isolated groups as the Irish Shehys of Youngstown and the Marylanders of Sapp's Settlement could retain a sense of church community without seeing a priest for a generation or more, but THEY WERE USED TO THIS LACK OF CHURCH LIFE FROM THEIR ENGLISH, IRISH, OR MARYLANDER EXPERIENCE.

In 1812, Father Fenwick had estimated "'fifty Catholic families in Ohio. . . .'"[41] By 1821, there were many more, and serving them was more difficult than in Kentucky, where people settled in colonies, which were formed from mother groups in Maryland. In Ohio, they were scattered throughout the state. Fenwick worked hard to secure money and priests. In 1819, he made a "begging tour" of Europe, visiting Rome, Florence, Livorno, Genoa, Turin, and Lyons to raise money for his Ohio mission.[42] The culture of Europe was a million miles away, but the funds brought joy to Ohio Catholics. In 1819, John Simon Dugan and his sister, Mrs. Harkins, welcomed the priests to the Green Tree Tavern in Zanesville. Dugan had been a hatter in Brownsville. Now, working with Father Young, he bought a brick warehouse and remodeled it for a chapel in Zanesville. Dugan was as enthusiastic a layman as was Dittoe. Dugan purchased land for a church and helped in the laying of the cornerstone by Stephen Hyacinth Montgomery, O.P. in 1823. Two years later, Dugan drove his stagecoach to Maryland to escort Bishop Fenwick, Father Young, and Father Gabriel Richard home from a church council. On this trip, an

---

40 *CRS*, XXVII, #7, July 2002.
41 McAvoy, p. 87.
42 Ibid.

accident near Cumberland, Maryland on March 11, 1825, took the life of Dugan and ended the positive energy of a great Catholic lay leader.[43]

In 1821, Pope Pius VII recognized the difficulty of serving the Catholic population in the American West, and created the Diocese of Ohio (Ohio, Michigan, and part of Wisconsin). Edward Fenwick was named Bishop of Ohio. He had only three churches under roof: St. Joseph's in Somerset, St. Mary's in Lancaster, and St. Patrick's in Cincinnati. He had at least 6,000 Catholics and two priests: himself and Father Nicholas Young. In Michigan, 12,000 Catholics–mostly Indians and French–were served by Gabriel Richard who, in 1823, was elected to Congress as the representative of the Michigan Territory. The road linking Detroit to Chicago was to be Father Richard's legacy. He died while treating cholera victims in Detroit in 1832.[44]

Father Gabriel Richard
Catholic Record Society, Columbus, Oh

From Somerset, Bishop Fenwick and Father Young carried out grueling schedules. In 1827, they traveled 2,500 miles on horseback, visiting Canton, Lancaster, New Lisbon, Danville, Beaver, and Johnathan's Creek on the Little Miami River–all for "trifling collections" and what was produced on the farm at Somerset. Frontier priests lived in true poverty.[45]

In the summer of 1827, Bishop Edward Fenwick, Father N. D. Young, and fellow Dominican, Father Mullon, set off through Ohio to preach the Jubilee Year. Bishop Fenwick moved up the Ohio River from Louisville to Wheeling on a steamer, then took the stage down the National Road to Zanesville and south via the Zane's Trace to Somerset. On the long journey, he "'visited the scattered flock along the road on either side.'"

The younger priests made the circuit through Muskingum and Guernsey counties and reported:

> on the way they preached at Washington [Old Washington]. The Church in Guernsey [St. Patrick's in Old Washington] is nearly finished. . .it is worthy of remark that 8 years ago there

---

43 Camillus Musselman, *St. Thomas Aquinas Church-125 Years* (Spencer-Waller Press: Zanesville, Ohio, 1967) pp. 11, 13, 15.
44 CRS, XX, #5. Louis Horton, "Portrait of an Ecumenist: Fr. Gabriel Richard," *The Catholic Digest*, March 1969, p. 60. *New Catholic Encyclopedia, First Edition*, , V. XII, p. 485.
45 CRS, XIV #4.

was not a Catholic in this neighborhood—it was about that time that the first convert to the Catholic faith was taken into the church. There are now about 40 families, chiefly converts [and] a few emigrant Catholics.[46]

The priests were describing the Leatherwood Creek/Gallagher settlements. Priests and people had finally connected. Together, they would lay a firm foundation for the Catholic Church in Ohio.

---

46 *The U.S. Catholic Miscellany*, Vol. VI, 390-91, quoted by Anthony Lisska in *CRS*, IXV, #7, July 1989.

Chapter Six

Scattered Flock–Few Shepherds
Fenwick's Ohio, 1825–1833 • Purcell's Ohio, 1834–1845

For a little less than two decades, the Dominicans had worked in the Ohio mission field, ministering to scattered families and tiny enclaves. Events in 1825 caused them to redouble their already exhausting efforts. The National Road project was reactivated by Congress and began to inch its way across Belmont County from the Ohio River. The Ohio legislature, seeking to secure some prosperity for a state absolutely savaged by the Panic of 1819, funded the building of the Ohio and Erie Canal. On July 4, 1825, at Newark, the first spade of dirt for the canal was turned. The 309-mile ditch would take seven years to build. As these two huge public works commenced, Irish laborers flooded into Ohio and the numbers of Catholics without a priest skyrocketed. Crossing at the cost

The Ohio and Erie Canal

Henry Howe, 1848

of £12 a person, the Irish flocked to American shores. By 1830, 207,381 had arrived; the number was 780,719 by 1850. Many were drawn by a Jacksonian idea of democratic life. They found work. Some 5,000 Irish worked on the canal, and 2,000 were working on the Wabash Erie Canal in Indiana in 1835. The Irish who "put something by" could purchase land.[1] Few wanted to return to the old world.

In the 1820's and '30s, Ireland suffered from economic depression. Unemployment soared as manufacturing jobs disappeared. The Poor Law Commission reported more than two million agricultural workers classed as "paupers."[2] These "shanty Irish" joined the flood to America, Canada, and Australia. Side by side with the Germans, the Irish–with their distinct "brogue"–gave the Roman Catholic Church in America what it had thus far escaped: a "foreignness."

When the British Empire's long war (1793-1815) with Revolutionary and Napoleonic France ended, Britain dominated the Atlantic world. Social transformation, rooted in the economic activity of the war decades, slowly changed England and Ireland. Daniel O'Connell, the Great Emancipator–the greatest leader of Catholic Ireland–as the Member of Parliament from County Clare, harnessed the masses to the Catholic Association. In his person, O'Connell blended Gaelic clansman and Catholic gentry and, through his efforts, the Catholic Emancipation Bill passed into law in 1829. The last vestiges of the old penal laws withered away.[3]

The Ireland that O'Connell championed was rapidly changing. Its population rose from 6.8 million in 1821 to 8 million in 1845, just when the great landowners embarked on a policy of "enclosure"–displacing tenants for beef and sheep pasturage. The old rural agrarian movements reorganized into "combinations" (farmer groups) resisting enclosures. Every eviction brought bitter resistance. Another Irish hemorrhage from the homeland began. Between 1815 and 1845, perhaps a million-and-a-half fled. In 1800, 1801, and 1802, six thousand left each year; in 1818, 20,000 boarded ships. Between 1820 and 1840, 33% of all immigrants to America were Irish. Then the potato crop began to fail: 1831, 1833, 1835, 1836, 1839, and 1842. In the 1840's, the number of Irish amongst total immigrants was 45%. Some of the emigrants sailed to Quebec, but most went to New York or Philadelphia; some were indentured.[4]

Most of the muscle that created the canal bed and the National

---

1 Foster, p. 345; McAvoy, p. 137.
2 Kathy Krepper, "Early Catholicism in Southeast Ohio," *CRS*, XIII #1/2, February 1988, p. 53.
3 Foster, pp. 298-300.
4 McAvoy, pp. 135-139; Blessing, pp. 528-529.

Road, belonged to the Irish. Sometimes, they left only deeds for land and potential churches in their wake, and moved along the surveyed trail.[5]

Edward Creighton joined his father, James, as a laborer on the National Road. The boy worked with young Phil Sheridan as a drover on the road. The Creightons moved west with the road builders.[6]

When an Irish road worker settled, he gravitated towards the company of his co-religionists. Thus, in Carlisle's old Catholic cemetery, tombstones bear the names McCune, Kennedy, Harkins, Butler, Cullen, and Doyle.[7] All these people were roughly of the same age (born c. 1795, probably in Ireland.) Irish names dominate the records of St. John the Evangelist Church (St. Thomas) in Zanesville: Donoghoe, McCarthy, O'Connor, Foy, and Mattingly are common entries. (St. Nicholas in Zanesville served German immigrants.) Church records in Zanesville and Temperanceville list legions of Irish-born. The tombstone evidence at St. Mary's tells the story graphically: Irish from many counties had settled in Ohio's southeast.[8]

Three other Irish families entered Belmont County during the road-building period: the Hughes, the Butlers, and the McCourts. Intermarriages tied them all together. John Butler (1799-1870) and his wife, Margaret Dorn, left Ireland in 1825 and settled on a farmstead in Washington County in 1827. With them were sons, Jamie (James) and John; their daughters would marry John Patterson and James McCourt. Michael Hughes buried his wife in Dungannon, Ireland. Their child, Isabel, joined Michael's in-laws on their voyage to America. A second marriage in Ireland produced John, Henry, and Frank, who immigrated as young men. Frank would marry Sarah Gallagher of Temperanceville. John McCourt and his wife, Sarah, settled in that area in 1825. Making the

---

5 Irish purchased two lots in Scotch-Irish Norwich for the "St. Joseph's Praying Society." When the Irish moved on, they left Norwich entirely Scotch-Irish Presbyterian and Methodist. John McCarthy, a canal engineer, left property for St. Frances de Sales (Newark) in his will. The Creightons set up a chapel in Linnville (1842-1856), but as the road-building progressed, the altar was moved to a church in Jersey.
6 Schlegel, "Creightons," *CRS*, XIX #10, October 1944.
7 Tombstones of oldest persons in Carlisle RC Cemetery.
   Charles McCune (1795-1853)
   Deborah Kennedy (1796-1852)
   Eleanor Harkins (1799-1884)
   Phillip Harkins (1797-1881)
   Harriet Cullen (1795-1830)
   Peter Cullen (1785-1841)
   Bridget Doyle (1792-1886)
   Michael Doyle (1812-1882)
   Edward Doyle (1819-1883 "born in Ireland, Co. Wicklow")
   Timothy Butler (1802-1867)
8 St. Mary's Cemetery/St. Mary's Birth and Death Records: Irish-born Settlers [See Chart next page.]

St. Mary's Cemetery/St. Mary's Birth and Death Records: Irish-born Settlers
[Note: Bold entries are material from genealogies.]

Armbruster, Francis	(1828-1923)		"saintly"	
Brown, Anna Hainey	(1815-1918)	Tyrone	"in NY few years"	"last of original Hainey *Jefferis"
Burk, Thomas	(1827-1865)			
Butler, John	(1799-1890)	Ireland		to area 1825, **Ohio 1827**
Butler, Margaret	(1806-1844)			
Carr, Susanna	(1780-1856)			
Creighton, Bridget	(1758-1842)	**Monaghan**		
Creighton, Mary Rachel ___	(1804-1870)			
Creighton, Sr., Michael	(1797-1882)			
Daugherty, Frances	(1838—)			
Daugherty, Jacob	(1827-1897)			
Doherty, Thomas	(1790-1848)	Donegal		
Doyle, Matthew	(1761-1836)	Wexford		
Forbes, Mary	(1803-1865)	Mayo		
Fordyce, Lemuel	**(1790-1862)**		[convert]	
Gallagher, Ann	(1797—)			
Gallagher, Edmund	(1772)	Meath		
Garvey, Bridget	(1827-1903)		[daughter of Thomas?]	
Garvey, Bridget	(1796-1889)			
Garvey, Thomas	(1798-1901)			
Hassion, John	(1716-1856)	Ballingrole, Mayo		
Hession, John (son?)	(1826-1856)	Ballingrole, Mayo		
Hughes, Francis	**(1847-1913)**	**Tyrone**		
Hyde, Frances (+Sarah Gallagher)	(1847-1879)	Tyrone		
Keenan, Jas	(1797-1842)			
Keenan, Margaret	(1803-1807)			
Lowe, Benedict	(1794—)			
Lowe, Henry	(1796-1844)			
Lowe, Stephen	(1759-1846)			
McCallion, James	(1813-1849)	Tyrone		
McClaughlin, Jane (Charles)	(1821-1883)	Derry		
McConnaghy, Hugh	(1778)	Ireland		to area in 1819
McCormick, Patrick	(1827-1853)			
McCourt, Bernard	**(1813-1893)**	**b. Ireland**		to T 1825
McCourt, John	(1779-1851)	Tyrone (?)		to area in 1825
McCourt, Sarah (John)	(1789—)			
Montgomery, Michael	(1833-1915)			
Mullen, Dennis	(1785-1856)	Tyrone		
O'Brien, Thomas	(1845-1915)	Wexford		to America 1867, age 22; blacksmith, NY 14 years; to Noble County 1881
Poulton, John	(1831-1917)	Ireland		
Slevin, Ann	**(1822-1905)**	**Ireland**		
Slevin, Edwin	(1813-1897)			
Slevin, Hannah	(1832-1832)			

Irish Names in Marriage Records-St. Mary's

1830's
Cronin   Hughes   Dilheny   [Burkhart   Schockling- -German]

1840's
Conayhe   Daugherty   Butler   McCoy   Coyle   McAleer

1850's
Malone   McGinnis   O'Donnell   O'Brien   Foley   Donahoe   Slevin   Connelly   Creighton

journey with them from Ireland were their children, Bernard, Sarah, Nancy, and James.⁹

Two other families joined the Catholic enclave: the Lowes and the Dillehays. Hannah Low (Lowe) and her husband, Lemuel Grimes, were in Morgan County in 1819. Her brother, Benedict, and his wife, Lucinda Dillehay, were in Guernsey County by 1831. Thomas Dillehey and Susanna Martin had their son, Benjamin, baptized in 1831. Henry Low and his wife, Ann Dillaghy, brought their daughter, Lucinda, to the Beaver church for the sacrament that year. Stephen Lowe, who was born in 1759, was the man mentioned by the priest as "old Mr. Lowe [who] took communion on Easter" in 1849.¹⁰

That priest–either R. P. Miles or C. P. Montgomery–made the long horseback trip to St. Dominic's once a year. Traveling east on the National Road to St. Clairsville, the priest would then turn south on a cattle path that ran through the valleys and along ridges until it climbed the hill overlooking the Leatherwood Valley. Families gathered around the log church at Beaver for the annual mass, baptisms, and marriages.

In 1832, Father Richard Miles was elected as prior of St. Rose's Convent in Springfield, Kentucky. Father Charles Montgomery was sent to tend the parish in Zanesville. His brother, Father Samuel Montgomery, came to Ohio to work as a secular priest. Both priests con-celebrated the first mass of the first Dominican ordained in Ohio–Father John George Alleman.¹¹

Father Richard P. Miles, O.P.
Bishop of Nashville
Catholic Record Society, Columbus, Oh

Bishop Fenwick traveled to Washington in 1831 to plead the cause of the Native Americans before the Secretary of War. (Ohio tribes were being removed to reservations in Oklahoma.) His greatest challenge remained the same: 24 priests and 22 churches to serve Catholics from the Ohio River to Lake Superior.¹² In 1832, he set out on the circuit to visit Detroit and the many thousands of Catholics under the care of Gabriel Richard, the Priest-Congressman.

---

9 Pearl Reischman genealogies.
10 Richard Lowe genealogies. St. Mary's Records.
11 Musselman, p. 44.
12 Donald Schlegel, "The Church in Ohio Prior to 1868," *CRS*, XX #4.

There, the bishop said mass in English at Holy Trinity Church and then visited Father Martin Kundig, who was caring for an influx of German miners. During this trip, Fenwick was exposed to cholera and typhoid. By the time he reached Canton, Ohio, he was physically exhausted; still, he pushed on to Steubenville where a church had "been built by [convert] Catholics most of whom live on the other side of the river in Virginia." The sick bishop rode on to Pittsburgh where the migration of workers on the National Road had established a Catholic presence in the Presbyterian-dominated town. Then he visited with Father Bonaventure McGuire in Wheeling. Fenwick returned to Ohio and held confirmations for two large Irish/German congregations at Lisbon. He was warmly received by the Ohio and Erie Canal workers at that town. Pushing on to Wooster, the venerable Apostle of Ohio finally gave in to the typhoid. He died on September 26, 1832. The pioneering era of Ohio's Catholic history ended.[13]

At the conclusion of an eight-day retreat, John Baptist Purcell knelt in the pew of St. Remigius Chapel in Conewago, Pennsylvania. The son of a nail-maker, Purcell was born in Mallow, County Cork, and had immigrated to Maryland, where he worked as a tutor. He enrolled at Mount St. Mary's College in Emmitsburg, and spent two years in France at Saint Sulpice before being ordained there in 1826. Back in Maryland, he taught philosophy at St. Mary's and was elected as its president. At the age of thirty-three, he was to follow in the footsteps of Edward Fenwick,

Father John Baptist Purcell, Bishop of Ohio
Henry Howes

---

13 John Martin Henni, "Last Days of Bishop Fenwick," *CRS*, XXVII, January 2002; R. P. Brennan, O. O., "Cradle of the Faith in Ohio, 1818-1968" (Rosary Press, St. Joseph Church: Somerset, Ohio, 1968).

"The Apostle of Ohio."

The new bishop-elect set off for Ohio on a stagecoach, along with seminarians, O'Mealy, O'Laughlin, and McCallion. Accompanying them was the old Ohio hand, Nicholas D. Young, the newly elected provincial of the American Dominicans. During the trip, Young and Purcell reviewed the status of the mission church of Ohio.[14]

Father Nicholas Dominic Young, O.P.
Catholic Record Society

Although he had never seen the Ohio terrain, Purcell could appreciate the veteran Dominican's description of the church's hard-won gains during the past twenty years. Purcell could count on sixteen churches under roof, and the labors of two dozen priests who served 6,000-7,000 people. Exhausting circuits lay ahead of the new bishop.[15]

Following his consecration in Cincinnati on October 13, 1833, John Purcell made the first of his many visits around the circuit of his diocese. With each trip, he became more and more concerned by the disastrous spiritual effects of the long-term absence of priests. Purcell's tenure in office, too, would be devoted to a search for priests, particularly to serve the increasing German population of the city of Cincinnati.

From top to bottom of the state, the story was the same. Incoming Roman Catholics were faced with maintaining their faith without the sacraments.

At Portsmouth, Purcell found

> many families which ought to be Catholic and who now have none, or only an erroneous faith; their defection, or rather falling off from the religion of their youth, being mainly attributal [sic] to the want of instruction. . . .

At St. Luke's in Sapp's Settlement (Danville–settled nearly thirty years before by the "Mountain Congregation" from St. Ignatius at Mount Savage, near Frostburg, Maryland), he discovered

> children grow up without instruction, the old are in danger of perversion and the sick often die without the consolation of religion. There were several hundred communicants, but few of

---

14 Lamott, pp. 76-77; Hartley, p. 114.
15 Ibid.

the young people were reputed sufficiently acquainted with the Catholic catechism to receive confirmation.

Purcell's heart was "oppressed with sadness at the impossibility of sending Pastors to the scattered sheep of the wilderness. . . ." He was echoing a lament once uttered by John J. Carroll and Edward Fenwick.[16]

Purcell was an eloquent preacher and relished opportunities to champion Catholicism on a broad scale. On June 2, 1834, he preached a sermon at the schoolhouse in Fairview (Guernsey County). In 1836, in Columbiana County, "the bishop preached in the Court-house to a large and attentive audience." But in Canal Dover (Tuscarawas County), he was refused permission to speak at the Methodist Meeting House–even though its deed opened it to all Christians. Some of the subscribers reportedly objected to barring Purcell.[17] In 1837, Purcell and fellow Irishman, Alexander Campbell, entered into Campbell's church for a weeklong debate on the theology of the Catholic Church versus that of the Church of the Disciples of Christ. Campbell's new church was but a single piece of the religious mosaic on the American frontier. A vast movement called "The Second Great Awakening," which began at the CaneBreak Revival in Kentucky in 1799, spread across the frontier, fed by emotional "fire and brimstone" sermons and gospel music. Much has been written about this frontier phenomenon, but the American convert movement toward Roman Catholicism occurred at the same time, underscoring a general quest for spiritual salvation. Responding to the expense of importing books from the East, the Dominican printing press at St. Rose produced cheap pamphlets that stimulated religious debate.[18]

The American Convert Movement in the first half of the nineteenth century reflected the fact that the American Catholic Church before 1825 was German–and restricted to enclaves–or American; that is, its adherents were old stock immigrants, dating from the 1700's. Most "old Catholics" were either Irish or English, and thoroughly American. With no foreign accent, and a common cultural tradition, these were "our" Catholics, led by American gentry such as the Carrolls and Fenwicks, somehow not so threatening as the "foreign, Popish" church of Europe.[19]

The early church leaders and clergy were also exceptional in that

---

16 *CRS*, XXI, #1, January 1996. The tour reached Danville on September 8, 1836.
17 Abstracted from the *Catholic Telegraph* in *CRS*, XX, #11, November 1995.
18 Lamott, p. 79; McAvoy, p. 155; V. F. O'Daniel, *The Right Rev. Edward Dominic Fenwick* (The Dominicana Press: New York, 1920) p. 175.

they were generally members of religious orders, either the highly trained Jesuits or the eloquent Dominicans. In entertainment-starved America, such priests were frequently found in public forums, or in pulpits of Protestant churches, where their sermons were held up to non-Catholic scrutiny. What was intended as entertainment frequently turned into spiritual search and a conversion.

The order priests contrasted well with the run-of-the-mill frontier preachers who

> were but pious pioneers who turned from weekday labors with ax and gun to conduct Sunday prayer service. Because such men had no knowledge of theology, and no schools of Protestant divinity appeared west of the Appalachians til long after the frontier days were past, this was a time of innumerable schisms from old sects and the foundation of as many entirely new creeds.[20]

Also, it was the European sophistication of the missionary priests that attracted early American converts, long before the Oxford Movement of the 1830's. The native-born nineteenth century converts were "products of American education and of American ideals" who found nothing foreign in the Catholic Church, as preached by the likes of Carroll, Fenwick, and Young.[21] Father John Austin Hill (1777-1828), an orator of "outstanding and charming eloquence," left a career in the British military (where he served as attaché in Rome) to become a Catholic, a Dominican, and a missionary to Ohio. Father Hill rode his circuit until his death, and was buried in Canton, Ohio. He and "Father Smith," aka Prince Demetrius Augustine Gallitzin, who converted in 1795 and served Pennsylvania Catholics until his death, were typical of the priest-convert from Europe.[22] Father Peter Augustine Anderson was a member of a Protestant family in Somerset, Ohio and "was a convert and the first parishioner of St. Joseph's to enter the Order." Father Joshua Moody Young was converted by the Dominicans in Lancaster in 1839 and served St. Mary's for fifteen years. In Zanesville, George Wilson was a Protestant who bought a pew in St.

---

19 Edward J. Mannix, S.T.L., *The American Convert Movement* (The Devin-Adair Company: New York, 1923) p. vi. McAvoy speaks to this phenomenon when he writes, "Catholics in America received acceptance socially only where these English and older Irish families in the country advanced and only where they lived." p. 43.
    Gaelic speaking Irish seem to have settled in enclaves and remained out of the public eye. There was one such settlement near Grassley in Pennsylvania and another near Bardstown, Kentucky.
20 Raphael N. Hamilton, "The Significance of the Frontier to the Historian of the Catholic Church in the United States," *The Catholic Historical Review*, V. 25 (2), July 1939, p. 171.
21 Mannix.
22 CRS, XXVI, #10, 2001.

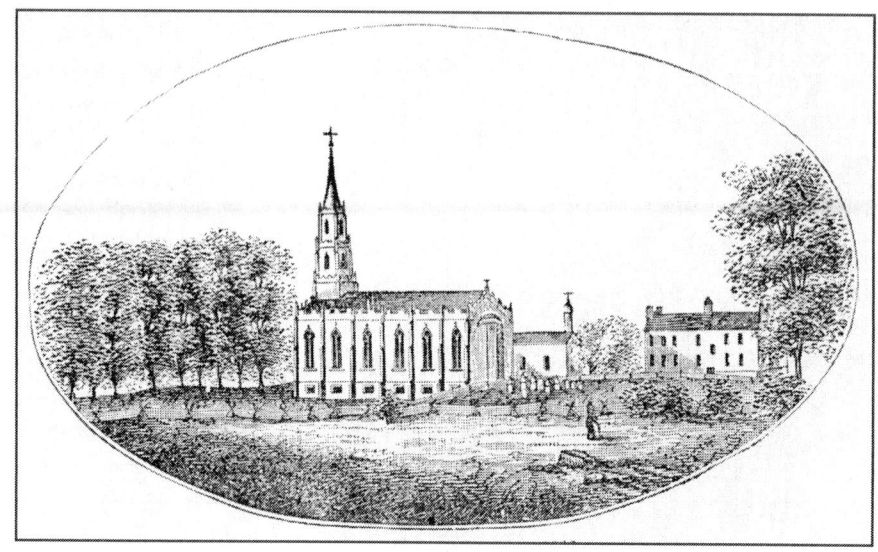

The second St. Joseph Catholic Church, Convent, and College in Somerset, Ohio.
Drawn by Henry Howe in 1848

John's. He converted to the church in 1827 and also entered the Dominican Order.[23]

Among the socially significant Catholic converts, Elizabeth Bayley Seaton, the granddaughter of an Episcopal rector and daughter of an anatomy professor at King's College (Columbia), stands out. Seaton was the widow of William McGee Seaton, who died while trying to recover his health in the climate of Italy. As a widow with five children, Elizabeth followed a long-held dream and converted in Rome in 1805. She was abandoned by her family. Churchmen invited her to establish a school for girls in Baltimore and, later, in Emmitsburg. Mother Seaton founded the Sisters of Charity in 1812.[24]

As the Dominicans began their labors in Ohio, conversion was frequent. Father Jean Baptiste Lamy, the French priest serving Danville, had a special gift for making converts. While at St. Luke's (1839-47), he brought a dozen families from the Methodist to the Catholic church, and converted an English-born Anglican family–the Brents–in Mount Vernon. Julius Brent would become a much-beloved priest at St. Vincent de Paul in that town.

Father Jean Baptiste Lamy
Catholic Record Society

23 O'Daniel, p. 175.
24 "Elizabeth Ann Seaton," *Catholic Encyclopedia*, XIII, p. 136.

In 1831, the "sectarian ministers" attacked the Catholic Church in newspapers, precisely because of the number of converts. Fenwick responded by initiating the *Catholic Telegraph*, the oldest Catholic newspaper in the country (October 22, 1831). To the "homegrown" converts came people profoundly affected by an upheaval in the Church of England in the 1830's.[25]

The Oxford Movement rose out of a reform movement in the Anglican Church. Clerics sought to avoid more government regulation of church life. While this battle was being fought in Parliament, a faction of clerics at Oxford University became engrossed in the quest for a spiritual renewal and found themselves leaning toward the liturgy and theology of Rome. John Keble, Edward B. Pusey, John Henry Newman, and Richard Froude led a movement dubbed the Tractarians, so named for the pamphlets (tracts) they published.

In 1833, Pusey published the influential Tract 18. A man with high political connections, Pusey's words lent decisive weight to the movement. Newman was vicar of St. Mary's Church at Oxford. His sermons between 1834 and 1842 provided the intellectual structure for the movement. Drawing on his reading of the Patristic Fathers, Newman's work–especially the *Apologia*–led him to a strong Anglo-Catholic position. By 1839, the once-hostile Newman had been drawn toward the Roman church. Deprived of his living (clerical post), he entered the Roman church in 1845, eventually becoming a cardinal. Pusey remained Anglican and was responsible for many "Catholic" movements

Cardinal John Henry Newman
Courtesy John Henry Newman Institue of Catholic Thought, Illinois

within that church, including the reestablishment of religious orders. In the 1850's, there was another flurry of the "return to Rome." Among the converts then was Henry Manning, later a cardinal.[26]

The English turmoil soon led to a debate in the American Episcopal Church. A number of its significant members "returned to Rome." Others

---

25 Kieppei, p. 48. *CRS*, XX, #5, May 1995, O'Daniel, p. 159.
26 "The Oxford Movement," *New Catholic Encyclopedia*, Vol. X, 1967, pp. 845-847.

Orestes Brownson
Courtesy Notre Dame Archives, Notre Dame University, Indiana

came from other traditions. Orestes Brownson was the most visible convert. He brought astonishing intellectual vitality to the Roman Catholic Church's lay movement. Brownson had been a Presbyterian, a Universalist, and a Unitarian. As a member of the Transcendental Movement, which was bubbling up in eastern intellectual circles, he even spoke of a "church of the future." In 1844, at the age of 41, he converted to Rome. His voice in the *Boston Quarterly Review* spoke not only for social reform, but also for an intellectual acceptance of Catholic dogma.[27]

James Roosevelt Bayley, the nephew of Mother Seaton and a graduate of Trinity College in Hartford, Connecticut, had been ordained an Episcopal priest. He entered the Roman church in 1842, studied at Saint Sulpice in Paris, and received his faculties as a Roman Catholic priest in 1844. Bayley served as secretary to New York Bishop John Hughes for seven years, and eventually became Archbishop of Baltimore.[28]

Bishop James Bayley
Seton Hall University Archives & Special Collections

The publication of pamphlets spread the Tractarian/Oxford Movement widely. A wave of conversions reached Ohio, produced by the influence of Newman and his Tractarians. Bexley Hall (the Episcopal Seminary) and Kenyon College in Gambier (near Danville and Mount Vernon) were dominated in the 1840's and '50s by Charles P. McIlvaine. Bishop McIlvaine was a staunch evangelist, and hostile to the liturgical practices advocated by the Tractarians. Yet Commodore Benjamin Franklin Bache, a great-grandson of Benjamin Franklin, and a noted surgeon who spent from 1838-41 as a professor of natural sciences at Kenyon, made his journey to Rome during that time.

McIlvaine assigned Henry Livingston Richards—a Bexley Hall graduate of 1838—as the rector of St. Paul's in Columbus, considered to be a plum assignment. However, Richards entered the Roman church; his son, J. Havens Richards, would become a Jesuit and, later, the president of Georgetown University.[29]

---

27 "Orestes Brownson," *New Catholic Encyclopedia*, V. 1, pp. 827-8.
28 "James Roosevelt Bayley," *New Catholic Encyclopedia*, V. I, pp. 182-183; McAvoy, p. 153.

Another student at Kenyon during this time was Sylvester Rosecrans. The conversion of this future bishop of Columbus did not depend on the theological life at Kenyon College. His conversion was a result of the influence of his brother, William Stark Rosecrans. The future Major-General Rosecrans was intrigued by the Oxford-leaning chaplain at West Point, and by his own study of the pamphlets. William converted in 1844; his classmate, *Mayflower* descendant, George Deshons, followed him in 1850. Deshons would become the superior of the Paulist Order.[30]

Georgetown College
Catholic Record Society, Columbus, Ohio

The Paulists consisted almost entirely of converts and were dedicated to missionary activity among fellow Americans. Issac Hecker, a convert in 1844, was a friend of Brownson, and he saw the need for an American religious order house that would address American issues. In 1856, the Vatican approved the founding of the Society of Missionary Priests of St. Paul the Apostle. Augustine Hewitt was another one of the founders; he was the grandson of U.S. Senator James Millhouse and the son of Nathaniel Hewitt, a Congregational minister in Fairfield, Connecticut. One of the elder Hewitt's colleagues in the Temperance movement, Judge Reuben Walworth, was the father of another convert–Paulist priest, Father Clarence Walworth. Augustine Hewitt became a priest after his conversion in 1846, and was instrumental in establishing the Paulist Press. Another Paulist, Francis Baker, journeyed from Methodism to the Episcopal Church to Rome, and converted in 1853.[31]

James Kent Stone, son of the dean of the Episcopal Theological School in Cambridge, Massachusetts, graduated from Harvard in 1861, and fought at the battle of Antietam. In 1863, he was on the faculty of Kenyon College, teaching Latin; he was elected as Kenyon's president in

---

29 O'Neill, pp. 89, 91. *Catholic Telegraph*, February 7, 1852, from *Catholic Record Society*, XXVIII, #1, January 2003, p. 30. "'On the feast of the Conversion of St. Paul, I had the happiness to receive into the Church Rev. H.C.L. Richards, former Rector of St. Paul's (Episcopalian) of this city. He very much edified the congregation by making the profession of faith publicly, after the ten o'clock mass.'"
30 "Sylvester Rosecrans," *New Catholic Encyclopedia*, V. IV, p. 798; *New Encyclopedia Britannica*, V. 8, pp. 657-8.
31 "Paulists," *New Catholic Encyclopedia*, V. VII, pp. 29-30; Sister Joan Bland, *Hibernian Crusade: the Story of the Catholic Total Abstinence Union of America* (The Catholic University Press: Washington, D.C., 1951) p. 4 fn. "Francis Baker," *New Catholic Encyclopedia*, V. II, p. 22.

1867. Stone and the Mount Vernon priest, Julius Brent, spent long evenings discussing theology as the Episcopal priest prepared for a journey to Rome. In 1868, Stone's graduation address aroused the wrath of fellow faculty members, John McElhenney and Sherlock Bronson, because of Stone's "Roman" treatment of the Doctrine of Incarnation. The uproar in the faculty forced Stone to resign. He spent a year at Hobart College, where his young wife died. In 1869, he entered the Roman Catholic Church. As Father Fidelis, he would serve as the provincial of the Passionist priests in the United States.[32]

Father Julius Brent
Catholic Record Society

Despite his perennial shortage of priests, Bishop Purcell was cheered by the continued influx of converts. In Lancaster, there were "many distinguished converts" among the other Catholics whom Purcell "had formerly served near Emmitsburg, Maryland." At St. Dominic's in Beaver, the 1833 baptismal records showed 30 baptisms in March; 20 of these were adults. In 1837, the record listed seven converts. At St. Dominic's, Purcell found 200-250 communicants; however, because of lack of preparation, he confirmed only eight persons–four of whom were converts.[33]

Margaret Douglas, wife of Nicholas Gallagher and daughter of Belmont County's state representative, William Douglas, was baptized in 1845. Sarah Winteringer DeLong made her first communion just before her death in 1845.[34]

Sarah Worthington King Peters
Henry Howe

Sarah King Peters, daughter of Thomas Worthington (Ohio's sixth governor) and the widow of General Edward King of Cincinnati, entered the Church through the Jesuits in Jerusalem in 1852. Mrs. Peters not only funded the Cincinnati Orphan Asylum, but she brought nuns to the diocese, and served as

---

32 "James Kent Stone," *New Catholic Encyclopedia*, V. XIII, p. 722; O'Neill, p. 89. (Stone ended his days as a missionary to South Americans.)
33 St. Mary's Records; *CRS*, XX, #8, August 1995.
34 Abstract of Purcell's letter, June 17, 1845, *CRS*, XXII, #7, July 1997.

a battlefield nurse herself, aboard a relief boat that she provisioned for the wounded at Shiloh.[35]

On the other hand, during the frequent Methodist revivals and tent meetings, at least some of the Catholics "fell away." In the year 1825, Nancy Archer Enochs convinced three of her brothers to attend a revival led by her husband, silver-tongued Elisha Enochs. The three brothers–Jacob, James, and Joseph–became Methodists, forever splitting the family.[36]

---

35 Howe, V. 1, p. 823; *CRS*, XX, #5, May 1995.
36 Archer, p. 227.

Chapter Seven

"New" Catholics and "Old" 1840–1900
The Struggle to Remain American

Converts aside, the Germans and the Irish provided the bulk of Purcell's population. The "old Catholics" and the "new" were mingling. On his first visit to Beaver in 1834, Bishop Purcell was delighted with the "wrought wood church" that the community had constructed on the south end of Edmund Gallagher's farm about a half-mile west of Batesville. The church was being served by the Dominicans from Zanesville. The priest, Father Richard Miles, visited the church once or twice a year.[1]

Following the mass at St. Dominic's, Purcell discussed visiting a new church that was being constructed for the German settlement ten miles over the hills from Beaver. The driving force was John J. "Door" (Dorr), a member of the St. Dominic's choir. Purcell visited first with the Jefferis family and found

> ten interesting converts, thence he proceeded, accompanied by Mr. DeLong, who numbers not fewer than 70 relatives, converted, like himself, to the Catholic faith on the road to St. Paul's church, in Columbiana County.[2]

Bishop Purcell had been recruiting foreign priests for the diocese. At Beaver, he introduced the people to Father Martin Kundig, a Swiss-born priest who was ordained in 1829 by Bishop Fenwick. Kundig built the log cabin church at St. Martin's in Brown County, which served as a way station on the western circuit. Purcell intended that Kundig would

---

1 The exact date of the creation of the church is impossible to reconstruct. The records of St. Dominic were kept at St. John's (Zanesville) and that church's records prior to 1828 are lost. There are occasional sacramental entries at St. Joseph in Somerset. Father Stephen Montgomery became a resident pastor at St. John's in 1823; sometime thereafter, he visited St. Dominic's. A traditional–and reasonable-date is 1822. Donald Schlegel, Father George Schlegel, "St. Dominic Parish, Beaver and St. Mary's Parish. CRS, XIII, #8, XIV, #9.
2 Ibid.

be the permanent priest at St. Dominic's, serving both the Irish and the Germans at Dorr's Settlement. It was to Kundig that Edmund and Lydia Gallagher deeded the two acres of land upon which St. Dominic's had been built. However, Kundig apparently could not adapt to the rigors of the terrain of Belmont County, and soon left the parish.[3]

In 1836, Bishop Purcell sent Fr. James Reid to pastor St. Dominic's, Dorr's Settlement church, and Archer's Settlement church. The forty-three-year-old native of Carrickmacross, County Monaghan, had been ordained by Fenwick in 1832. Riding a Canadian pony given to him by Robert Gallagher, the Dominican rode his circuit from Beaver to Woodsfield and beyond. In 1835, on a

> special invitation...[he spoke in Woodsfield] and the Court House was placed at his disposal. He ascended the Judge's Bench. The audience was large, almost entirely Protestant. The attention was profound and respectful. The text was "Our Lord, one faith, one baptism."

In Barnesville, a fear of "romanish plots" surfaced when Reid received a package of odds and ends from St. James's Seminary, which closed at St. Martin's in 1835. Two globes were in the package, and their stands protruded from the package. Fear that "some kind of 'Roman artillery' or fire arms" were inside rattled up and down Main Street in Barnesville.

Reid remained at Beaver for two years and was replaced by another Irishman, James Quinlan, who was ordained in 1834. Tending the scattered flock of his charge, "he may have been instrumental in the erection of St. Peter and Paul Church at Doherty Settlement on Crane's Nest Creek in Monroe County."[4]

Having made the circuit of the state twice, John Purcell was thoroughly prepared for the needs and wants of his people when he undertook his third visitation in July of 1836. His party steamed up the Ohio River from Cincinnati to Wheeling, where he bid adieu to two seminarians–James McCallion and William Peter Murphy–who were bound for the long journey to Rome. Purcell and German-born Joseph Stahlschmidt (ordained in 1835) traveled by coach down the National Road. At St. Clairsville, they mounted horses for the winding trails across the ridges into the valley where St. Dominic's lay. There, on July 7, 1836,

---

[3] Kundig is not listed in the official history of this parish, nor as its pastor in the *Catholic Almanac*. Howe, V. 1, p. 340; Schlegel, *CRS*, XIII, #8, August 1988; Guernsey County Direct Deed Book, 1-H-525.

[4] *CRS*, XIII, #6, June 1993. Reid became pastor of Beaver, Pennsylvania's church (1846-1866), *CRS*, XIII, #9, September 1988.

the bishop confirmed nineteen persons. He also "preached to a large audience, chiefly Protestant, in a grove near the church, the building being too small to contain one half the assembled multitude."

Purcell and Stahlschmidt then crossed the Leatherwood Valley to the point where Robert Gallagher had built his gristmill. James DeLong had also opened a blacksmith shop and served as both grocer and postmaster. The population of the western Leatherwood Valley had found its economic center. Robert Gallagher, a strong Temperance man, would soon plat the village (1842) and name it Temperanceville.[5]

On Tuesday, July 19, the bishop blessed the church near Malaga that had been built by Dorr's efforts. Crowning a hill south of the village, with a cemetery spilling down the hill and a devotional crucifix by the road, it mirrored Dorr's German homeland.

As Father Stahlschmidt mounted the pulpit, elation swept the church as the people heard their first German-language sermon in years. On the occasion, the bishop confirmed nineteen persons at the new St. Joseph's.

The following day, the two clerics continued on to Archer's Settlement on Duck Creek—eighteen hilly, difficult miles farther. There the bishop

> was gratified by the fidelity of the Catholics of the place to their old faith, notwithstanding that they had been for a long time deprived of religious instruction and pastoral consolation.

The priests were then piloted through the intricate

> winding of the hills and vales by the good Mr. Archer, rode thirty one miles on horseback to Mr. Sherlock's near Meigs Creek—where he was cordially welcomed by a considerable number of Catholics [who] were under the care of C. P. Montgomery of Zanesville, 36 miles away.[6]

Around 1831, Patrick Sherlock moved his family from Guernsey County into Morgan County, to a farm on Hackney Ridge. Eventually, the children would number twelve. The site of St. James/St. Margaret's Church was on their farm. The Irish in the church community would include names of Kennady, Kennedy, Kelly, Waters, Cahill, Mager, Callaghan—all in America by 1827. By the 1830's, the roster expanded to include Lowe, McHugh, Kearnes, Molyneaux, Powers, Geary, McDonald,

---

5 CRS, XX, #11, November 1995. Abstract from *Catholic Telegraph*. Mirroring wider American society, and aided by the pamphleteering of the Irish Temperance leader, Brother Mathew Talbot, the Temperance Movement swept both the Irish and German parishes of the area. Churches in Somerset and Zanesville enrolled 1,700 members in the Total Abstinence Society. CRS, XXI, #12, December 1996.
6 CRS, XX, #11, November 1995. Abstract of *Catholic Telegraph*.

Owens, McCarty, Canning, and the English-born Pilkingtons. The immigrants represented Counties Clare, Cork, Tipperary, Tyrone, Queens, Donegal, and Louth.[7]

Young Father William Peter Murphy, home from his studies in Rome and ordained in 1839, celebrated mass at St. Dominic's on Christmas Day, 1839. Father Murphy was affable and energetic, and soon solidified a parish feeling at Beaver. He encouraged the construction of the brick church of St. Michael's at Archer's Settlement. The elation of security, growth, and availability of the sacraments turned to sorrow when the priest died of fever in 1841. Grieving parishioners carried the body over the hill to Beaver, intent on taking it to Wheeling. Stifling summer heat made the plan impossible. The two congregations buried Father Murphy in the graveyard at St. Dominic's and erected a stone in his honor:

> He was a man of singular purity of mind and goodness of heart, a Christian who faithfully followed in the footsteps of his Divine Master and a priest of the most high God who sought no consolation on his arduous mission but in sacrificing himself with the salvation of the immortal souls of his people.[8]

In his continual search for more priests, Purcell and Provincial President Young visited St. John's in Zanesville, and ordained Joseph Sadoc Alemany, whose studies in Spain had been interrupted by political upheaval. After a flight to Italy, Alemany made his way to America. Although Purcell needed the new priest, he agreed to Young's request that Alemany go to Somerset to deal with the increasing German population. In 1850, Alemany would become the Bishop of San Francisco.[9]

Conversion continued to be a source of priests. Morgantown (Virginia) stonemason, George Wilson, was a convert. He was ordained at St. Rose in 1837. The burley frontiersman was a "gifted cleric in bringing persons into the Catholic Church." It was Wilson who constructed St. Thomas Aquinas Church in Zanesville (on the site of St. John's) to meet the needs of the Irish in Zanesville.[10]

Seven times, Purcell made a journey to Europe seeking priests. Purcell secured the services of the Jesuits for Cincinnati and recruited a number of able French priests, including Jean Baptiste Lamy. Lamy arrived in Ohio in 1839 and would build St. Francis de Sales in Newark, and St.

---

7 *CRS*, XXVII, #8, August 2002.
8 *CRS*, XIII, #9, September 1988. Also, Joseph Stahlschmidt died in 1839 in Mexico City.
9 "Joseph S. Alemany," *New Catholic Encyclopedia, First Edition*, , Vol. I, p. 284.
10 Anthony J. Lisska, "Father George Augustine Joseph Wilson, Temperance Preacher, Parish Missionary, and Church Builder," *CRS*, XVII, #4, April 1988.

Vincent de Paul in Mount Vernon. Here, the Frenchman would become the beloved pastor of the Marylander community in Knox County.[11]

The Marylanders of Sapp's Settlement (Danville) settled in Knox County in 1805. Without a priest for a generation, they retained a semblance of a faith community. They may have been visited by the Somerset Dominicans as early as 1819.[12] Their log church was probably erected in 1822, and blessed in October of 1824 while Bishop Flaget was on his two-year "begging tour" of Europe (May 1823–1825).[13]

Excitement washed over the Knox County Catholics when, in 1839, Bishop Purcell appointed a resident pastor for St. Luke's. Jean Baptiste Lamy was born in Lampdes, France in 1814, and was one of the recruits that Purcell welcomed into the Ohio mission field. The young Frenchman was welcomed by the familiar "old Catholic" names in Danville and by the few resident Catholics in Mount Vernon: William Brophy–"the little Irish Tailor"–and Timothy and William Colopy, David Morton, and Charles Colerick. The old-line Protestant establishment of Mount Vernon– Judge Anthony Banning, Banning Norton, Dr. J. M. Burr, and Henry B. Curtis–also welcomed him and encouraged his dream of erecting a church in the town.[14]

The foundation for St. Vincent de Paul was begun in 1843 on a lot across the street from the Colopy and Morton cottages. On March 2, 1844, the church burned under mysterious conditions. Local residents– mostly Protestant–subscribed $600 toward the rebuilding campaign.[15]

Lamy burned with zeal for his first assignment. Mastering English and seeking citizenship, he became a forceful missioner with sites in Mansfield, Ashland, Loudenville, Canal Dover, Newark, and Massillon. He baptized so many people into the church that, on January 7, 1844, he wrote to Purcell of some "converts about which the Methodists are furious." Other converts were spouses of Catholics who entered the church, such as old Danville settler, Issac Dial (born in Hampshire County, Virginia in

---

11 Hartley, p. 114.
12 On September 20, 1834, Father N. D. Young wrote to Purcell, recommending that the church in Danville be transferred to diocese priests, as it was 50 miles from Somerset. The Dominicans had served it "these 15 years." That would put their priests on the Danville circuit in 1819. *CRS*, XIX, #7, July 1989.
13 See the closely-reasoned articles by Anthony J. Lisska on the foundation of St. Luke's, *CRS*, XI, #9, September 1986, and XIV, July 1989.
14 Purcell complimented Judge Banning "to whom he had been indebted, some years before for much kindness." Banning had opened the Methodist church building to Purcell when the courthouse was refused. *CRS*, XXI, #10, October 1996; Hartley, p. 416; Paul Horgan, *Lamy of Santa Fe* (Farrar, Straus & Girous: New York, 1975) p. 39.
15 Hartley, p. 385.

1799). He'd been married to Nancy Durbin since 1818. He would be baptized in the presence of his daughters, Mrs. Arron McKenzie and Mrs. David Shafer, and their husbands–both converts.[16]

A number of Lamy's converts were of Mount Vernon's "substantial class," a fact reflecting the Oxford Movement and the importance of the Catholic press. Eliza Plimpton was an influential matron in the town; Francis Xavier Hurd and Mary Hurd were the son and wife of the common pleas judge. Dr. Lewis Porter and his wife donated the land for Mount Calvary Cemetery on October 14, 1849. Porter had been born to a Marylander Catholic family, but orphaned at an early age and raised Presbyterian by his uncle, George Porter, the former Governor of Michigan. Lewis Porter graduated from Princeton's Divinity School and became a minister in the German Reformed Church, and then became a physician. He converted to Catholicism at this time. Seven members of the Brent family entered the church, and Lamy prevailed on the bishop to accept Julius Brent as a seminarian. Brent would pastor St. Vincent de Paul from 1851 to 1880.[17]

Baptisms more than doubled during Lamy's pastorate. However, the bishop transferred the priest to St. Mary's in Covington, Kentucky at the end of 1847. The young priest looked out over his congregation one last time on Christmas Day that year and marveled that, even with horrendous weather and deep snow, a hundred people filled the pews for the 5 a.m. mass at St. Luke's.

Lamy was only in Covington a short time before the national needs of the church called. The War with Mexico transferred the southwest into American hands, and the American bishops were then responsible for that region, too. Jean Lamy became the Archbishop of Santa Fe, with a diocese that covered New Mexico, Arizona, Colorado, Nevada, Utah, and California.[18]

Of necessity, foreign-born priests dominated the American clergy. In 1829, when Edward Fenwick traveled to Baltimore for the first council of American bishops, he and his cousin, Benedict Fenwick (Bishop of Boston), were the only native-born men in the American hierarchy.[19]

16 Lamy Letters, University of Notre Dame Archives, January 7, 1844; Horgan, pp. 46-47, 36.
17 St. Vincent de Paul Baptismal records; Frank Hurd was a freshman at Kenyon College when he converted. He would become a prominent attorney in Toledo and a Congressman. Hurd donated the pipe organ when the new St. Vincent's was built in 1922. *Centennial of St. Vincent de Paul Church*, Mount Vernon, Ohio, 1949; Porter, *Catholic Telegraph*, December 15, 1860.
18 Lamy Letters, December 25, 1847, University of Notre Dame; Horgan, p. 68. In 1844, Lamy baptized 144 people at St. Luke's; in 1846, the number was 72.
19 Lisska, *CRS*, XVII, #11, November 2000.

St. John Nepomucene Neumann CSSR
*Courtesy Notre Dame Archives
Notre Dame University, Indiana*

Purcell was Irish-born, and Lamy was French. Purcell recruited others from St. Omer (France) who became bishops: Louis Amadeus Rappe (Cleveland), Louis DeGoesbrian (Burlington, Vermont), Joseph Macheboeuf (Denver), Joseph S. Alemany, O.P. (Monterrey, and Archbishop of San Francisco), and St. John Nepomucene Neumann, C.S.S.R. (Philadelphia). All these men worked for Purcell's Ohio missions.[20]

In America, Irish-born seminarians studied alongside Americans. In 1838, Purcell was able to ordain Joshua Moodie Young, a native of Shapleigh, Maine (the future bishop of Erie), Irish-born James Whelan, O.P. (the future bishop of Nashville), Irish-born Edward Purcell (the bishop's brother), Irish-born Joseph MacNamera, and American-born James McCaffrey and William Peter Murphy. By 1843, Purcell had fifty priests: 9 Americans, 12 Germans, 11 Frenchmen, 10 Irishmen, 4 Italians, 3 Belgians, and 1 Spaniard. These men served 50,000 people.[21]

Purcell was also successful in persuading religious communities to locate in his diocese to establish schools and hospitals. English convert, Mother Julia Chatfield, brought French Ursulines to Cincinnati and settled into the log cabin compound at St. Martin's in Brown County in 1845. At the bishop's invitation, a number of Belgian families relocated to the area. The Ursuline convent became a favored boarding school for local Catholic families: the Shermans, Rosecranses, and Sheridans sent their children there. Mother Elizabeth Seaton's Sisters of Charity would eventually serve a large portion of the state with schools.[22]

These schools served people who poured into Ohio on the National Road and the Ohio & Erie Canal. The Irish who built both transportation avenues literally pulled the nation behind them. As the road crept across Belmont County and to the west, James and Bridget Creighton moved

---

20 Lamott, pp. 351, 354; Hartley, p. 127.
21 *CRS*, XXI, #3; #4, April 1996; Lamott, p. 354. In 1847, the Diocese of Cleveland was split off.
22 Howe, Vol. I, p. 380. Sherman papers, University of Notre Dame, Sister Monica, *The Cross in the Wilderness, a Biography of Pioneer Ohio* (Longmans, Green and Co.: London, 1930) pp. 74-76. The Ursuline Convent is today known as Chatfield College. Bishop Purcell is buried there.

on, living beside the road as James worked on its construction. Their son, Edward, would gain fame as the force behind Western Union and its transcontinental telegraph. Ohioan Zane Grey would celebrate Creighton's achievements in his novel, *Western Union*. Edward Creighton would endow Creighton University in Omaha, Nebraska.[23]

As products of economic hardships at home, the newly-arriving 1840's Irish began to settle in remote parts of the southeastern Ohio area. William and Jane McGinnis Fox, and his brother, Patrick, left County Tyrone in 1843 and settled on Archer's Run in Washington County, thirty miles south of Temperanceville. Their sugar camp would be on the circuit from Temperanceville until they consecrated their own church, St. Paul, in 1863.[24]

The Irish Slevin clan left County Tyrone and settled on farms in the Leatherwood Valley. There, Edward married Hannah Gallagher, daughter of John and Mary Gallagher. Her cousin, Sarah, daughter of Christopher and Mary Gallagher, married Edward Slevin's brother, Michael, in St. Mary's in 1841. Sarah's brother, Thomas Gallagher, married Mary Slevin. Ann and Rose Slevin married into the Creighton family, and Edward Joseph Slevin married Mary Ann Butler, connecting the Slevins to yet another Catholic link in the family tapestry of the Leatherwood Valley. Mariah Fordyce, daughter of area pioneer, Lemuel Fordyce, married John Slevin. Both she and her brother, Lemuel, converted to Catholicism.[25]

The recent Irish immigrants were part of the "famine fled" migration. The Irish potato crop failed completely in 1845; between 1845 and 1851, the island lost two million people to migration and another million to starvation. Of the emigrants, fifty-percent died on the journey. The desperate flight of starving poor brought another element of Irish-ness to America–the "shanty Irish" who clustered into tenements in cities, too poor to continue on. "Irish" became synonymous with poverty and crime. A virulent anti-Catholicism was spawned. The Ursuline Convent in Charlestown, Massachusetts (endowed by Father Thayer) was burned in 1834, and similar events punctuated riots in several cities. Competition for menial work generated an Irish/black hostility. By 1850, most urban Irish were isolated culturally and socially from the rest of society.[26]

---

[23] Schlegel, "The Creightons," *CRS*, XIX, #10, October 1994; #11, November 1994.
[24] Donald Schlegel, "St. Patrick's Mission, Fox Settlement, Ludlow Township, Washington County, Ohio, 1863-1954," *CRS*, XVII, #3, March 1992;.
[25] Slevin Genealogy, Pearl Reischman.
[26] Blessing, pp. 529, 533. Only 10% of the Irish in America in 1870 were farmers. Blessing, p. 530.

The Irish refugees themselves were confused and frightened. The Church was the only thing they recognized in the new world. Catholic social work saved many, many lives. In New York–with its sudden, enormous Catholic minority–Archbishop John Hughes emerged as the leader of an increasingly "foreign" church. The world faced by Hughes and John Purcell in Ohio was far different from the world of John Carroll and Edward Fenwick.

Even the Irish who were long resident in America and migrated to Ohio in the 1840's, faced a different atmosphere. The Gildeas, for example, found it advisable to settle with co-religionists. Nationally, the All American Party–commonly called the Know Nothings–tried to curb immigration and wanted to deny citizenship to all immigrants–no matter how long they had been in America. The 1854 election was particularly nasty. In Cincinnati, an anti-Catholic frenzy broke out and an attempt to burn the cathedral was just barely averted.[27]

Michael Gildea was born in 1789, the son of Cormack Gildea of County Donegal, Ireland. He arrived in Baltimore in 1806 and soon married Baltimore-born Ruth Gist. When she died in 1819, Gildea was left in straited circumstances, and their children, George Washington Gildea and Susanna Gildea, were brought up as itinerants by "comparative strangers" and "afforded few advantages." Young Gildea worked as a shoemaker in Emmitsburg, Maryland. Observing the educated Catholic elite of that town, he determined "to better himself." While working his trade as a cobbler through Pennsylvania and Ohio, he also cobbled together an education. He began to read medicine with a physician in Berwick, Pennsylvania. Gildea moved on to Ohio in 1844 and then married into a Belmont County Gallagher family.

Margaret Gallagher was the daughter of "Long Jim" Gallagher, a native of County Donegal. Long Jim and his brother, Patrick, had staked out their claim in 1811, and worked tobacco farms in the Leatherwood Valley. Jim's wife was Ann Carr of German-dominated New Gottingen. G.W. and Margaret Gildea settled in nearby Temperanceville in 1845. There, he traveled periodically to Old Washington to read medicine with Dr. John McFarland. Gildea enrolled in the Ohio Medical College in Cincinnati in 1847, and hung out his shingle in New Gottingen in 1850. There, his patients were the farming Irish and the Germans who turned

---

27 In 1840, the foreign-born population in Ohio was 3%; in 1850, it was 7%. Embrey B. Howson, *The German Element in Ohio, 1803–1830* (Ohio State University: Columbus, Ohio) p. 2; Bland, p. 300.

tobacco into cigars, shipping them out to the world market through the railroad station at Gibson Station.²⁸

In 1855, Dr. Gildea and his children, Ruth, James, and John, stood in St. Mary's Cemetery as Margaret was laid to rest. Seven years later, Dr. Gildea would marry her sister, Anne.

The steady increase of Catholics along the National Road led to the laying of the cornerstone for St. Patrick's church in Old Washington in1844. Forty-two German families at Fulda began to build their church that same year.²⁹ It became more difficult to serve smaller sites. St. Dominic's reverted to a stop on the circuit. In the 1840's, Fathers Joseph Alemany of Zanesville, James McCaffrey of Marietta, Charles McCallion, Philip Foley, and Timothy Foley of Zanesville entered sacramental information into St. Dominic's records. Clearly, the influx of Germans would dominate the area, and Irish Beaver and Archer would fall to the status of missions. In 1849, John Christian Kraemer, a German native, would be assigned to serve the church at Miltonsburg, and the missions around it.³⁰

Following the collapse of Napoleon's Europe in 1815, a flood of conservative Catholic Germans began arriving in America. Many of them settled in Ohio, particularly along the Ohio/Indiana border. Cincinnati began to sport a German face. Butcher shops, sausage houses, and breweries sprang up "over the Rhine" as the immigrants settled into the city. Forty different German language guides to Ohio were sold at the port city of Baltimore. Catholics in the eastern Ohio area, desirous of securing Catholic marriages, encouraged German settlement in the Sunfish and Duck Creek valleys. St. Joseph's, Wills Creek (outside Malaga), Immaculate Conception in Fulda, and St. John's in Miltonsburg are the result of that settlement.

Bishop Purcell now sought German speaking priests to assist his few veterans. Father John Martin Henni, long a fixture in Ohio, established the first German language Catholic newspaper in Ohio (1837): *Der Wahrheits Freund*. Another priest, Father Hieronymous Vogeler, preached the first German sermon at the church in Zanesville in 1838, bringing his people "long sought consolation."³¹

Purcell also faced the difficult problem of culture clash, and a demand

---

28 Marie Gildea. *Jeffersonian*, December 22, 1982.
29 *CRS*, XXII, #8, July 1997.
30 St. Mary's Records.
31 *CRS*, XXV, #6, June 2000. Another of the German-speaking priests was "Father Serge" (Sergius de Stckoulepmkoff), "the son of a noble Russian family" who would serve in the diocese after 1857, both in Coshocton (1858-62) and Circleville (1869-72). Hartley, p. 499; Lamott, p. 366.

for ethnic churches that would plague the American Catholic Church during the wave of immigration. In Dresden (Muskingum County), German Catholic canal workers and Irish Catholics demanded separate churches. In Wills Creek Valley in southern Coshocton County, two mission churches—St. Nicholas and St. Mary's—were built to serve Germans and French Catholics. In Zanesville, Germans agitated for another church separate from St. John's/St. Thomas. In 1836, Purcell and Father Stahlschmidt visited the city to ascertain needs. A small gray church on the corner of Main Street and Greenwood Avenue was dedicated to St. Nicholas by Purcell on December 1, 1842. At Christmas-time, German-born Father Joseph Gallinger arrived to take up his duties.[32]

German names began to appear in St. Dominic's records as immigration spilled into that end of the Leatherwood Valley: Francis Xavier Leger and his wife, Ursala, once of Hohenzollern, Germany (to America in 1854); Helen Poulton, born in Germany; Anton Schaefer, born in Hohenzollern, Germany; Herman Clouse, born in Hesse, Germany. Peter "Ambrose" (Armbruster) and his wife, Lena, and three children, along with his mother-in-law, Mary Rapp, a native of Prussia, and Joseph and Elizabeth "Ambrose" and George and Frances Rapp Armbruster—all German-born—were recorded in the 1860 census. George was a stonemason and grocer in Temperanceville.[33] The old families slowly intermarried with the Germans. In 1859, Eliza Jane Daugherty married Joshua Poulton.[34]

German became the dominant language in town and church.[35] In 1852, German-born Father John W. Brummer was transferred from Dayton to St. Dominic's. The twenty-seven-year-old priest saw it as banishment, and complained of being forced to exist on "cornbread and creeks...tumbling about on horseback...." The terrain was difficult and the people were scattered. Brummer shared the duty with Father John Christian Kroemer, who was "weak and infirm"; their circuit was St. Dominic's, St. Patrick's in Old Washington, Sts. Peter and Paul at Crane's Nest, St. Joseph at Wills Creek, St. Michael's at Archer's, Immaculate Conception at Fulda, St. John's at Miltonsburg, and the railroad towns of Bellaire and Bridgeport. Brummer appealed for more help. He voiced the

---

32 Musselman, pp. 39, 43.
33 St. Mary's Records, 1860 Census. Also in that record are Leo "Pickering" (Pekari), a native of Westenbourg, Germany, a wagon-builder and carpenter, and his wife, Victoria, a native of Prussia. Their son, "Fincey" (Vincent) was born in Ohio.
34 Ibid.
35 German was the first language for many in Elk Township, Noble County (Fulda) until the 1930's. Keith Schockling.

lament heard in Ohio for half a century—too few priests, too much work:

> the priest always running about is always distracted becomes careless to his own prayers, meditation and even breviary...his mind is occupied with his worldly temperary [sic] material difficulties & troubled more and more he becomes a man of worldly mind & how can such a person bring & lead these poor....people to become good catholics [sic] & save their souls....If things go on this way most of these missions will become what Archer's is now, died away....[36]

Even with his disheartened state of mind, the priest baptized forty-five during his first year. Despite his frustrations, Brummer made some important decisions. At Beaver, he built a new church east of the old one and, on the Feast of the Assumption (August 15) in 1855, St. Mary's Church was consecrated. Father Brummer was granted a respite and stationed in Zanesville at St. Nicholas; French-born John Mary Jacquet was assigned to St. Mary's. Jacquet began to reconstruct the parish records. He found no records for 1845-1849, and what he recorded, he described: "I have transcribed this from various documents which I found here on my arrival."[37]

Purcell had recruited Jacquet for Ohio. He was another in the line of many French priests who served the American missions after John Carroll's time. Purcell visited St. Omer and inspired the young seminarian Jacquet to seek out the distant mission field. Jacquet sailed for America ten weeks after his ordination in 1845. Dominican Father Richard Miles, who once served St. Dominic's from Zanesville, had been elevated to the bishopric of Nashville. Jacquet went to him, apparently having given a promise for ten years of service. Miles sent the burly Frenchman to work among the Irish railroad builders and miners around Chattanooga. Jacquet was

Father John Mary Jacquet
Catholic Record Society, Columbus, Ohio

---

36 Quoted in *CRS*, XIV, #6, June 1989.
37 Father Brummer would be sent to Miltonsburg and Fulda in 1858. He would later assume Archer's and Crane's Nest parishes. During this decade, Woodsfield grew in population, while Dougherty's Settlement and Crane's Nest withered away. In Woodsfield, the Germans build St. Sylvester's in 1869. German Evangelicals had opened their church in 1856. *CRS*, XIV, #6, June 1989. Donald Schlegel believes the church records for this period are inscribed at Miltonsburg, where Father Kroemer resided.

one of nine priests in the state. His appetite for hard physical labor and his working class attitude endeared him to the tiny Tennessee Catholic community.

In 1855, with a recommendation from Bishop Miles, the big French priest boarded a steamer and traveled up the Cumberland River to the Ohio, and on to Purcell's parsonage in Cincinnati. He joined the other 109 priests in the diocese. The Irish bishop sent the French priest to the Irish at St. Mary's in Temperanceville. It was a marriage made in heaven.

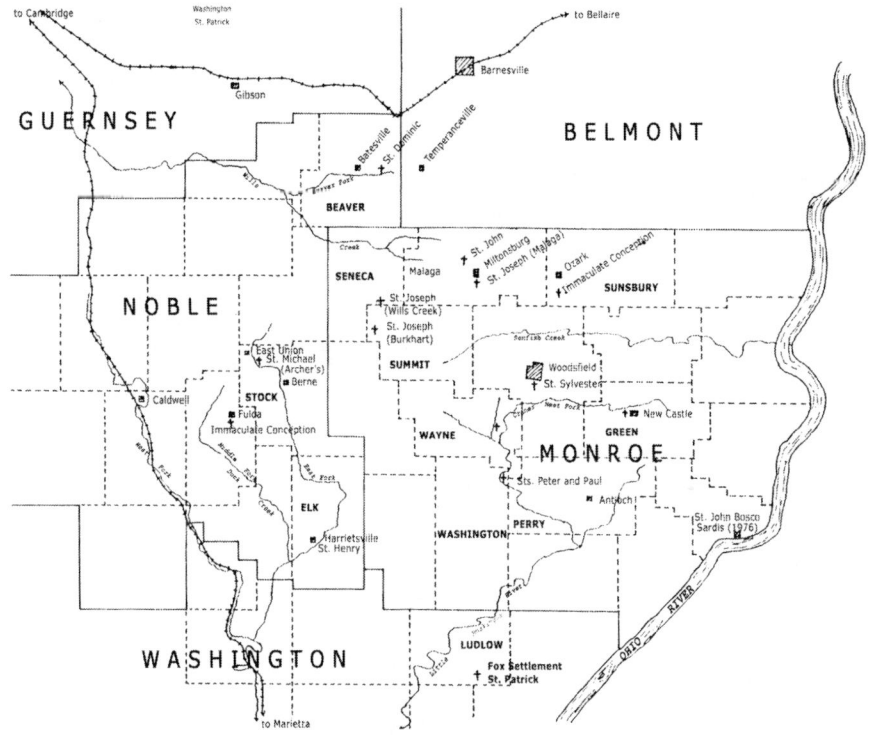

MONROE/NOBLE COUNTY CATHOLIC COMMUNITIES

Courtesy Donald Schlegel

Jacquet arrived in the village with his mass kit, his books, and a maul too heavy for other men to lift. The priest merrily set about splitting rails, sawing lumber, building a spring house, and then a school. During the first year, the priest familiarized himself with his circuit: Sts. Peter and Paul in Monroe County (where he baptized Leches, Shephards, and many Daughertys); McMahon Creek, St. Patrick's at Gibson Station, Barnesville, Bellaire, Archer's, New Gottingen, and Cambridge. Jacquet recorded 127 people making their Easter Duty at Beaver, and 100 in the missions; in

1859, it would be 149 in Beaver, and 252 in the missions.

Jacquet's parish report of 1857 reported 128 communicants at St. Mary's, 38 at St. Patrick's, 22 at Sts. Peter and Paul, 14 at Archer's, 15 at Miller's Run, 17 at Lewis Mill, 8 "at Mr. Burns," and 10 at Barnesville. He also reported the opening of a mission at Bellaire. Jacquet's work in Tennessee's mining towns had prepared him for the conditions created by the oil boom at Sistersville, (West) Virginia, and the railroad frenzy around Bellaire. Twice a month, he went to the river town "via ferrea" to serve the

Bellaire Railroad, 1887

Henry Howe

Irish railroaders. By 1865, he would report 500 attached to his mission there, and another 750 in his entire charge.[38]

Young Nicholas Gallagher accompanied the priest on his circuit. Gallagher, who was training to enter seminary, experienced first-hand the arduous work and the need for discipline and self-sacrifice required for his chosen life. At 16, Nicholas began his spiritual journey at St. Mary's of the West Seminary. His vocation was a source of great pride for his family. The patriarch, Edmund Gallagher (who died on November 22, 1860), had left a rich tradition in the valley. Father Jacquet reported to the *Catholic Telegraph*: "Under the guidance of Providence he was the chief cause of a congregation having been formed here in the woods." Gallagher's settlement was thriving, and his grandson was training to serve his beloved church, but the uncertainty of the approaching constitutional crisis reached down into his valley.[39]

As the Civil War engulfed the country, area men donned blue and marched off to war. Many of them served in the 78th Ohio Volunteer

---

38 St. Mary's Records, abstracted by the author. Donald Schlegel, "St. Dominic's Parish," *CRS*, XIII, #8, XIV, #9.
39 *CRS*, XXI, #1, January 1989. *Catholic Telegraph*, December 15, 1860, p. 4.

The Squirrel Hunters of Ohio and Indiana, crossing the Ohio at Cincinnati
Henry Howe, 1862

Infantry, one of the most valiant–and bloodied–units. John Jefferis enlisted at eighteen; Pius Jefferis at 37. John J. Jefferis was shot in the face and demobilized; he reenlisted. John R. Jefferis of Company K died at Shiloh. Joseph Jefferis, Sr. died at his home in Temperanceville from the effects of his service. His son, Joseph, Jr., received a surgeon's dismissal order at Crumps Landing on March 18, 1862.

Edmund DeLong served as a sergeant in Company K, 78th O.V.I. Thomas DeLong died at Shiloh at the age of 20. William DeLong died at 21 at Bolivar, Tennessee. All of the Gallagher boys except Nicholas–who was in the seminary–served in the 78th. Their mother sat by the window daily, staring towards the south and saying the rosary. James D. was a sergeant; John J., William, and Edmund rounded out the family group in blue. Edmund was mortally wounded at the battle of Atlanta. His body was hit again by a shot as his brother James carried him to the aid station. Edmund died at the hospital in Marietta, Georgia on July 21,

James D. Gallagher (1838–1917)
Courtesy Pearl Gallagher Reischman

1864. His brother, William, died at home on March 10, 1865, as a result of his service. Austin joined the 9th Ohio Volunteer Cavalry, Company B, and served under the reckless "Kilcavalry" Kilpatrick in the Carolinas. Cousin Charles Gallagher died at Campach on April 15, 1864. He, too, rode in the 9th O.V.C., Company B. Another Sergeant James Gallagher died on July 26, 1862 at Bolivar, Tennessee.[40]

Owen DeLong was in Company D, 60th O.V.I., and was wounded at Mary's Bridge, Nye River, Virginia. Charles DeLong served in the 176th O.V.I. Another St. Mary's parishioner, Sergeant Daniel McDaniel, was killed at Monterey, Tennessee on May 16, 1862. William and Levi Poulton of St. Mary's, and Hugh, Daniel, and Jerra McCaughy enlisted. Jerra died at St. Louis, Missouri on August 16, 1862.[41]

Nine of the Archers went to war; Absolom, Simon, Ambrose, Aaron, Thomas, Sebastian, Nathan, and James came home; Issac died in Nashville. William Henry Enochs was in Company B, 2nd O.V.I. Having enlisted as a private on April 17, 1861, he was brevetted a brigadier general of volunteers on March 13, 1865. Post war, he would graduate from a Cincinnati law school in 1866, practice law in Ironton, and serve one term in Ohio's General Assembly and one term in Congress. George Crow (son of Martin, the Indian Fighter) was a colonel in the Confederate Army.[42]

Returning from the War

Henry Howe

40 *Official Rosters of the Soldiers of the State of Ohio in the War of the Rebellion.* Cincinnati, 1886.
41 Ibid.; *CRS*, XIII, #9, September 1988.
42 *Biographical Guide to Congress.* Internet. Archer, p. 230.

Far removed from the battlefield, another area man played a role in the war. James DeLong made a career in politics. Elected as a probate judge in Guernsey County (1852–1856), DeLong rejected his heritage, joined the Presbyterian Church, and became a Mason. Active in the emergence of the Republican Party, DeLong was rewarded by newly elected President Abraham Lincoln, and appointed as Consul for Tangier, Morocco.

DeLong's sojourn in North Africa assumed importance when Confederate privateer–and Roman Catholic–Captain Ralph Semmes brought his ship, the *CSS Alabama*, into port for coal. The *Alabama* had been creating havoc among Union ships in the Mediterranean and the English Channel. DeLong arranged for the arrest of two of the ship's officers, thus delaying the vessel long enough for the *USS Kearsarge* to overtake and destroy it.[43]

Sister Anthony O'Connell (center, behind two girls).
Courtesy Sisters of Charity of Cincinnati

At home, the unprecedented carnage of the war shook the population. Perhaps no action during the war did more to mitigate anti-Catholic prejudice than the selfless action of the many orders of nuns who cared for the wounded from both sides, in hospitals and on the battlefield. Thirty-eight Sisters of Charity from the Cincinnati Diocese–led by Sister Anthony O'Connell–and the Sisters of Charity of Nazareth, Kentucky, were part of a truly heroic action during the war. An entire generation of soldiers would never forget them.[44]

The Herculean efforts expended in the Civil War radically changed American life in the North. A steady march toward urbanization began during the war and continued rapidly afterwards. Small farming communities began to contract. This national movement affected the Church. A new Diocese of Columbus was created in 1868, and Purcell's

---

43 "James DeLong," Wichita, Kansas obituary, 1890, unknown paper. DeLong moved to Independence, Kansas after the war and was twice elected mayor.
44 Bland, p. 315.

auxiliary bishop, Sylvester Horton Rosecrans, was put in charge of the new jurisdiction, which included all of Ohio, south and east of Delaware and Morrow counties.[45]

Rural parishes and missions began to disappear. By 1864, Dougherty's Mission was attached to Fulda and served by newly ordained, German-born Nicholas Pilger, who lived at Miltonsburg. On Easter in 1868, Pilger oversaw the Easter Duty of 25 people at Crane's Nest, and a hundred Germans at St. Sylvester's in Woodsfield. As the population continued to shift toward the logging town of Woodsfield, the log church at Crane's Nest would be abandoned.[46]

The railroad had been of paramount importance during the war; it continued to siphon off trade from the National Road. The need waned for St. Patrick's in Old Washington. In 1868, Father Jacquet and other carpenters dismantled the abandoned church (which had bullet holes from Confederate John Hunt Morgan's raid in 1863) and rebuilt St. Patrick's at Gibson Station. Thereafter, the valley residents attended mass at either St. Patrick's or St. Mary's.[47]

After Father Jacquet's decade in the hills of eastern Ohio, Bishop Rosecrans reached out to him for a delicate mission. He appointed Jacquet as the first pastor of St. George's in Coshocton, with an additional charge of five missions. Leave-taking in Belmont County was difficult, and the priest and his people kept in touch with frequent letters. Jacquet followed with joy the career of his altar server, Nicholas Gallagher, who was the administrator for Columbus in 1878, and the administrator for Galveston in Texas in 1881. However, all of Jacquet's quiet strength was needed in Coshocton County to mediate an ethnic feud.

One of his missions was St. Ann's in Linton Township–German; nearby was St. Nicholas in Franklin Township–French. Animosities from Europe–including the savage Franco-Prussian War–made brotherly harmony impossible. Jacquet took up his challenge. Having made a pilgrimage to Lourdes in France in 1878 before assuming his new charge, the priest worked to create an atmosphere of trust among his disparate flock. In 1886, he successfully combined St. Nicholas's and St. Mary's into one: Our Lady of Lourdes.[48]

---

45 *CRS*, XX, #5, May 1995.
46 Ibid.
47 *Jeffersonian*, December 22, 1982.
48 *CRS*, IX, #4, April 1983.

Demographic changes took a toll on Temperanceville. In 1873, when Father Patrick Heery, late of Ireland, rode his horse down the winding hill into the valley, he found the parish in disrepair. Jacquet's school was closed and the population was gravitating to the flourishing railroad town of Barnesville. Heery labored for a decade to stabilize the parish. Then, in 1882, George Montag (born in Canal Dover, Tuscarawas County) set up shop in the cold log cabin rectory. Montag rode the rails to serve his parish: ten families at St. Patrick's, Gibson Station; 22 in Cambridge; 14 in Barnesville, and 12 at Trail's Run, as well as the 55 families in Temperanceville. In 1891, Montag supervised the construction of the new St. Mary's in Temperanceville.[49]

In January 1900, the decision was made to move the church at Archer Settlement to Carlisle, a mile-and-a-half to the south, and to assign it to St. Henry's in Harrietsville as a mission. This was a bitter pill to some at Archer's. However, it was a realization that the German-ness of the region was paramount. Of the 191 parishioners at Archer's in 1912, twenty-eight were English-speaking and 163 spoke German.[50] The Leatherwood and Duck Creek valleys had changed in the century. Now largely German, the eastern part was called the Little Switzerland of Ohio. Still, the

ST MARYS CATHOLIC CHURCH, BEAVER TWP, NOBLE CO OHIO
Courtesy Catholic Record Society, Columbus, Ohio

---

49 CRS, XIII, #11, November 1988. The twelve families in Trail's Run were the first of a wave of Slavic immigrants who came to work during the coal boom. Their earliest records are at St. Mary's. Montag spoke German. The 1899 census of Catholic families in the diocese listed 49 in Miltonsburg/Burkart; 35 in Barnesville; 73 in Cambridge and its missions; 120 in Fulda; 67 in Harrietsville, Fox, and Archer Settlements; 80 in Temperanceville; 71 in Woodsfield and Ozark. CRS, III, #11, November 1977.
50 *St. Mary's Catholic Church*, Temperanceville, Ohio, 1972.

Irish Catholic immigrants had planted the seeds of the ancient faith in the area. In the early years, their "strange" faith had been accepted because they were Americans. The "foreign" faith of the Germans, the famine-fled Irish, and the later Slavic coal miners would hold these groups apart for many years, and be the source of friction with their neighbors. Still, the identity of the "old Catholics" remained, and continues to live through their descendents in the valleys.

First Communion and Confirmation at St. Mary's in Temperanceville.
Pearl Gallagher Reischman

Bibliography

Primary Sources

COUNTY RECORDS
Chester County, PA   Citizen Petition #252, Edmund Gallagher
                            Deed Book 43, V. 119, p. 151
                            Direct Deed Book 1, V. H, p. 525
Noble County, OH   Ohio Will Book, V. 6, Case 383, Box 39. Edmund
                            Gallagher
Guernsey County, OH   Guernsey County Deed Records
Muskingum County, OH   Muskingum County Marriage Records, 1804-1835;
                            1835-1848
                            Tax Lists, 1806, 1807, 1810

STATE RECORDS
Ohio Census   1820, 1830, 1840, 1850, 1860

CHURCH RECORDS
Archbishopric of Cincinnati, University of Notre Dame, Lamy File.
St. Joseph Church, Philadelphia, Baptism Records
St. Joseph Church, Somerset (Perry County), Ohio
                            Reprinted in *Catholic Record Society*, V. 1, #1,
                            January 1975.
St. Luke, Danville, OH   Birth, Marriage Records
St. Mary's, Temperanceville, OH
                            Baptisms, 1832-1846; 1849
                            Marriages, 1833-1845; 1853-1859; 1873
                            Deaths, 1833-1844; 1853-1860; 1906
                                In 1855, Fr. J.M. Jacquet recorded what
                                he could from various scraps of paper.
                                Otherwise, the missing years are lost.
St. Vincent de Paul, Mount Vernon, OH
                            Birth and marriage records
University of Notre Dame   Parish Histories
                            PPHC   090/17
                                    092/15
                                    090/05
                                    093/15
Kanely, Edna Agatha, "Directory of Ministers and the Maryland Churches They
    Served, 1634-1990," Family Line Publications, Westminster, Maryland.
"Holy Rosary Industrial School, Notes on Galveston," Typescript, Sisters of the Holy
    Family Motherhouse Archives, New Orleans, Louisiana.

CEMETERY RECORDS AND TOMBSTONE HEADINGS
Guernsey County: Catholic Cemetery, Richland Township
Noble County: St. Michael's Cemetery, Berne
                            Old Roman Catholic Cemetery, Stock Township
                            (Road 303 off SR 78)
                            Beaver St. Dominic Cemetery

Muskingum County: Old Catholic Cemetery, Harrison Township
St. Ann's Catholic Cemetery, Harrison Township
St. Mary's Cemetery (Mattingly), Muskingum Township
Stine Catholic Cemetery, Madison Township

CIVIL WAR SOURCES
Official Roster of the Soldiers of the State of Ohio in the War of the Rebellion, 1861-1865. Cincinnati, Ohio, 1886.
1890 Enumeration of Union Veterans (Belmont County, Ohio).

GENEALOGIES
George W. Archer, "The Archer Family," McLean, Virginia, 1983.
George W. Archer, "Patrick Archer and His Descendents," McLean, Virginia, 1999.
Ira Archer, "The Archer Family," *The Jeffersonian*, January 2 & 6, 1964.
Catherine Foreaker Fedorchak, "Sketches of Family Research in Monroe County, Ohio," *The Spirit of Democracy*, Woodsfield, Ohio, 1970-1980.
Ruth Fox, The Creighton Family.
Marie Gildea, Gallagher Family Memories, oral history with Kathy Kreppner.
Eugene L. Jefferis, Jr., Jefferis Genealogy, typescript, 1986.
Richard Lowe, Lowe Family Genealogy.
James Logsdon, Sapp Settlement research.
Lorle Porter, Sapp Settlement research
Samuel Doak Porter, *A Genealogy of the Porter Family of Maryland, West Virginia, and Michigan*, Kerrville, Texas, 1971.
Pearl Gallagher Reischman, Gallagher and related families.
Francis Sapp, Sapp Family research.
Raymond F. Stephens, DeLong Family research.
Patricia McCourt Yanchak, McCourt Family research.

NEWSPAPERS
Barnesville Enterprise, "Agnes Gallagher White," July 29, 1990.
The Catholic Messenger, "Slander Answered," Davenport, Iowa, April 2, 1914.
Catholic Telegraph and Advocate
   July 28, 1836; December 15, 1860,
   "Diocese of Cincinnati Episcopal Visitation,"
   October 18, 1849, *Catholic Record Society*, XVII, #4.
   CRS, XXIV, #9, September 1999.
   CRS, XXIII, #11, November 1998.
   "Bishop John Purcell's Letter," June 17, 1843, *CRS*, XXII, #7, July 1997.
Catholic Times, Diocese of Columbus
   February 26, 1993, Supplement
   "A Layman Founds a Parish," March 3, 1968.
   "Bishop Fenwick, The Apostle of Ohio," March 3, 1968.
   "Bishop Rosecrans: Laying the Foundation," March 3, 1968
   "Suppression of the Diocese Proposed," February 26, 1993.
Galveston Daily News, "Bishop Nicholas A. Gallagher," January 23, 1918.
Jeffersonian, Cambridge, Ohio. "Austin Gallagher," May 6, 1931.
The Pittsburgh Catholic, "Historic Record of Pioneer Priest in Western Pennsylvania," November 1, 1923.

The Register, Diocese of Steubenville, "Strong in the Faith," September 22, 1995.
    Supplement, 40th Anniversary, November 2, 1984
    M.B. Archer, "Genealogical History of the Archer Family from 1803-1919," November 2, 1984.
Times Recorder, Zanesville, Ohio, "First Catholic Mass Held in the Green Tree Tavern," July 8, 1973.
U.S. Catholic Miscellany
    "A Missioner," "The 1827 Journey of the Ohio Missionaries Proclaiming the Jubilee of Pope Leo XIII," *CRS*, XIV, #7, July 1989.
    "The Catholic Church in Ohio in 1823," *CRS*, XIV, #7, February 1989.
_____ Wichita, Kansas, 1890, "Judge James DeLong."
Pearl Reischman, Collection of obituaries scrapbook.

ARTICLES
Archer, M.R. "First Catholic Church in Ohio." *Ohio Archaeology and Historical Publication*, XXIV. 1915, Columbus, Ohio.
Blessing, Patrick J. "The Irish," *Harvard Encyclopedia of American Ethnic Groups*. Belknap Press: Harvard University, 1980.
Carmel of Port Tobacco Almanac. Sisters of Carmel, La Plata, Maryland, 1990.
New Catholic Encyclopedia, First Edition
    "Joseph S. Alemany," Vol. I, p. 136.
    "Francis Asbury Baker," Vol. II, p. 22.
    "James R. Bayley," Vol. I, pp. 182-183.
    "Orestes Brownson," Vol. I, pp. 827-828.
    "John Carroll," Vol. III, pp. 151-154.
    "The Oxford Movement," Vol. X, pp. 845-847.
    "The Paulists," Vol. VII, pp. 29-30.
    "Sylvester Rosecrans," Vol. IV, p. 798.
    "Elizabeth Ann Seaton," Vol. XIII, p. 126.
    "James Kent Stone," Vol. XIII, p. 722.
    "Gabriel Richard," Vol. XII, pp. 484-485.
    "James Talbot," Vol. XIII, p. 918.
    "Joseph Thayer," Vol. XIV, p. 3
    "England," Vol. V, pp. 359-368.
Catholic Record Society. Diocese of Columbus, Ohio.
    Vol. XIX, #7, July 1989.
  John Martin Henni, Translated by Msgr. Joseph A. Hakel. "A Glimpse of the Ohio Valley."
    Vol. XXVII, #1, January 2002.
    Vol. XVII, #5, May 5, 2002.
    Vol. XXV, #10, October 2000.
  Forbes, John H. and Rev. Bede Hansen. "History of the Church of the Assumption, Barnesville, Belmont County, Ohio." V. XV, #8, August 1990.
  Lisska, Anthony J.
    "Father George Augustine Joseph Wilson, Temperance Preacher, Parish Missionary and Church Builder," Vol. XIII, #4, April 1988.

"O'Daniel and Mulhane on the Second Oldest Church in Ohio," Vol. XI, #9, September 1986.
"Bishop Fenwick's Apostolate to the North Americans," Vol. XVII, November 2000.
"The Catholic Church in Ohio in 1823 from the *U.S. Catholic Miscellany*," Vol. II, 1823; Vol. XIV, #2, February 1989.
"Notice on the State of the Catholic Religion in the State of Ohio," from the *U.S. Catholic Miscellany*," Vol. VI, 1827; Vol. XIV, #4, April 1989.

Kreppner, Kathy. "Early Catholicism in Southeastern Ohio," Vol. XIII, #1 and #2, February 1988.

Mattingly, Herman.
Vol. I, "Early Baptism Records of St. Joseph, Somerset, Ohio." (Msgr. arranged the records in chronological order.)
Vol. III, #4, April 1977.
Vol. III, #5, May 1977.
Vol. III, #7, July 1977.
Vol. III, #8, August 1977.
Vol. III, #9, September 1977

Schlegel, Donald.
"The Church in Ohio Prior to 1868."
Vol. XX, #4, April 1995.
Vol. XX, #5, May 1995.
"The Creighton or McCraren Family, Catholic Pioneers in Ohio and Omaha."
Vol. XIX, #10, October 1994.
Vol. XIX, #11, November 1994.
"The Dominican Sisters of the Sacred Heart and Sacred Heart Academy."
Vol. XVIII, #6, 7, 8, 10, June, July, August, October 1993.
"The Religious Vocations in the Gallagher Family of Beaver St. Dominic's Parish."
Vol. XIV, #1, March 1992.
"St. Patrick Mission, Fox Settlement, Ludlow Township, Washington County, Ohio, 1863-1954."
Vol. XVII, #3, March 1992.

Schlegel, Donald and Rev. George Schlegel
"St. Dominic Parish, Beaver and St. Mary's Parish, Batesville, Beaver Township, Noble county, 1819-1891." Vol. XIII, #8 and Vol. XIV, #9, 1989.
"Monroe County Churches: Dorr's Settlement, St. Joseph, St. John." Vol. XIV, #6, 1989.
"Dougherty's Settlement, Wills Creek." Vol. XXIV, #12, December 1989.

Davison, Alan. "Sources of Church History, Recusant History," *The Local Historian*, Vol. 9, No. 6, 1971, 283-289.

Haig, Christopher. "The Fall of a Church or the Rise of a Sect? Post Reform Catholicism in England," *The Historical Journal*, 21, 1, 1978, 181-186.

Hamilton, Raphael N. "The significance of the Frontier to the Historian of the Catholic Church in the United States," *The Catholic Historical Review*, Vol. 25 (2), July 1939.

Hennessey, James. "Catholicism in the English Colonies," *Encyclopedia of American Religious Experience*. Charles Schreiber's Sons, New York, 1988.
Hibbard, Caroline M. "Early Stuart Catholicism: Revisions and Re-revisions," *Journal of Modern History*, 52, March 1980. I, 1-34.
The Historical Times. Newsletter of the Granville, Ohio Historical Society, "The Church Builder of Newark who became the hero of a Willa Cather novel," X 2, Spring 1996.
Horton, Louis. "Portrait of an Ecumenist: Fr. Gabriel Richard," *The Catholic Digest*, March 1969, 56-60.
Lowery, Jack. "The Storm of the Century," *Texas Highways*, August 2000.
McGrath, Patrick and Joy Rowe. "The Elizabethan Priests: Their Harbourers and Helpers," *Recusant History*, 19, #3, 1989, 209-233.
O'Neill, Scannell. "Convert Sons of Kenyon," *Rosary Magazine*, January 1908.
"Puseyism," *Dictionary of American History*, Vol. 4, 194.
Williams, J. Anthony. "Sources for Recusant History, 1559-1791," *Recusant History*, Catholic Record Society, London 1957.

PAMPHLETS
Brennan, R.E., (O.P.), "Cradle of the Faith in Ohio, 1818-1968," Rosary Press, St. Joseph Church, Somerset, Ohio, 1968.
Hennessey, James (S.J.), "John Carroll, American Educator," John Carroll University Centennial, Cleveland, Ohio, 1986.
LaHue, William O., "The Carlisle Story," privately published, Ft. Lauderdale, Florida, 1984.
McCann, M.A., "Archbishop Purcell and the Archdiocese of Cincinnati," unpublished dissertation, Catholic University of America, 1918.
Mulhane, L.W., "History of St. Vincent de Paul Church," Mount Vernon, Ohio, 1896.
Musselman, Camillus (O.P.) *St. Thomas Aquinas Church-125 Years*, Spencer-Waller Press, Zanesville, OH, 1967.
"St. Mary's Catholic Church," Commemoration, Temperanceville,, Ohio, 1972.
"Centennial of St. Vincent de Paul Church," Mount Vernon, Ohio, 1949.
"Souvenir of the Golden Sacerdotal Jubilee of the Rt. Rev. Msgr. A. P. Gallagher, St. Agnes Church," Mena, Arkansas, 1947.
Spielman, Richard M., "Bexley Hall: 150 Years, a Brief History," Colgate Rochester Divinity School, Rochester, New York, 1974.

BOOKS
Anonymous. *The House of Honored Men: The Bishop's Palace, Galveston, Texas*, privately published, 1998,
Anonymous. *Belmont County History*, Walsworth Press, Inc., Salem, WV, 1988.
Abramson, Harold J. *Ethnic Diversity in Catholic America*, John Wiley & Sons, New York, 1973.
Allitt, Patrick. *Catholic Converts: British and American Intellectuals Turn to Rome*, Cornell Press, Ithaca, NY, 2000.
Adams, Edmund and Barbara Brady O'Keefe, *Catholic Trails West: The Founding Catholic Families of Pennsylvania*, V. II, Gateway Press, Inc., Baltimore, 1989.
Bailey, Thomas A. *The American Pageant: A History of the Republic*, D.C. Heath and Company, Boston, MA, 1956.

Bates, Samuel F. *History of Greene County, Pa.*, Nelson, Rishforth & Co., Chicago, IL, 1888.
Beitzell, Edwin Warfield. *The Jesuit Missions of St. Mary's County, Maryland*, second edition, privately published, Abell, MD, 1976.
Bland, Sister Joan. *Hibernian Crusade: The Story of the Catholic Total Abstinence Union of America*, The Catholic University Press, Washington, DC, 1951.
Bosey, John. *The English Catholic Community 1570-1850*, Oxford University Press, New York, 1976.
Caldwell, J.A. *History of Belmont and Jefferson Counties, Ohio*, J.H. Beers and Company, Chicago, IL, 1880.
Diocese of Columbus, Ohio: The History of Fifty Years, 1868-1918. Columbus, Ohio, 1918.
Connolly, S.J. *Priests and People in Pre-Famine Ireland, 1780-1845*. Gill and MacMillan, St. Martin's Press, NY, 1982.
Dolan, Jay P. *The Immigrant Church: New York's Irish and German Catholics, 1815-1865,* The Johns Hopkins University Press, Baltimore, MD, 1983.
Ellis, John Tracy. *Catholics in Colonial America*, Benedictine Studies, Helicon, Baltimore, MD, 1965.
Foreman, Harry. *Conocheague Headwaters of the Amberson Valley*, np, nd.
Foster, R. F. *Modern Ireland*, Penguin Putnam, 1990.
Fraser, Antonia. *Faith and Treason: the Story of the Gunpowder Plot*, Nan A. Talese, Doubleday, NY, 1996.
Guernsey County, Ohio, *Collection of Historical Sketches and Family History,* Guernsey County Historical Society, Cambridge, Ohio, 1979.
Guernsey County, Ohio, *Portraits and Biographical Records*, E.O. Owens and Company, Chicago, IL, 1895.
Hackett, Sheila (O.P.) *Dominican Women in Texas: From Ohio to Galveston and Beyond*, D. Armstrong Co., Inc., Houston, TX, 1986.
Haig, Christopher. *Reformation and Resistance in Tudor Lancashire*, Cambridge University Press, Cambridge, 1975.
Hardy, Beatriz Bentancourt. *Papists in the Protestant Age: The Catholic Gentry and Community in Colonial Maryland, 1689-1976*, University of Maryland, College Park, MD, 1993.
Hartley, James J. *History of the Diocese of Columbus,* Vol. I & II, Diocese of Columbus, Ohio, 1918.
Harvard Encyclopedia of Ethnic Groups, 1980.
Hill, N.N., Jr. *History of Knox County, Ohio: Its Past and Present*. A.A. Graham & co., Mount Vernon, Ohio, 1881.
Horgan, Paul. *Lamy of Santa Fe*, Farrar, Strauss & Giroux, New York, 1975.
Howe, Henry. *Historical Collections of Ohio*, Vol. I, C.J. Krenbiel & Co., Cincinnati, Ohio, 1904.
Howson, Embrey B. *The German Element in Ohio, 1803-1830*, The Ohio State University, Columbus, Ohio, 1950.
Hughes, Philip. *The Catholic Question and Rome and the Counter Reformation in England,* London, 1944.
Kelly, Michael J. and James M. Kirwin. *History of Mount St. Mary's Seminary of the West*, Keating & Co., Cincinnati, Ohio, 1894.
Kline, Omer U. (O.S.B.) *The Sportsman's Hall Parish Later Named Saint Vincent, 1790-1848*, St. Vincent Arch Abbey Press, Latrobe, PA, 1990.

Koch, Richard T. and Phyllis I. Davidson. *Western Maryland Catholics, 1819-1851,* Clearfield Company, Inc., Baltimore, MD, 1998.
    St. Luke's Records, 1829-early 1900s, Danville, Knox County, Ohio, Clearfield Company, Inc., Baltimore, MD, 2001.
Lambing, A.A. *A History of the Catholic Church in the Diocese of Pittsburgh and Allegheny,* Benziger Bros., New York, 1880.
Lamers, William M. *The Edge of Glory: A Biography of General W. S. Rosecrans,* Harcourt, Brown & World, New York, 1961.
Lamott, John H. *A History of the Archdiocese of Cincinnati,* F. Pustet Co., New York, 1921.
Lecky, Howard L. and Hilda Chance. *Index to Tenmile Country and Its Pioneer Families: Genealogical History of the Upper Monongahela Valley,* Liberty, PA, np., nd.
Maguire, John Francis. *The Irish in America,* Arno Press and *The New York Times,* New York, 1969.
Mannix, Edward J. (S.T.L.) *The American Convert Movement,* The Davin-Adair Company, New York, 1923.
Matthew, David. *Catholicism in England, 1535-1935: Portrait of a Minority, Its Culture and Traditions;* London, Eyre Spottiswoode, 1948(1936) 2nd ed.
Mattingly, Sister Mary Ramona (S.C.N.) *The Catholic Church on the Kentucky Frontier, 1785-1812,* The Catholic University of America: Studies in American Church History XXV, Washington, DC, 1936.
Monica, Sister (O.P.) *The Cross in the Wilderness, A Biography of Pioneer Ohio,* Longmans, Green and Co., London, 1930.
McAvoy, Thomas T. *A History of the Catholic Church in the United States,* University of Notre Dame Press, Notre Dame, IN, 1969.
McGee, Thomas D'Arcy. *A History of the Irish Settlers in North America from the Earliest Period to the Census of 1850.* Patrick Donahoe, Boston, 1852.
Norman, Edward. *Roman Catholicism in England from the Elizabethan Settlement to the Second Vatican Council,* Oxford University Press, London, 1985.
O'Daniel, V.F. *The Right Rev. Edward Dominic Fenwick,* The Dominicana, New Library, New York, 1920.
O'Rourke, Timothy J. *The Catholic Church on the Frontier: The Missouri and Texas Settlements of Maryland Catholics,* Brifney Press, Parsons, KS, 1973.
Pakenham, Thomas. *The Year of Liberty,* Prentice Hall, Inc., Englewood Cliffs, NJ, 1969.
Payne, John Orlebar. *Records of the English Catholics of 1715,* Burnes & Oates, Limited, New York, Catholic Publication Series, 1889.
Petit, Loretta. *Friar in the Wilderness: Edward Dominic Fenwick,* Project OPUS, Chicago, IL, 1994.
Scharf, John Thomas. *History of Maryland from the Earliest Period to the Present Day,* I.II.III, Tradition Press, Hatboro, PA, 1957 (reprint of 1879).
Schlegel, Donald M. *The Ancestors of the McDonalds of Somerset,* privately published, Columbus, Ohio, 1998.
Shea, John Gilmary. *The History of the Catholic Church in the United States,* D.H. McBride & Co., New York, 1886.
Shepherd, William R. *Historical Atlas,* 7th Edition, Henry Holt & Co., New York, 1928.
Smith, G. Wayne. *History of Greene County, Pennsylvania,* Cornerstone Genealogical Society, Waynesburg, PA, 1996.

Spalding, H.S. (S.J.) *Catholic Colonial Maryland, a Sketch*, Bruce Publishing Company, Milwaukee, 1931.

Spalding, Martin J. *Sketches of the Early Catholic Missions of Kentucky from their Commencement in 1787 to the Jubilee of 1826-7*, Arno Press, New York, 1972.

Stanton, Thomas J. *A Century of Growth: The History of the Church in Western Maryland*, I, II, John Murphy Company, Baltimore, 1900.

Steel, D.J. and Edward R. Samuel. *Sources for Roman Catholic and Jewish Genealogy and Family History*, Phillimore Publishing, London and Chichester, 1974.

Stevens, Sylvester K. *Pennsylvania: Birthplace of a Nation*, Random House, New York, 1964.

Walch, Timothy. *Catholicism in America: A Social History*, Robert E. Krieger Publishing Co., Malabar, FL, 1989.

Walsham, Alexandra. *Church Papists: Catholicism, Conformity and Confessional Polemic in Early Modern England*, The Royal Historical Society, The Boydell Press, 1993.

Watkins, L.H. *History of Noble County, Ohio*, J.H. Beers and Company, Chicago, IL, 1887.

Wolfe, William G. *Stories of Guernsey County, Ohio*, W.G. Wolfe, Cambridge, Ohio, 1943.

Index

A

Alemany, Father Joseph Sadoc 9, 18
Allen, Cardinal William 11
Altham, John 9, 11
Anderson Family 24
Anderson, Father Peter Augustine 11
Anderson, Jane Frew Wilson 24
Anderson, John 24
Anderson, Lucinda 24, 108
Anderson, William 24
Archer, Aaron 18
Archer, Absolom 18
Archer, Adah 110
Archer, Ambrose 18
Archer, Ann 110
Archer, Cynthia 110
Archer, Eliseus 110
Archer, Elizabeth 8, 69
Archer Family 9, 8, 11, 22, 18, 69
Archer, George 110
Archer, Hannah 110
Archer, Henry (1) 110
Archer, Henry (2) 110
Archer, Issac 18
Archer, Jacob 8, 69, 110
Archer, James 8
Archer, James (Junior) 8, 18, 69, 110
Archer, James (Senior) 8, 69
Archer, Jane 8, 69
Archer, Joseph 8, 69, 110
Archer, Lucinda 110
Archer, Margaret 110
Archer, Mary 8, 110
Archer, Michael 8, 69, 110, 111
Archer, Nancy 8, 69
Archer, Nathan 8, 18, 69, 110
Archer, Patrick 8, 69
Archer, Polly 8, 69
Archer, Rachel 69
Archer, Rebecca 110, 111
Archer, Robert A. 110
Archer, Roda 111
Archer, Rudy 110
Archer, Samuel 111
Archer, Sarah 69, 110
Archer, Sebastian 18
Archer, Simon 8, 18, 69, 110, 111

Archer, Sophia 8
Archer, Susan 69
Archer, Thomas 18
Armbruster, Elizabeth 18
Armbruster Family 18
Armbruster, Francis 120
Armbruster, George 18
Armbruster, Joseph 18
Armbruster, Lena 18
Armbruster, Peter 18
Armstrong, Colonel John 8
Arnold, Archibald 22
Arnold, Catherine 22
Arnold Family 22
Ashley, Captain Thomas 11

B

Badin, Father Stephen 9, 10, 15, 11, 22
Baker, Rachel 11
Banning Family 9
Banning, Judge Anthony 9
Barrett, Michael 24
Barriere, Father Michael Bernard 10
Barrighman, Anna Mary 22, 103
Barry, John 10
Beecher, Frances 107
Beecher, Maria 107
Beecher, Gen. Philemon 107
Beymer, George 11
Biedenbach, Henry 27
Biedenbach, Sr. Mary Eloise 27
Blaine, Ephraim Lyon 107
Blaine, James G. 107
Boarman, William 13
Bouquet, Colonel Henry 8
Boyle Family 22
Boyle, Hugh 11, 107
Boyle, Maria Wills 107
Braddock, General Edward
    13, 8, 10, 11, 22
Brady, Mary 110
Brady, Michael 103, 110
Brent Family 11, 9
Brent, Father Julius 11, 9
Brinton, Deborah Darlington 22
Brinton Family 22
Brinton, Mary Ann 12, 24, 27
Brinton, Sarah Darlington 22
Brooke, Elizabeth 13
Brooke Family 11
Brooke, Robert 9, 11, 13
Brooke, Thomas 13
Brophy, William 9
Browers, Father Theo 9, 10, 15

Brown, Anna Hainey 9, 120
Brown Family 9
Brummer, Father John W. 24, 18
Burk, Thomas 120
Burns Family 18
Burns, Martha (1) 111
Burns, Martha (2) 111
Burns, Mary 111
Burns, Michael 111
Burns, Walter 111
Burns, Patrick 22
Burr, Dr. J. M. 9
Burr Family 9
Butler Family 24, 8, 15, 11
Butler, James 11
Butler, John 8, 15, 11, 120
Butler, Margaret Dorn 8, 15, 11, 120
Butler, Mary Ann 9

C

Cackler, Elizabeth 69
Cahill Family 9
Calvert, Cecil 9, 11, 13
Calvert, George 11, 13
Campbell, Alexander 11
Campbell Family 11
Campion, St. Edmund 9, 11
Canning Family 9
Carr, Ann 18
Carr, Susanna 120
Carrol, Ann 110
Carrol, Elizabeth 110
Carrol, George 110
Carrol, Margaret 110
Carrol, Mary 110
Carroll, Bishop John J.
    9, 11, 13, 10, 15, 11, 22, 11, 18
Carroll, Charles (1) 11, 13
Carroll, Charles (2) 13
Carroll, Charles (3) 13, 10
Carroll, Daniel 11
Carroll, Dr. Charles 13
Carroll Family 9, 11, 13, 10, 15, 11, 11
Carroll, Jack 10
Carroll, Jackie 13
Cause, Father John Baptist 10, 15
Cecil, Sir Robert 11
Chandler, Jane 22
Chase, Samuel 10
Church Family 8, 69
Church, George 8, 69
Church, Henry 8, 69
Church, Jane 8
Church, Margaret 8, 69

Church, Nancy 8, 69
Churches
    Holy Cross, Columbus 12, 10
    Holy Rosary, Galveston 12
    Sacred Heart, Galveston 12
    St. Agnes, Arkansas 25
    St. Dominic, Beaver 12, 24, 11, 9, 18
    St. Joseph, Somerset 11
    St. Joseph's Cathedral, Columbus 24
    St. Mary's Basilica, Galveston 12
    St. Mary's, Temperanceville 12
    St. Patrick, Galveston 12
    St. Patrick's, Columbus 24, 25
Clark, General George Rogers 8, 10
Clary, Ann 22
Cline Family 12
Cline, Issac 12
Clitheroe, St. Margaret 13
Clouse, Herman 18
Coffey, Father Dan 24
Colerick, Charles 9
Collin, Frances 110
Colopy Family 9
Colopy, Timothy 9
Colopy, William 9
Condon, Mary Rachel 103, 110
Convents
    Good Shepherd, Kentucky 12
    Sacred Heart, Galveston 12
Coode, Jack 9, 11
Copley, Father Thomas 11
Cornwallys, Governor Thomas 11
Cox, Ellen 107
Crawford, Lt. William 8
Creighton, Andrew 22, 103
Creighton, Angeline 103
Creighton, Ann Slevin 9
Creighton, Anna Mary Barrighman 22
Creighton, Bridget 24, 9, 103
Creighton, Bridget (1) 22, 103, 120
Creighton, Christopher 22, 103
Creighton, Edward 9, 103
Creighton Family 25, 11, 9, 103
Creighton, Francis 22, 103
Creighton, James 22, 103
Creighton, John 22, 103, 110
Creighton, Josephine 24
Creighton, Mary 22, 103, 120
Creighton, Mary McKiggan 22, 103
Creighton, Michael 22, 103, 120, 110
Creighton, Priscilla 27, 103, 110
Creighton, Rachel Conden 110
Creighton, Rose Slevin 9
Creighton, Sarah 103
Creton, James 110

Creton, Joseph 110
Creton, Mary 110
Cromwell, Oliver 11, 13
Crossin, Manuel 110
Crossin, Mary 110
Crossin, Roseanna 110
Crow Family 9, 8, 69
Crow, Christina 69
Crow, Elizabeth 69
Crow, Frederic 69
Crow, George 18
Crow, Jacob 69
Crow, John 69
Crow, Katherine 69
Crow, Martin 18, 69
Crow, Michael 69
Crow, Suzanna 69
Cullen Family 11
Curtis, Henry B. 9

D

Darlington, Deborah 22
Darnall, Eleanor 11, 13
Darnall Family 11
Darnall, Henry 13
Darnall, Mary 13
Daugherty, Eliza Jane 18
Daugherty Family 18
Daugherty, Frances 120
Daugherty, Jacob 120
Davidson Family 11
Davidson, Mary DeLong 11
de Rohan, Father William 10
DeGoesbrian, Father Louis 9
Delille, Henriette 24
DeLong, Angelina 11
DeLong, Ann 11
DeLong, David 11, 108
DeLong, Dr. Edward 25, 108
DeLong, Edmund 18
DeLong, Edward 24, 11, 108
DeLong, Elizabeth 11, 108
DeLong Family 9, 25, 9, 18
DeLong, Frank 25, 108
DeLong, George 11, 108, 98
DeLong, Issac 11, 108
DeLong, James (Senior) 11, 108, 98
DeLong, James (Junior) 24, 108, 98
DeLong, Jane 25
DeLong, Jean Law 11
DeLong, Col. John Frances 108, 98
DeLong, Dr. John 108, 98
DeLong, Joseph 11, 108
DeLong, Lucinda Anderson 24

DeLong, Mary 25, 11, 27
DeLong, Nancy 11
DeLong, Nancy Simpson 11
DeLong, Owen 18
DeLong, Rachel 11
DeLong, Sarah Gallagher 12, 24, 11
DeLong, Sarah Winteringer 11
DeLong, Thomas 24, 25, 18, 108
Denman, Sam, Jr. 107
DeRymacher, 22
Dial, Issac 9
Digges Family 11
Digges, John 13
Dillehay Family 11
Dillehay, Benjamin 111
Dillehay, Henrietta 111
Dillehay, Lucinda 11
Dillehey, Susanna Martin 11, 111
Dillehey, Thomas 11, 111
Dinwiddie Governor 8
Dittoe, Catherine 11
Dittoe Family 9, 11, 22
Dittoe, Henry 11
Dittoe, Jacob 11, 22
Dittoe, Peter 11
Doherty Family 9
Doherty, Thomas 120
Dominica, Sister 12
Donoghoe Family 11
Dorn, Margaret 11
Dorr, John J. 9
Dorsey, Anna 22, 27
Dougherty, David 22
Dougherty, Eleanor 107
Dougherty Family 18
Dougherty, Patrick 22
Dougherty, Rose McTeague 22
Dougherty, Sarah Maloy 22
Douglas, Margaret 24
Douglas, Mary ann 27
Doyle Family 11
Doyle, Matthew 120
Doyne, Joshua 13
Drexel, Mother Katherine 12
Dubuis, Bishop Claude Marie 12
Duffy, Honora 22
Duffy, John 22
Dugan Family 22
Dugan, John Simon 22
Dugan, Peter 22
Dunmore, Lord 8
Durbin Family 9
Durbin, Elinor 111
Durbin, Honora 111

E

Emmet, Robert 15
Enochs, Amy 69
Enochs, Colonel Henry 8
Enochs, Elisha 8, 69
Enochs, Enoch (Senior) 8, 69
Enochs, Enoch (Junior) 69
Enochs Family 8, 11, 69
Enochs, Hannah 69
Enochs, Henry 69
Enochs, Lydia 69
Enochs, Nathan 69
Enochs, Phoebe 8, 69
Enochs, Rachel 8, 69
Enochs, Rebecca 8, 69
Enochs, Rhoda 8 69
Enochs, William Henry 18
Ewing Family 25
Ewing, Charley 107
Ewing, Thomas 107
Ewing, Ellen 107
Ewing, Hugh 107
Ewing, Fr. Hugh 107
Ewing, Nellie 107
Ewing, Tom 107
Ewing, Maria Theresa 107

F

Fabian, Sister 12
Farmer, Father Ferdinand 10
Fee Family 8
Fee, George 8
Fenwick, Bishop Benedict 9, 9
Fenwick, Bishop Edmund 18
Fenwick, Bishop Edward 22, 11
Fenwick, Cuthbert 11, 10, 15
Fenwick Family 11
Fenwick, Father Edward
    9, 15, 11, 22, 11, 9
Fenwick, Ignatius 15
Fenwick, Joseph 10, 15
Finck, John 11
Finck, Mary 11
Fink Family 9, 11
Finley, Angelina DeLong 11
Finley, Robert 11
Fitzgerald, Bishop Edward M. 12, 25
Flaget, Bishop Benedict Joseph
    9, 10, 15, 11, 9
Foley, Father Philip 18
Foley, Father Timothy 18
Forbes Family 25
Forbes, Mary 120

Fordyce, Lemuel (1) 9, 120
Fordyce, Lemuel (2) 9
Fordyce, Mariah 9
Foster, Charlotte 24
Fowler, M. O. 24
Fox Family v, 25
Fox, Jane McGinnis 9
Fox, William 9
Foy Family 11
Franklin, Benjamin 8, 10
Frew, Jane 24
Fromm, Father Francis 10, 15
Frost, Rebecca 22
Froude, Richard 11
Frye, Amanda 103

G

Gallagher, Angeline 27
Gallagher, Ann Carr 18
Gallagher, Anna (1) 12, 24, 25, 22
Gallagher, Anna (2) 24, 27
Gallagher, Anna Dorsey 22
Gallagher, Anne 18, 120
Gallagher, Augustine 24, 27
Gallagher, Austin 18
Gallagher, Bishop Augustine Patrick 25, 27
Gallagher, Bishop Nicholas Aloysius
    12, 24, 18
Gallagher, Bridget Ann 22, 110
Gallagher, Bridget Creighton 24, 9, 110
Gallagher, Charlotte Foster 24
Gallagher, Christopher 25, 22, 9, 27, 110
Gallagher, Clara 27
Gallagher, Edmund v, 12, 25, 22, 9, 18
Gallagher, Edmund (1)
    v, 12, 25, 22, 9, 18, 27
Gallagher, Edmund (2) 22, 120
Gallagher, Emma 27
Gallagher, Eugene 24
Gallagher, Frank 24
Gallagher, Hannah 27, 103
Gallagher, Ignatius 24, 27
Gallagher, "Long Jim" 9, 11, 18
Gallagher, James D. 24, 27
Gallagher, John 22, 9, 27, 110
Gallagher, John Augustine 110
Gallagher, Juleann (Sister Mary Ann) 12, 27
Gallagher, Lydia 24, 9
Gallagher, Lydia McGinnis 22
Gallagher, Margaret 18
Gallagher, Margaret Douglas 24
Gallagher, Mary 24, 25, 9, 27, 110
Gallagher, Mary (Mame) 12, 25
Gallagher, Mary Ann 24

Gallagher, Mary Ann Brinton 12, 24, 110
Gallagher, Mary DeLong 25, 108
Gallagher, Mary Slevin 9
Gallagher, Michael 24
Gallagher, Nicholas 22, 27, 27
Gallagher, Patrick 11
Gallagher, Robert 24, 22, 9, 103, 110
Gallagher, Rosa 110
Gallagher, Rosanna 22, 110
Gallagher, Rose Montag 24
Gallagher, Sarah 12, 24, 22, 11, 9, 108, 27
Gallagher, Thomas 22
Gallagher, William 25, 22, 27, 103, 110
Gallinger, Father Joseph 18
Gallitzin, Prince Father Demetrius Augustine 9, 15, 22, 11
Garvey, Bridget 120
Garvey, Thomas 120
Geary Family 9
Gervase, Brother Thomas 11
Gibbons, Cardinal James 12
Gildea, Anne Gallagher 18
Gildea, Cormach 18
Gildea, Dr. George Washington 24, 25, 18
Gildea Family 18
Gildea, Margaret 18
Gildea, Margaret Gallagher 18
Gildea, Michael 18
Gildea, Ruth Gist 18
Gildea, Sussanna 18
Gillespie, Eleanor 11, 107
Gillespie, Elizabeth 107
Gillespie Family 25, 8, 22, 107
Gillespie, John Purcell 107
Gillespie, Margaret 107
Gillespie, Maria 107
Gillespie, Mary 107
Gillespie, Neal 22, 107
Gillespie, Neal (Junior) 107
Gillespie, Susan 107
Gist, Ruth 18
Graham, Ezra 11
Grandon, Bernard 8
Grandon, Henry 69
Grandon, Rhoda 8, 69
Grandon, Sarah 69
Grant, General Ulysses S. 12
Gray, Matthew 69
Greathouse, Daniel 8
Greatin, Father Josiah 13
Grimes, Hannah Low 11
Grimes, Lemuel 11
Grubb, Charity 22
Guillett, Urbain 11

H

Harding, Robert 9
Harkins Family 11
Harris, George 69
Hartley, Bishop James 24
Hassion, John 120
Hayes, General Rutherford B. 12
Heed, Anna Gallagher 24
Heed, Jacob 24
Heideman, Mrs. William Henry 12
Heideman, William Henry 12
Helbron, Father Peter 9, 10, 15
Helbron, John Baptist 10, 15
Henni, Father John Marie 18
Hession, John 120
Hight, David 11
Hight, Elizabeth 11
Hill, Father John Austin 11
Howard, Cardinal Philip Thomas 15
Hughes Family 10, 15, 22, 11, 18
Hughes, Bridget 103, 110
Hughes, Constance 27
Hughes, Felix 9, 10
Hughes, Frances 120
Hughes, Frank 11, 103
Hughes, Henry 11
Hughes, Isabel 11
Hughes, John 11
Hughes, Joseph 27
Hughes, Michael 11
Hupp, George 8, 69
Hurd, Francis Xavier 9
Hurd, Mary 9

I

Irwin, Eleanor 107
Irwin, Susan 107
Irwin, William 107

J

Jacquet, Father John Marie 12, 18
Jefferis, Ambrose 108
Jefferis, Charity Grubb 22
Jefferis, Charles 108
Jefferis, Edward 108
Jefferis, Elizabeth Taylor 22, 110
Jefferis, Elizabeth Tull 22
Jefferis, Emmor (1) 22
Jefferis, Emmor (2) 22
Jefferis Family 11, 22, 9, 18
Jefferis, Frances 108
Jefferis, James 22

Jefferis, Jane Chandler 22
Jefferis, John J. 18, 108, 110
Jefferis, John R. 18, 108
Jefferis, John Shippen 22
Jefferis, John Shippen (2) 22
Jefferis, Joseph (Jr) 18, 108
Jefferis, Joseph (Sr) 18, 108
Jefferis, Mary Louise 25, 27
Jefferis, Nathan 108
Jefferis, Pius 18, 108
Jefferis, Robert 22
Jefferis, Sarah Darlington Brinton 22
Jefferis, Simeon 108
Jefferis, Thomas 108
Jefferis, William 108
Jefferson, Thomas 10
Jeffries, Charity 111
Jeffries, John 111
Jeffries, Sara Brenton 111
Jones, Anna 110
Jones, Elizabeth 110, 111
Jones, Farrel 110
Jones, John 110, 111
Jones, Mary 111
Jones, Sara 110

K

Kearnes Family 9
Keble, John 11
Keen, Captain Laurence 11
Keenan, James 120
Keenan, Margaret 120
Keller, Father Phillip 25
Kelly Family 9
Kennady Family 9
Kennedy Family 11, 9
Kerrigan Family 24
kings
    Charles 15
    Charles Edward 15
    Charles I 9, 11
    Charles II 11
    Edward VI 9, 11
    Henry II 11
    Henry VIII 9, 11
    James 11
    James I 9, 11, 8
    James the Pretender 13, 15
    Robert the Bruce 11
    William III 11, 13
Kirwin, Father James M. 12
Kraemer, Father John Christian 18
Krepps, John 107
Krepps, Eleanor 107

Kundig, Father Martin 11, 9

L

Lamy, Father Jean Baptiste 11, 9
Law, Jean 11
Leche Family 18
Leger, Francis Xavier 18
Leith, Ann 11
Leith, Sam 11
Lewis, Sarah 110
Lincoln, Abraham 12, 18
Linicome, Jane 8, 69
Linicome, Nathan 8
Linicome, David 110
Linicome, Mary 110
Linicome, Simon 110
Logan, Bridget 22
Logsdon Family 22
Lonergan, Father Patrick 9, 15
Longstreth, Bartholomew 22
Low, Anna 111
Low, Henry 11, 111
Low, Lucinda 11, 111
Lowe, Benedict 11, 120
Lowe Family 24, 11
Lowe, Henry 120
Lowe, Hannah 11
Lowe, Lucinda Dillehay 11
Lowe, Stephen 11, 120
Lucas, Sara 69

M

MacNamera, Father Joseph 9
Mager Family 9
Magevney, Eugene 25
Majors, Ann 111
Malone, Clara 12, 27
Malone Family 12, 24
Malone, Genevieve 27
Malone, Mary ann 27
Malone, Michael 27
Malone, Sarah Gallagher 12
Maloy, Sarah 22
Manners, Matthias 9
Manning, Cardinal Henry 11
Maring, Sara 111
Martin Family 8, 22, 9
Martin, Susan 111
Martin, Susanna 11
Mathis, Sarah 11
Matthews Family 9, 13, 10
Matthews, Father Ignatius 13, 15
Matthews, William 9, 13

Mattingly Family v, 15, 22, 11
Mattingly, Henry 111
Mattingly, John 22
Mattingly, Samuel 111
Mattingly, William 22
Maxwell, Jane 22, 110
McBride, John 69
McCabe, Edward 25
McCaffrey, Father James 9, 18
McCallion Family 11, 9
McCallion, Father Charles 18
McCallion, James 120
McCarthy Family 11
McCarty Family 9
McCaughy, Ann 110
McCaughy, Daniel 18
McCaughy, Hugh 18, 110
McCaughy, Jane 110
McCaughy, Jerra 18
McCaughy, John 110
McClaughlin, Jane 120
McClaughlin, Charles 120
McCleland, Sophia 69
McConnaghey Family 22
McConnaghey, Daniel 110
McConnaghy, Hugh 22, 110
McConnaghy, Hugh (2) 22, 120
McConnaghy, Jane Maxwell 22, 110
McConnaghy, John 22
McConnaughy, Elizabeth West 110
McConnaughy, John 110
McConnaughy, Mary 110
McConnaghy, Mary 110
McConncoughy, Hugh (1) 110
McConncoughy, Hugh (2) 110
McCormick, Patrick 120
McCourt, Bernard 11, 120
McCourt, Edna Rose 27
McCourt Family 11
McCourt, James 11
McCourt, James (2) 11
McCourt, John 11, 120
McCourt, Loretta 27
McCourt, Nancy 11
McCourt, Sarah 11, 120
McCourt, William 24, 27
McCrearen Family 22
McCune Family 11
McDaniel, Catherine 110
McDaniel, Daniel 18
McDaniel, John 110, 111
McDaniel, Mary 111
McDaniel, Sara Maring 111
McDonald, Bridget Logan 22
McDonald Family 13, 9

McDonald, Felix 11
McDonald, James 11
McDonald, Patrick 11
McDonald, Philip 11, 22
McDonald, Susan Ward 11
McDonnell, James 22
McFadden Family 11
McFarland, Dr. John 18
McGinnis, Lydia 22, 27
McGuire Family 15, 22
McGuire, Father Bonaventure 11
McHugh Family 9
McKenney, Mary Ward 11
McKenney, Michael 11
McKenzie Family 22
McKenzie, Gabriel 22
McKenzie, Mrs. Arron 9
McKiggan, Mary 22, 103
McLain, Jane 11
McNamara, Michael 111
McNulty, Mrs. J. F. 24
McTeague, Rose 22
McWilliams, Martha 111
Meahan, Christina 111
Meahan, Elizabeth Ward 111
Meahan, Peter 111
Meigs, Gov. Return Johnathan 11
Meyer, Elizabeth 24
Meyer, Minnie 24
Miers, Mary 107
Miles, Bishop Richard P. 18
Miles, Father Richard P. 11, 9, 18
Miller, Eli 107
Miller, John Krepps 107
Miller, Virginia L. 107
Miller, Thomas Ewing 107
Moeller, Bishop Henry 24
Molyneaux Family 9
Montag Family 24
Montag, Father George 24
Montag, Rose 24, 27
Montgomery, Father Charles P. 11, 9
Montgomery, Father Samuel 11
Montgomery, Michael 120
Montgomery, Stephen Hyacinth 22
Moore, Governor F. 107
Moore, John 8, 69
Morgan, Anna 110, 111
Morgan, Enoch 110
Morgan, George 111
Morgan, Isaac 111
Morgan, John Hunt 18
Morgan, William 110
Morris, Rebecca 8, 69, 110
Morton, David 9

Morton Family 9
Mucheboeuf, Father Joseph 9
Mullen, Dennis 120
Murphy, Father William Peter 9

N

Napoleon 12, 10, 18
Neale, Charles 13
Neale Family 11
Neale, Father Charles 10
Neale, Francis 13
Neale, Leonard 13
Neale, Sister Ann 13
Nerinckx, Father Charles 11
Newman, John Henry 11
Norton, Banning 9

O

Oates, Titus 9, 11
O'Brien, Thomas 120
Oden, John Mary 12
O'Connell, Daniel 15, 11
O'Connell, Sister Anthony 18
O'Neill, Honora Duffy 22
O'Neill, John 22
Owens, Captain David 8
Owens Family 25, 8, 9

P

Parsons, Robert 11
Patterson, John 11
Pekari, Anthony 24
Pekari, Carolina 27
Pekari, John 27
Pilger, Father Nicholas 18
Pilkington Family 9
Pitt, William 8
Plimpton, Eliza 9
Plunkett, Father Robert 10
Plunkett, St. Oliver 11
popes
    Clement XIV 11
    John Paul II 13
    Leo XIII 12
    Pius IX 12
    Pius VII 15, 11, 22
Porter, Dr. Lewis 9
Porter Family v, 9
Porter, Gabriel 22
Porter, Governor George 9
Porter, Rebecca Frost 22
Poulton, Eliza Jane Daugherty 18

Poulton Family 24, 18
Poulton, Helen 18
Poulton, John 120
Poulton, Joshua 18
Poulton, Levi 18
Poulton, William 18
Poulton, William C. 24
Powers Family 9
Preples, John 69
Purcell, Archbishop John 24, 11, 9, 18
Purcell, Bishop Edward 9
Purcell, Bishop John Baptist v, 11, 9, 18
Purcell, Bishop John J. 18
Pusey, Edward B. 11

Q

queens
    Elizabeth I 9, 11
    Henrietta Marie 11
    Mary 11, 13
    Mary, Queen of Scots 11
    Mary Tudor 9, 11
Quinlan, Father James 9

R

Rapp, Father Louis Amadeus 9
Rapp, Frances 18
Rapp, Mary 18
Reasbeck, Barbara 27
Reid, Father James 9
Rhodes, Rudy 110
Richard, Father Gabriel
    9, 15, 11, 22, 11, 9, 18
Rinehart, Moyiia 111
Robbin, Father William 24, 25
Rosecrans, Bishop Sylvester Horton
    12, 24, 18
Rosecrans, Bishops Sylvester Horton 24, 18
Rosecrans, Charles Wesley 24
Rosecrans Family 9
Rosecrans, Major-General William Starke 24
Rosecrans, Mamie 24

S

Sapp, Catherine Arnold 22
Sapp Family 9, 22, 11, 9
Sapp, Fanny 22
Sapp, George (Jr) 22
Schaefer, Anton 18
Schmuesser, Frances Viola 12, 27
Schmuesser, Henry 27
Schneider, Theodore 9

schools
>   Holy Rosary School for Colored
>   Children 24
>   Sacred Heart Academy 24, 25
>   St. Elizabeth's School for Colored
>   Children 24
>   St. Mary's of the West Seminary
>   12, 18
>   St. Mary's Seminary, Galveston 24

Seals, Captain James 8
Seams, Abraham 111
Seams, Michael (1) 111
Seams, Michael (2) 111
Seams, Sara 111
Seaton, Elizabeth Bayley 9, 11, 9
Seaton Family 9, 11
Seaton, William McGee 11
Semmes, Captain Ralph 18
Sewall Family 11
Shafer, Mrs. David 9
Shannon, Jane DeLong 25
Shannon, Willson 25
Shannon, Willson (Jr) 25
Sheehy, Edmund 11
Sheehy Family 11
Sheehy, Father Nicholas 11
Shehy, Daniel 11
Shehy Family 9, 11, 22
Shephard Family 18
Sheridan Family 9
Sheridan, General Phil 12, 11
Sherlock, Ann Clary 22
Sherlock, James 110
Sherlock, Patrick 22, 9
Sherman Family 9
Sherman, Tom 107
Sherman, Gen. William T. 107
Simpson, Nancy 11
Sister Agnes (Clara Malone) 12, 25
Sister Imelda 24
Sister Mary Isadore 24
Sister Mary St. Rita 12, 25
Sister Philomena (Frances Viola Schmuesser)
    12
Slevin, Ann 9, 103, 120
Slevin, Charles 24
Slevin, Edward 9, 27
Slevin, Edward Joseph 9
Slevin, Edwin 120
Slevin Family 24, 22, 9
Slevin, Hannah Gallagher 9, 103, 120
Slevin, John 9
Slevin, Mariah Fordyce 9
Slevin, Mary 9
Slevin, Mary Ann 9

Slevin, Mary Ann Butler 9
Slevin, Michael 9, 103
Slevin, Rose 9, 103
Slevin, Sarah 103
Slevin, Theresa 27
Smith, Mary 111
St. Clair Family 11, 22, 11, 9
St. Clair, Governor Arthur 11
St. Mary's Orphanage, Galveston 12
Stahlschmidt, Father Joseph 9, 18
Stanbury, Henry 107
Steele, Colonel 107
Steward, John 110
Steward, Martha 110
Steward, Sarah Lewis 110
Stuart Pretenders 15

T

Talbot, Father Gilbert 13, 15
Talbot, Father James 15
Taney, Sara 15
Taylor, Elizabeth 22
Temple, Bridget 110, 111
Temple, Catherine Ann 110
Temple, Elenora 110
Temple, Jane 111
Temple, Mary 111
Temple, William 110, 111
Thayer, Father 15
Thayer, Father John 10, 15, 9
Timoney, Ann 110
Timoney, Denis 110
Timoney, Elizabeth 110, 111
Timoney, Margaret 111
Timoney, Mary 110
Timoney, Peter 111
Tone, Theobald Wolfe 9, 10
Trogus, Father Otto P. 24, 25
Tull, Elizabeth 22
Tuohey, Rev. J. 24

V

Van Trump, Fannie 107
Van Trump, Philadelphia 107
Vogeler, Father Hieronymous 18

W

Wallace, William 11
Walmsley, Right Rev. Charles 10
Walpole, Luke 107
Ward, Edward 11
Ward, Elizabeth Ann 110

Ward, Elizabeth Jane 11
Ward, Elizabeth Timoney 110
Ward Family 11, 22
Ward, John 11
Ward, Mary 11
Ward, Morning Dove 11
Ward, Peter
Ward, Philip 11, 22
Ward, Susan 11
Ward, William 11
Wareham, Lucretia 103
Washington, General George
    13, 8, 10, 22, 18
Waterhouse, Eleanor 110
Waterhouse, William (Senior) 110
Waterhouse, William (Junior) 110
Waters Family 9
Watterson, Bishop John A. 24
Weld Family 11, 10
Weld, Thomas 10
Wells, Elizabeth 8, 69
Wells Family 8
Wells, William 8
Wetzel, Lew 9
Whelan, Bishop James 9
Wheland, Charles Maurice 10
White Family 24, 25, 11, 13, 22
White, Father Andrew 9, 24, 11, 13
Wilson, George 11, 9
Windal, William (1) 111
Windal, William (2) 111
Windal, Effa 111
Windell, Daniel 110
Windell, Effa 110
Windell, William 110
Winteringer, Sarah 11, 98
Wolfly, Dr. William 107

Y

Young, Henrietta 107
Young, Father Joshua Moody 11
Young, Bishop Nicholas Dominic 9
Young, Father Nicholas Dominic 15, 22
Young, John 11

Z

Zane, Ebenezer 11
Zocchi, Father Nicholas 22